DECISIONS OF THE
RED RIVER CAMPAIGN

OTHER BOOKS IN THE COMMAND DECISIONS IN AMERICA'S CIVIL WAR SERIES

Decisions at Stones River
Matt Spruill and Lee Spruill

Decisions at Second Manassas
Matt Spruill III and Matt Spruill IV

Decisions at Chickamauga
Dave Powell

Decisions at Chattanooga
Larry Peterson

Decisions of the Atlanta Campaign
Larry Peterson

Decisions of the 1862 Kentucky Campaign
Larry Peterson

Decisions at The Wilderness and Spotsylvania Court House
Dave Townsend

Decisions at Gettysburg, Second Edition
Matt Spruill

Decisions of the Tullahoma Campaign
Michael R. Bradley

Decisions at Antietam
Michael S. Lang

Decisions of the Seven Days
Matt Spruill

Decisions at Fredericksburg
Chris Mackowski

Decisions at Perryville
Larry Peterson

Decisions of the Maryland Campaign
Michael S. Lang

Decisions at Shiloh
Dave Powell

Decisions at Franklin
Andrew S. Bledsoe

Decisions of the 1862 Shenandoah Valley Campaign
Robert Tanner

Decisions at Kennesaw Mountain
Larry Peterson

Decisions of the Vicksburg Campaign
Larry Peterson

Decisions of the Galveston Campaign
Edward T. Cotham Jr.

DECISIONS
OF THE
RED RIVER CAMPAIGN

The Fifteen Critical Decisions
That Defined the Operation

Michael S. Lang

Maps by Tim Kissel

COMMAND DECISIONS
IN AMERICA'S CIVIL WAR
Matt Spruill and Larry Peterson,
Series Editors

The University of Tennessee Press / Knoxville

Copyright © 2025 by The University of Tennessee Press / Knoxville.
All Rights Reserved.
First Edition.

All images are from the Library of Congress unless otherwise noted.

Library of Congress Cataloging-in-Publication Data

Names: Lang, Michael S., author.
Title: Decisions of the Red River Campaign : the fifteen critical decisions that defined the operation / Michael S. Lang.
Description: First edition. | Knoxville : The University of Tennessee Press, [2025] | Series: Command decisions in America's Civil War | Includes bibliographical references and index. | Summary: "At the time of the Red River Campaign, between March 10 and May 22, 1864, Federal victory was nearly assured. However, this final Trans-Mississippi offensive was launched to capture Shreveport, a strategic port and military complex for the Confederate Army. The fall of Shreveport would split the Confederate lines, allowing the Federals to encircle and destroy the Confederate military forces in Louisiana and southern Arkansas as well as open a gateway to potentially invade Texas. But the dense forests and swamps of Louisiana made for difficult maneuvering, and both sides made severe tactical mistakes, leading General William Tecumseh Sherman to infamously exclaim the Red River Campaign was simply 'one damn blunder from beginning to end.'"— Provided by publisher.
Identifiers: LCCN 2024047419 (print) | LCCN 2024047420 (ebook) |
ISBN 9781621909163 (paperback) | ISBN 9781621909170 (kindle edition) |
ISBN 9781621909187 (adobe pdf)
Subjects: LCSH: Red River Expedition, 1864. | Strategy—History—19th century.
Classification: LCC E476.33 .L36 2025 (print) | LCC E476.33 (ebook) |
DDC 973.7/36—dc23/eng/20241017
LC record available at https://lccn.loc.gov/2024047419
LC ebook record available at https://lccn.loc.gov/2024047420

CONTENTS

Preface	xi
Acknowledgments	xix
Introduction	1
Chapter 1. The Campaign Begins: January 1863–April 1864	11
Chapter 2. The Battles of Mansfield and Pleasant Hill: April 6–9, 1864	63
Chapter 3. The Aftermath: April 9–April 30, 1864	99
Chapter 4. Conclusions and Consequences	115
Appendix I. Driving Tour of the Critical Decisions of the 1864 Red River Campaign	127
Appendix II. Union Order of Battle	189
Appendix III. Confederate Order of Battle	205
Appendix IV. Red River Campaign: Unit Strength and Naval Vessels	219
Notes	225
Bibliography	251
Index	261

ILLUSTRATIONS

Photographs

Maj. Gen. Nathanial P. Banks, USA	4
Maj. Gen. Richard (Dick) Taylor, CSA	7
Birds' eye view of New Orleans	8
Lieut. Gen. Edmund Kirby-Smith, CSA	13
Lieut. Gen. Theophilus H. Holmes, CSA	20
Maj. Gen. Henry W. Halleck, USA	21
Smith's & Porter's expedition begins	27
Maj. Gen. William Tecumseh Sherman, USA	28
The Red River	33
Brig. Gen. William Robertson Boggs, CSA	34
Converted Ironclad USS *Eastport*	38
Lieut. Gen. Ulysses S. Grant, USA	39
Mansfield State Historic Site	43
President Abraham Lincoln	44
The Inauguration of George Michael Decker Hahn	49
Fortifications at Grand Ecore	51
The Red River at Grand Ecore	56
Maj. Gen. Frederick Steele, USA	57
Battlefield at Poison Springs, AR	61
Rear Admiral David D. Porter, USA	65
Battle of Mansfield	71

Maj. Gen. John G. Walker, CSA	73
Rebel attack on Gen. Lee's wagon train at Mansfield	78
Maj. Gen. William B. Franklin, USA	80
The Battle of Pleasant Hill	85
Brig. Gen. Thomas James Churchill, CSA	86
Pleasant Hill Battlefield Park	92
Brig. Gen. Andrew Jackson Smith, USA	93
The Battle of Pleasant Hill	97
Brig. Gen. Thomas Kilby Smith USA	101
The Battle at Blair's Landing	107
Confederate President Jefferson Davis	109
Admiral Porter's Flotilla on the Red River	113
Capt. Elijah Parsons Petty, CSA	117
Confederates attack Union Gunboats	122
Ironclad USS *Essex*	124
United States Custom House, New Orleans, LA	130
United States Custom House, New Orleans, LA	137
Jackson Square, New Orleans, LA	138
Jackson Square, New Orleans, LA	142
Fort DeRussy State Historic Site	144
The Capture of Fort DeRussy	146
The Red River at Forts Randolph & Buhlow State Historic Site	148
Porter's Fleet passing Baily's Dam	151
The Red River at Grand Ecore, LA	152
View of Natchitoches, LA	155
Russell B. Long Lock and Dam – Blair's Landing, LA	157
Neosho-class river monitor - USS *Osage*	159
Pleasant Hill Battlefield Park	161
The Battle of Pleasant Hill	166
Mansfield State Historic Site	168
Mansfield State Historic Site	173
Mansfield Cemetery	174
Confederate Grave	177
The Red River at Stoner Avenue Park	179
Ironclad gunboat USS *Louisville* on the Red River	184
Jenkins Ferry Battleground State Park	185
Brig. Gen. Samuel Allen Rice, U.S.A.	186

Maps

Union Offensives in 1863	6
Theatre Map of the Red River Campaign	14
Grant's Spring 1864 Spring Offensives	23
Tones Bayou & The Defensives of Shreveport	36
The Capture of Fort DeRussy	46
Banks' Advance From Grand Ecore	52
The Camden Expedition	58
Banks Advances at Shreveport	66
The Battle of Mansfield, April 8, 1864, 4:00pm to 5:00pm	75
The Battle of Mansfield, April 8, 1864, Dusk	82
The Battle of Pleasant Hill—Churchill's Advance (4:30 to 5:00 pm)	88
The Battle of Pleasant Hill—Smith's Counter-Attack, Dusk	95
Banks Withdraws to Grand Ecore	102
The Battle of Jenkins Ferry	110
Bank's Retreat to Simmesport	120
Red River Campaign Decisions Tour Map	128

PREFACE

If you study the American Civil War long enough, you eventually come to realize that there are any number of recognizable themes. One of the more fascinating and perhaps least understood of these is that the war in the Western and Trans-Mississippi Theaters can appropriately be described as a conflict by way of and for control of rivers.

From the capture of Ship Island, New Orleans, Forts Henry, and Donelson in 1862 to the fall of Arkansas Post, Vicksburg, Port Hudson, and Chattanooga in 1863, the war west of the Appalachian Mountains was fundamentally decided by who controlled the Mississippi and its vast interconnected system of rivers. Almost every campaign conducted in these theaters was influenced in some way by this massive river system. The thousands of miles of navigable waterways enabled the Union to project force along very secure lines of advance. Conversely, the Confederacy was compelled to expend enormous amounts of its limited resources defending them.[1]

The Mississippi River meanders some 2,300 miles directly through the continent, beginning its course roughly 200 miles north of Minneapolis and ending its journey 70 miles below New Orleans, splitting the country in two. By the middle of the nineteenth century, the Mississippi had become an essential transportation and logistical tool for the burgeoning republic. In the decade before the Civil War, more than 1,200 steamboats operated up and down the river's length, transporting people and goods from as far north as

Minnesota to the Gulf of Mexico. As one of the largest seaports in the nation, New Orleans served as a vital link to international commerce.

In 1864, the entirety of the Mississippi watershed ran through or defined the borders of thirty-three current and future states. Five major rivers, the Arkansas, Illinois, Missouri, Ohio, and Red, made up this enormous system. Ohio River tributaries like the Allegheny, Tennessee, Cumberland, and Wabash are considered essential arms of the Mississippi system. The fourth largest in the world, the Mississippi basin drains an area of over 1.2 million square miles, or 40 percent of the current contiguous United States.[2]

In 1803, Pres. Thomas Jefferson finalized the Louisiana Purchase, doubling the nation's size. This act made much of the land west of the Mississippi River more relevant to the rest of the country. At about this same time, we first see the term Trans-Mississippi used in writings, surveys, and communications to denote all the lands west of the river.

As soon as the Civil War began, both sides quickly recognized the Mississippi River system as a critical component to victory. Union General-In-Chief Maj. Gen. Winfield Scott believed control of the Mississippi was vital to bringing the Confederacy to heel. Scott proposed that a massive naval blockade was the best and least costly way to defeat the South. The Union would cordon off Southern seaports and work to control the entire length of the Mississippi, essentially strangling the South and denying the industrially deprived region the means to make war. Admonished by a Northern press who demanded more decisive and immediate action, Scott saw his proposal pejoratively labeled the Anaconda Plan. However, Scott and his plan were ultimately proved correct.[3]

While all these facts in and of themselves are interesting, how do they help us better understand the 1864 Red River Campaign?

Beginning its own journey deep in the Texas panhandle and the eastern plains of New Mexico, the Red River flowed almost 1,400 miles along the border of Texas and Oklahoma, then briefly into Arkansas, entering Louisiana just above Shreveport. The Red then meandered across Louisiana, connecting to the Mississippi near present-day Angola, Louisiana. During the twentieth century, several public works projects sought to control the damage flooding caused at the confluence of the Red and Mississippi Rivers. Flood mitigation necessitated a course change, and the Army Corps of Engineers severed the Red River's direct connection to the Mississippi. As part of the Old River Control Structure, the Red now intersects the Atchafalaya River, emptying into the Gulf of Mexico separate from the Mississippi.[4]

In the summer of 1863, the notion of a Federal campaign up the Red River was partially conceived from the Union army and navy's exclusive capability to support large land operations with a modern and powerful river fleet. A Union general in New Orleans at this time would find the Red River the most reliable and logical way to capture Shreveport as a prelude to an invasion of Texas. Conversely, any reasonably competent Confederate commander in Shreveport understood that any Union invasion into western and northern Louisiana would likely come via the Red River.

Still, the Red River Campaign of 1864 remains one of the least understood significant campaigns of the American Civil War, often overshadowed by more consequential operations east of the Mississippi. With a few exceptions, commanders on both sides of the campaign are often considered second-rate generals banished to the Trans-Mississippi, where they could be out of sight and out of mind.

Also, it is not controversial to state that the most significant aspect of the Red River Campaign is that it was one of the worst Union debacles of the war. Never at a loss for words, William T. Sherman labeled the Union effort "one damn blunder from beginning to end."[5] Whether you consider the actions in the Red River Campaign little more than an interesting sideshow of the Civil War or critical to its outcome, the operation provides some of the most intriguing narratives the war produced.

The Red River Campaign was the most extensive in the entire history of the Trans-Mississippi Theater. It was also the largest combined-arms operation attempted by Union forces west of the Mississippi. Furthermore, it is fair to say that the entire Federal high command completely underestimated their Confederate opponents and the difficulty of an offensive campaign in western Louisiana. Ultimately, the ill-fated operation proved a significant black eye for the Lincoln administration, ending an almost unbroken string of Union military victories since July 1863.[6]

Additionally, the Red River Campaign was heavily influenced by politics and greed. When considering the command decisions of America's Civil War, one quickly observes that these critical decisions often originate from military necessity. In other words, they are often a response to an opponent's action or decision at the strategic and tactical levels. However, as military strategy undergirds the civilian government's policy and war aims, choices made of political necessity frequently influence military actions. To fully understand this particular campaign, one must recognize that politics and avarice helped drive some decision-making and influenced the operation's course.

As with the other volumes in the Command Decisions in America's Civil War series, *Decisions of the Red River Campaign* applies the critical-decision methodology. This methodology asserts that as we study the course of a particular campaign or battle, we need to ask, "Why did these events happen the way they did?" We often believe that history is a series of random events mixed together to make up the past. As a matter of fact, history is almost always determined by human beings' conscious and deliberate decisions. The Red River Campaign is a perfect example of this phenomenon.

A study of the critical decisions of this campaign requires us to look at a particular series of events and then contemplate why they happened or what caused them to happen. We must also ask, "What might have changed had this decision not been made in favor of another?" When this critical-decision concept is understood, it can be applied to any campaign in any war.

During the Red River Campaign, participants on both sides made thousands, if not tens of thousands, of decisions. Most of these are typical of any military campaign. While many of these choices can be considered significant, only a handful are deemed critical. Critical decisions are not only consequential in their own right, but also so important that they substantially shape the decisions and events that follow, thus forming the course of history.

The chart below illustrates the decision hierarchy. At the bottom are the many and various decisions. Above those are a lesser number of important decisions, and at the top are a very few critical decisions.

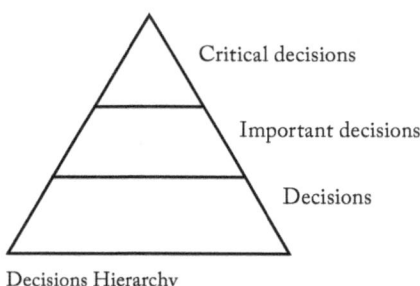

Decisions Hierarchy

The fifteen critical decisions made during the Red River Campaign are arranged in three specific time periods.

The Campaign Begins: January 1863–April 1864
    Edmund Kirby-Smith Takes Command
    The Union Advances Up the Red River
    The Availability of A. J. Smith's Command
    The Confederates Divert the Red River

>   The Command of the Union Operation
>   Banks Remains in New Orleans
>   Banks Changes His Line of March
>   Steele Advances at Shreveport
>
> The Battles Of Mansfield And Pleasant Hill: April 6–9, 1864
>   Banks's Order of March
>   The Confederate Stand at Mansfield
>   Banks Retreats to Pleasant Hill
>   Churchill Fails to Find the Union Flank
>   A. J. Smith Counterattacks
>
> The Aftermath: April 9–May 30, 1864
>   Banks Withdraws to the Red River
>   Kirby-Smith Moves Forces to Arkansas

Studying these critical decisions quickly reveals that they are made at every command level. Critical decisions can be strategic, operational, tactical, organizational, personnel related, or logistical. Some choices appear trivial at first glance, but they can be judged highly critical under more scrutiny, impacting future events.

Simply stated, the study of critical decisions examines the why of a historical event instead of the what. Concentrating on the critical decisions, this analysis presents the basic facts in an outline of a highly complex affair. In the situational narrative, the pertinent details and biographical and topographical information provide the reader with an overview of why the events developed as they did. The account also presents the situational awareness and options of the decision-maker, along with the decision made and the repercussions of an alternate choice.

Judgments about what constitutes a critical decision may differ, and many readers' opinions will undoubtedly diverge from my own. The critical-decision analysis is somewhat subjective. For example, cases like the struggle for Mansfield and Pleasant Hill involved countless determinations. Still, after extensive research, I have reduced the list to the most critical decisions discussed in this narrative.

This book looks at decisions made during the battles and those that occurred before and after the fighting. While Mansfield and Pleasant Hill are significant, they are only parts of the sum that is the 1864 Red River Campaign.

This book is not intended to retell or reinterpret the Red River Campaign completely. For example, I only briefly reference the very complicated and relevant political aspects of the operation and touch on a few material points of the overall narrative. This book covers those events and details pertinent to the various decisions discussed. Any number of excellent books provide a more detailed analysis of those topics. They are not listed here, so the reader should refer to the bibliography as a possible introductory study guide.

Where applicable, modern terminology and concepts are inserted into the text to bring perspective, but the vocabulary of 1864 is also employed when that approach makes sense.

As you read, you will notice that the Union and Confederacy used similar but often differing methods to identify units. Both sides similarly identified units at the company, battalion, and regimental levels. Companies were distinguished by a letter—e.g., A Company, B Company, and so on. Regiments and battalions were usually designated by a number—e.g., Twelfth (or 12th) Texas, Thirty-Second (or 32nd) Iowa. Above the regimental level, the Union and Confederacy took different approaches to identify units.

The official Union brigades, divisions, and corps designations were numeric and began with a capital letter. Examples include First Brigade, Second Division, Nineteenth Corps, Brig. Gen. James W. McMillan's Second Brigade, Brig. Gen. William H. Emory's First Division, Maj. Gen. William B. Franklin's Nineteenth Corps. Lowercase letters refer to a brigade or division belonging to or commanded by an individual. Examples include Nickerson's brigade, Hubbard's division, Smith's corps, etc.

Early in the war, the Confederacy simultaneously used both numbering and naming systems for unit designations. As the war progressed, the numbering system was used far less often than the naming system. Confederate brigades, divisions, and commands/corps were officially designated by the commanders' last names, followed by Brigade, Division, or Corps. Examples include Crawford's Brigade and Marmaduke's Division.

Of course, as with most things related to the Civil War, these rules always have exceptions. Additional details on unit designations and leadership are referenced in the orders of battle located in appendixes II and III.

Determining the specific facts and events during the Civil War can be highly problematic. As a result, understanding the precise number of combatants on each side of the conflict becomes a circular discussion with no clear answer. New research contradicting earlier assertions seems to be published daily to complicate this situation further. Additionally, as many students of the war understand, exact and standard timekeeping was not generally practiced in the nineteenth century. Therefore, readers can add or subtract an hour from any stated time and increase or decrease every head count by 15 percent.

A complete and thorough grasp of mid-nineteenth-century warfare often requires studying the ground where these events took place. Topography plays a critical role in the comprehension of a decision or event. Knowing what a decision-maker saw can often provide valuable, otherwise obscured insight. Exploring the geographic area where the campaign took place perfectly illustrates this fact. A campaign guide (appendix I) includes tour stops correlating with many critical decisions discussed in this work to better facilitate such understanding.

I sincerely hope you find this a valuable work, and a welcome addition to your library and your study of this most remarkable and often overlooked campaign of the American Civil War.

ACKNOWLEDGMENTS

No work of this type is ever done in a vacuum, as countless authors before me can attest. It requires assistance, guidance, suggestions, and feedback from friends, colleagues, and experts.

I wish to thank series editors Matt Spruill and Larry Peterson. Together, they encouraged me while providing valuable comments on this manuscript.

I would also like to thank the talented and hardworking staff of the University of Tennessee Press. This dedicated team is always a pleasure to work with. I could not have completed this project without their guidance and professionalism.

Thanks to Scott Dearman former manager of the Mansfield State Historic Site and William Bozic of the United States National Park Service. Scott was invaluable to my understanding of the campaign and generous with his time and vast knowledge. William provided helpful feedback on the initial draft of this manuscript.

I would like to collectively thank all the extraordinary people I have met since moving to Texas. Traveling through the world of Civil War enthusiasts and roundtables in Texas, Arkansas, and Louisiana has allowed me to connect with keepers of diaries, letters, and resources that I would not have been able to access otherwise. All of these individuals have contributed to this manuscript.

Thanks to Ron A. Viskozki of Shreveport for sharing his knowledge of the area in and around this incredibly fascinating and historically significant city.

I must also give a big thank-you to Tim Kissel. This is the third manuscript Tim has contributed to with his extraordinary talent as a cartographer. His maps have elevated the overall credibility and aesthetic of this manuscript.

Of course, I want to thank my loving wife, Rebecca. Her tireless support in following me to countless Civil War sites, roundtables, and symposia has been invaluable. I could not have completed this project without her encouragement.

Last, I want to thank all the talented writers and historians of the Red River Campaign who have come before me. Inspiration derived from gifted individuals like Ed Bearss, Ludwell H. Johnson, and Gary Joiner, to name a few, helped lay this book's foundation.

INTRODUCTION

On Wednesday, May 13, 1864, as his army prepared to break out of Alexandria, Louisiana, Union Major General Nathanial P. Banks sat alone in his headquarters, penning a letter to his wife in New Orleans. Barely two months had passed since his much-anticipated Red River Campaign was inaugurated. When he departed the Crescent City, leaving his beloved Mary behind, Banks believed nothing but glorious victory and profits from confiscated cotton lay in his future. Unfortunately for Nathaniel Banks, providence had other plans.

The fortunes of war turned against him when Richard Taylor's Confederate army routed him at Mansfield on April 8, forcing the Union commander to fall back to the small town of Pleasant Hill. The next day, the Confederates were themselves driven from the field. Believing his command was at risk, Banks turned victory into defeat by retreating to the Red River that evening. Falling back again from Gand Ecore on April 21, Banks slipped a Confederate trap at Monett's Ferry. His retreating army then marched into Alexandria and dug in.

For the better part of the next month, this mighty Union force designed to capture Shreveport and take the war into Texas was besieged by a mere 5,000 Confederates. Nathaniel Banks outnumbered his opponent by five to one, but somehow, the politician-turned-general had convinced himself the opposite to be true. Adding to Union frustrations, the level of the Red River had dropped so low that several warships in Admiral Porter's flotilla had become trapped above the falls at Alexandria. As Banks readied his army for another retreat downriver, an unconventional scheme devised to save the flotilla might yet provide some positive news in what was an otherwise disastrous campaign.

In his solitude, Banks undoubtedly contemplated his predicament. His grand opportunity for glory, launched with much fanfare and anticipation, had somehow evaporated before his eyes. Finishing his letter, the general opened his heart to his wife, whom he often referred to in the third person. He lamented, "Thanks to my dear wife, she is a proud woman. I want to see her—to breathe my soul into hers. I have nobody to talk to, nobody to embrace . . . I am alone."[1]

One can imagine a dejected Banks gazing intently at his words as if to glean some divine revelation, replaying his recent decisions over and over, wondering how it had come to this, who was to blame, and where it had all gone wrong.

The circumstances that delivered Nathanial Banks to this moment began the previous summer. On July 4, 1863, the Confederate cause was dealt a staggering one-two blow. Robert E. Lee's ignominious retreat after the loss at Gettysburg, combined with the surrender of the Confederate bastion of Vicksburg, Mississippi, marked a critical turning point in the Civil War. Whereas the Confederate loss at Gettysburg was undoubtedly a stunning blow to Confederate hopes, the fall of Vicksburg was even more devastating. Strategically located at a great bend in the Mississippi River, Vicksburg was the most crucial Confederate strongpoint on the river. Vicksburg's surrender, combined with the Confederate defeat 135 miles downstream at Port Hudson just days later, meant the Union now effectively controlled the entire length of the Mississippi, severing the embattled Confederacy in two, just as Union general Winfield Scott predicted. Every Confederate state west of the Mississippi was now officially on its own until the war ended. Even though the Civil War would go on for almost two more years, many historians cite these concurrent defeats as the beginning of the end for the Confederacy.

Following his hard-earned victory at Vicksburg, Union general Ulysses S. Grant relocated northeast, orchestrating the end of the Confederate siege and the ultimate defeat of Braxton Bragg's army at Chattanooga, Tennessee, in November 1863. Rewarded by Lincoln for his cumulative victories, Grant was subsequently summoned to Washington, DC, and promoted to lieutenant general; he was then made general-in-chief of all Union armies in March 1864.[2]

The spring of 1864 was a time of immense transition for the Civil War. The relative lull in the previous winter's fighting was soon to dissipate. U. S.

Grant now conceived a plan to attack every significant Confederate army simultaneously. Determined to keep the various Confederate commands from supporting one another, Grant devised multiple concurrent offensives. Maj. Gen. Benjamin Butler's Army of the James was to advance along its namesake river at Richmond, while Maj. Gen. Franz Sigel was to march his forces through the Shenandoah Valley. Maj. Gen. William T. Sherman and the Army of the Tennessee were to advance at Atlanta and Joseph Johnston's army. In the east, Maj. Gen. George Meade and the Army of the Potomac were to attack Robert E. Lee's forces in northern Virginia. In addition, another campaign west of the Mississippi set sights on northwestern Louisiana and Texas. For the record, Grant disapproved of this particular campaign, believing it a waste of resources and preferring an operation at the port city of Mobile, Alabama.[3]

New Orleans, Louisiana, the largest city in the Confederacy, had been under an uneasy Federal occupation since May 1862. No sooner than New Orleans fell to Union forces, Abraham Lincoln cast a covetous eye on the rest of Louisiana and neighboring Texas. The conquest of the Mississippi was to begin here, as was Lincoln's reconstruction experiment for the soon-to-be defeated South. To these ends, in late 1862, Lincoln sent political general Nathaniel Prentiss Banks to New Orleans to command the newly established Department of the Gulf. The forty-six-year-old Banks replaced another political general, the wildly unpopular Maj. Gen. Benjamin F. Butler. Known by the locals as "The Beast."

It was no accident that Lincoln selected Banks for this position. Born in Waltham, Massachusetts, in 1816, Banks rose from a simple bobbin boy in New England's textile mills to a nationally prominent and influential political figure. This included holding the offices of Speaker of the US House of Representatives and governor of Massachusetts.[4]

After his election to the presidency, Abraham Lincoln, seeking to shore up support for his administration within the political power apparatus of New England, considered giving Banks a position within his cabinet. As this did not pan out, the president decided to commission Banks, a major general in the Union army, shortly after the firing on Fort Sumter. Banks, who had no serious previous military experience, was suddenly the fourth-highest-ranking general in the United States Army, outranked only by Winfield Scott, John C. Frémont, and George McClellan at the time of his appointment.[5] One of the first so-called political generals to serve in the war, Banks took a command in Maryland as his first assignment, eventually arresting several secessionist state legislators on orders from Lincoln.

In March 1862, Lincoln ordered corps to be formed within the Union

Introduction

Major General N.P. Banks, full-length portrait, standing, facing left, Mathew Brady, circa 1861, Library of Congress Prints and Photographs Division Washington, DC 20540.

armies. The Second Corps was summarily organized from the divisions of Banks and Alpheus Williams. Its command now fell to Banks, who accumulated a less-than-stellar record on the battlefield. From 1861 until his transfer to the Department of the Gulf in late 1862, a common refrain on his leadership was that he was personally brave, and his men fought well despite being poorly led.

While Banks was Commanding the Department of the Shenandoah, his forces were defeated by Stonewall Jackson's troops in the Shenandoah Valley in the spring of 1862, and then again at Cedar Mountain in August. Banks first faced his future Red River opponent Richard Taylor at the Battle of Front Royal. Taylor commanded a brigade in Ewell's Division. Banks's Second Corps was stationed at Bristoe Station, Virginia, and did not participate in the Second Bull Run battle in August. During the Maryland Campaign, the general cooled his heels for several weeks in Washington, DC, as garrison commander until Lincoln sent him to New Orleans in December 1862. Banks's Second Corps was redesignated the Twelfth Corps and folded into the Army of the Potomac.[6]

Circumstances in Louisiana necessitated leadership from an individual proficient in the political nuances of the war and how to navigate them. Banks was that individual. Despite his questionable military skills, the general, a potential presidential opponent, was conveniently exiled far from the

Washington, DC, political scene with a stroke of Lincoln's pen. At the same time, Lincoln was inserting a politically shrewd general into an assignment he was well suited for. In addition to opening the Mississippi and conquering Texas, Banks was charged with disseminating Lincoln's reconstruction policies into the rest of Louisiana and Texas. This included installing Union-friendly governments in the area.

Over the next year, the Union made several efforts to seize this cotton-rich Confederate territory. But it was not just cotton to feed the starving New England textile mills that Lincoln and Banks were after. Like many in the North, Lincoln believed that a robust pro-Union population resided in places like Texas, just waiting for the right time and opportunity to cast secession aside and rejoin the Union. Additionally, since late 1861, the French government had been overtly scheming to displace the current Mexican regime and seize control of the country. Texas's border with Mexico was among the few places Confederate cotton could effectively pass through the Yankee blockade. A solid Federal presence in southwest Texas would signal to the French that the Union would not tolerate foreign interference while blockading a Confederate revenue source. In 1863, Union forces under Banks launched offensives at Galveston, Sabine Pass, and Brownsville in Texas, as well as Bayou Teche in Louisiana. For various reasons, none of these actions were successful for the Union.[7]

Banks was more successful in Louisiana from May to July 1863, when he commanded the Federal force besieging Port Hudson on the Mississippi downstream of Vicksburg. When Vicksburg fell, the defenders of Port Hudson saw their cause as lost, surrendering to Banks's army on July 9, making more than 6,500 Confederates prisoners. The victory cost Banks over 5,000 battlefield casualties and between 4,000 and 5,000 men overcome by disease and heatstroke.[8]

In the meantime, the fall of Vicksburg and Port Hudson created a real challenge for the Confederate command and control of the Trans-Mississippi. This department, comprising Arkansas, Missouri, Texas, western Louisiana, Arizona Territory, and the Indian Territory (Oklahoma), occupied over five hundred thousand square miles. Defending this vast region was no straightforward assignment, as the aggregate of all Confederate forces in the theater by the winter of 1863–64 was fewer than forty thousand men of all arms. Moreover, after Port Hudson's fall, every Trans-Mississippi command was, in effect, severed from the rest of the Confederacy by the Mississippi River.[9]

The previous summer, to help the region's defense, Confederate president Jefferson Davis sent his former brother-in-law, the aggressive and irascible

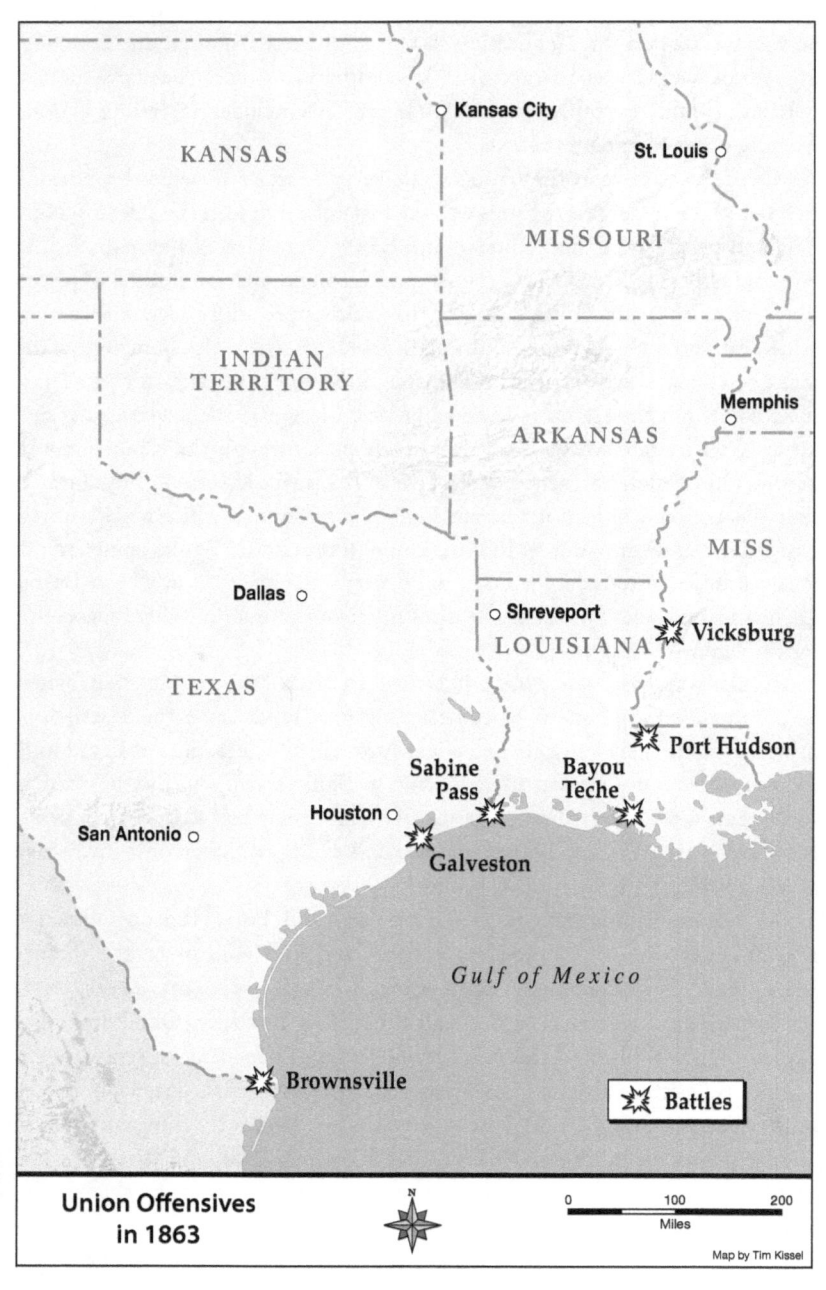

Maj. Gen. Richard Taylor, to command the District of Western Louisiana.[10] Born in 1826 at his family's plantation in Springfield, Kentucky, Richard "Dick" Taylor was the sixth child of war hero turned president Zachary Taylor. As a boy, the younger Taylor attended private schools in Kentucky and Massachusetts, eventually graduating from Harvard University in 1845. While at college, Taylor spent his spare time reading classical and military history books. He furthered his exposure to army command by serving on his father's staff during the Mexican War. In July 1850, Richard Taylor inherited the family plantation in St. Charles Parish, Louisiana, just west of New Orleans, after his father's death. In 1855, he formally entered the world of politics by winning an election to the Louisiana State Senate.

Taylor, a strict disciplinarian, has been described as one of the hardest-fighting Confederate generals of the war. He is depicted as dogged, profane, and personally brave, often inspiring his men while cussing out a stubborn mule in the same breath. Taylor, who never received a formal military education, reportedly never fought a battle where he was not outnumbered. To say he and Edmund Kirby-Smith did not get along is an understatement. Their long-running, acrimonious feud was a prominent thread running through the overarching story of the Red River Campaign.[11]

After Louisiana seceded and war broke out, Taylor was initially asked to act as secretary to Braxton Bragg in Florida. However, in July 1861, he was

Richard Taylor, CSA, Unknown, circa 1860–870, Library of Congress Prints and Photographs Division Washington, DC 20540.

commissioned colonel of the Ninth Louisiana Infantry Regiment. Sent to Virginia, the Ninth arrived too late on the field at Manassas to participate in the first great battle of the war. In October 1861, primarily due to this relationship with Jefferson Davis, Taylor was promoted to brigadier general, eventually commanding a Louisiana brigade under Richard S. Ewell in Stonewall Jackson's Shenandoah Valley Campaign. Taylor subsequently traveled with the rest of Jackson's Command to participate in the Seven Days Battles around Richmond. However, illness kept him from leading his brigade during these engagements. In July 1862, supported by a recommendation by Stonewall Jackson, the thirty-five-year-old Taylor was promoted to major general, the youngest in the Confederacy at that time. That same month, ordered to Opelousas, Louisiana, Taylor was tasked with building troop strength in the District of Western Louisiana while posting forces to defend the Red River and western Louisiana from potential Union incursions. He spent the rest of 1862 and most of 1863 rebuilding the mismanaged District of Western Louisiana while fending off multiple enemy offensives.[12]

As 1863 gave way to 1864, The Union army and navy now busied themselves planning their next strategic moves for the Western and Trans-Mississippi Theaters. Despite all previous setbacks, the Lincoln administration still wanted the national flag "hoisted in some point of Texas."[13] Union leadership now considered a path making better use of its superior riverine

Birds' Eye View of New Orleans. John, Bachmann, circa 1851, A. Guerber & Co., Library of Congress.

naval fleet. After resisting these notions for over a year, Nathaniel Banks also became convinced that it might be best to invade Texas by way of the Red River. Scant few senior Union generals besides Banks believed the benefits of such a campaign were worth the men and resources needed to execute it. Nevertheless, the overarching political objectives of the Lincoln administration and the opportunity to seize valuable Confederate cotton made the operation too tempting to resist.[14]

CHAPTER 1

THE CAMPAIGN BEGINS

JANUARY 1863–APRIL 1864

The Battles of Mansfield and Pleasant Hill were without question the climax of the 1864 Red River Campaign. To fully understand these engagements, we must first appreciate the decisions made beforehand. The following choices facilitated the actions that eventually brought the armies of Richard Taylor and Nathaniel Banks face-to-face in the woods and hills south of Shreveport. While not as well documented, the decisions made in the first four months of 1864 are essential to comprehending this Civil War campaign. Eight critical decisions were made from January 1863 to April 1864.

If you have skipped the preface, please return to it and read the definition of a critical decision to better understand the format in which this book is presented.

Edmund Kirby-Smith Takes Command

Situation

On January 20, 1864, two months before the onset of the Red River Campaign, Edmund Kirby-Smith sent a departmental update to Pres. Jefferson Davis in Richmond. In this communication, he predicted what the Confederacy in the Trans-Mississippi might expect come that spring. More accurate than he knew, Kirby-Smith's forecast might have been fully realized had it not been for a few men making a few critical decisions. He wrote in part:

The only true line of operations by which the enemy can penetrate the department is the valley of Red River, rich in supplies; with steamboat navigation for six months in the year, it offers facilities for the co-operation of the army and navy, and enables them to shift their base as they advance into the interior. The enemy are fully aware of the importance of this line of operations, and I have reliable information from more than one quarter that as soon as the river rises a formidable expedition of land and naval forces will be employed in that direction. This, taken in connection with the reluctance evinced by the enemy in sending troops to Texas, and with the formidable fleet collected in the Mississippi, would point to active operations on Red River this spring. The facilities which the enemy possess in transportation and operating on interior lines give him advantages which, with his superiority of numbers, will tell in all the early operations of a campaign.

The works and obstructions in Red River and the Washita are being pushed as rapidly as the limited means at our disposal will admit. We are sadly embarrassed by the want of heavy artillery.

The enemy this spring will make vigorous efforts to possess themselves of Red and Washita Rivers, and, fortifying the strategic points, Monroe and Alexandria, they will control the navigation and effectually separate the department from the Government east of the Mississippi.[1]

Edmund Kirby-Smith was born in 1824 in St. Augustine, Florida, graduating from the US Military Academy in 1845, twenty-fifth out of a class of forty-one. His graduating class contained such notable personalities as William "Baldy" Smith, Fitz-John Porter, Bernard Bee, John Hatch, Gordon Granger, and Charles Stone. Infamous as the scapegoat of the Ball's Bluff affair, Charles Stone later served as Nathaniel Banks's chief of staff during the Red River Campaign.[2]

After West Point, Second Lieutenant Kirby-Smith served in Mexico and Texas and then briefly taught at his alma mater. Promoted to captain in 1859, he was severely wounded fighting Comanches on the Texas frontier, and in 1861 he was promoted to major.

Initially unenthusiastic about secession, Kirby-Smith believed caution and coolheadedness were the best courses of action. He even refused to surrender his US Army command to Texas forces after that state left the Union. This soon changed as state after state seceded. Stating, "Right or wrong, I go with the land of my birth," Kirby-Smith resigned from his army commission

Portrait of Gen. Edmund Kirby-Smith, Unknown, circa between 1860–1865, Library of Congress Prints and Photographs Division Washington, DC 20540.

in April 1861 and threw his lot in with the Confederacy. Soon rising to the rank of brigadier general, he was wounded while leading his brigade at the Battle of First Bull Run.[3]

In February 1862, Kirby-Smith was sent west to command the eastern division of the Army of Mississippi. Cooperating with Gen. Braxton Bragg in the invasion of Kentucky, he was victorious at the Battle of Richmond, Kentucky, in August 1862. On October 9, he was promoted to the newly created grade of lieutenant general, commanding the Third Corps, Army of Tennessee. This unit was subsequently broken apart, with one division participating in the Battle of Stones River.[4]

As 1862 drew to a close, Confederate forces under Robert E. Lee achieved a stunning win over the Army of the Potomac at Fredericksburg in December of that year. However, Jefferson Davis and his Confederacy faced far more uncertain times in the West. By January 1863, Braxton Bragg and the Army of Tennessee had been forced to fall back to Tullahoma, Tennessee, after losses at Perryville and Stones River. To add to Confederate misfortunes, Union forces under U. S. Grant had begun their dogged advance at the Confederate stronghold of Vicksburg.

Gen. Braxton Bragg presented one of Davis's primary dilemmas in the West. Dissatisfied with his handling of the Kentucky and Stones River Campaigns, several of Bragg's most senior lieutenants demanded his removal.

They included Edmund Kirby-Smith. Determined to find a solution to the rapidly disintegrating situation, Davis sent Western Department commander Gen. Joe Johnston to investigate and report.[5]

West of the Mississippi, affairs were not much better. Davis's overall commander of the Trans-Mississippi since October 1862 was the equally problematic Lieut. Gen. Theophilus H. Holmes. Holmes was banished to the theater, a victim of Robert E. Lee's purge of army commanders he had no further use for after the Seven Days Battles. From his headquarters in Little Rock, the lieutenant general constantly complained about the inferior quality of his troops, the weapons he was provided, and the general lack of support he received from the Confederate War Department in Richmond. Holmes also refused to send troops to support Vicksburg and was primarily blamed for the Confederate losses at Prairie Grove and Dripping Springs in December 1862, resulting in the Union occupying most of northern Arkansas.[6]

Options

With the situation on both banks of the Mississippi seeming to worsen by the moment, Jefferson Davis, who often functioned as his own secretary of war and general-in-chief, pondered a solution to his command woes west of the Mississippi. He could keep Holmes in place, move Bragg or Johnston to the Trans-Mississippi, divide command responsibilities, or give the job to Edmund Kirby-Smith. Davis had a critical decision to make.

Option 1

Davis's first choice was to keep Theophilus H. Holmes in command of the Trans-Mississippi. With limited options, the president might conclude that leaving Holmes in place was his best option. The pool of experienced Confederate officers who could also lead at the theater level was somewhat limited. While the Trans-Mississippi was critical to the overall Confederate strategy, other regions also required Davis's attention and his most competent commanders. Moving anyone else to that department might weaken other vulnerable areas of the Confederacy. In his short tenure, Holmes had become a challenge for the Confederate high command. As head of the Department of North Carolina in 1862, Holmes often complained that he was unsuited for the complexities of departmental command, repeating these same objections while serving in the Trans-Mississippi. This fact alone might justify Holmes's removal in Davis's mind. Additionally, Holmes often clashed with the area's governors and his commanders in the field.

On the other hand, Davis and Holmes had known each other for almost forty years, since their days at West Point. At some point, Davis seemed to believe in the officer's abilities, giving him a command early in the war. Holmes was already the department commander, and Davis might have considered that, despite his shortcomings, Holmes was best suited to carry on this isolated and challenging role.[7]

Option 2

Davis's second option was to send Joe Johnston west of the Mississippi to command. Joseph E. Johnston was one of the highest-ranking generals in the Confederate army. He had commanded the main eastern Confederate force from the summer of 1861 until his wounding at the Battle of Seven Pines (Fair Oaks) in May–June 1862. After a long and difficult rehabilitation, Johnston was made overall commander of the Western Theater in November of that same year. A West Point classmate of Robert E. Lee's, Johnston had been an officer for almost forty years, amassing extensive command experience. He was one of a few generals on either side who was actually a brigadier general before the war, functioning as quartermaster general for the US Army. Joe Johnston was intimately familiar with departmental command's administrative complexities and demands. Additionally, Davis and Johnston did not get along at all. Their mutual dislike and distrust began soon after the first shots were fired at Fort Sumter and lasted until the war's end. The Confederate president might have considered the Trans-Mississippi an ideal place to further exile this bothersome thorn in his side.[8]

Conversely, Johnston already had a job. Managing the convoluted and drama-filled Department of the West was no straightforward assignment. Moreover, if Davis sent Johnston west of the Mississippi, he had to wonder who might take the general's place. Last, Johnston was extremely prickly when it came to seniority. His numerous ongoing quarrels concerning his rank defined his entire Civil War career. Davis had to ask himself whether Johnston would quietly submit to a command that might appear to him as a demotion.[9]

Option 3

Davis's third option was to send Gen. Braxton Bragg to the Trans-Mississippi. Bragg was one of the most experienced Confederate generals in the West at this time. He had previously fought in the Second Seminole War and with distinction in Mexico. Once the Civil War began, he quickly rose through the Confederate ranks from colonel to full general by April 1862. Bragg took over command of the Army of the Mississippi after the Battle of Shiloh. When the force was renamed the Army of Tennessee in November of that same year, Bragg continued as its leader. In the late summer of 1862,

Bragg and Kirby-Smith cooperated in simultaneous invasions of Kentucky. Davis had known Bragg since their time in Mexico, and the administration's praise of his early successes was crucial to his ascension. Furthermore, Bragg was familiar with command at this level and was a strict disciplinarian. His command style might be just the ticket for the badly mismanaged Trans-Mississippi.

However, the embattled Bragg came with his unique form of baggage. The discontent within the high command of the Army of Tennessee was becoming a real challenge for Jefferson Davis. The grumbling within that army that began in late 1862 and continued until the end of 1863. The Southern press had also started to throw multiple accusations and criticisms at the beleaguered general. Davis had to consider whether the risk of further discontent within the Trans-Mississippi Department could be offset by the benefits of Bragg's presence.[10]

Option 4

Jefferson Davis might have decided it made sense to divide the department's vast area into two or more parts, with separate commanders responsible for each. The advantage of this decision would be that each commander would lead a smaller and presumably more easily managed territory. The officers' respective communication and logistical problems might be reduced as well. Moreover, the stress and difficulties of managing a department with so many moving parts might decrease for the individuals picked for this assignment.

On the downside, each of these separate department commanders would be expected to cooperate for the mutual good of the Confederacy. Given the potential list of candidates and the drama they seemed to thrive on, voluntary cooperation might be too much to ask.

Option 5

Davis's final option was to send Edmund Kirby-Smith to the Trans-Mississippi. By the end of 1862, Kirby-Smith had essentially become a general without a job. After the Confederate loss at Perryville, Bragg retained command of a large portion of Kirby-Smith's army. This was the last straw for Kirby-Smith, who complained vociferously about Bragg's competency and the loss of his command to anyone who cared to listen. Kirby-Smith certainly possessed the needed experience and organizational skills for departmental leadership. He was a seasoned combat commander, leading Confederate troops from the first days of the war. As Kirby-Smith was one of the loudest voices railing against Braxton Bragg, Davis might have seen this as an ideal opportunity to separate and distance these two quarrelsome generals.[11]

Decision

After some consideration, Davis decided Kirby-Smith was best suited to lead the Department of the Trans-Mississippi (Option 5). Initially, it was determined to divide the responsibilities of the far-flung region (Option 4). On January 14, 1863, Kirby-Smith received orders to command the newly created Department of Western Louisiana and Texas, while Holmes retained control of the department's balance, including Arkansas, Missouri, and the Indian Territory. After further contemplation, the Davis administration had a change of heart. Before he could reach his new command, Kirby-Smith received countermanding orders on February 9, 1863. Edmund Kirby-Smith was now to assume control of the whole of the Trans-Mississippi, placing him over Holmes and that general's dramatically reduced command.[12]

Results/Impact

The effect of Davis's decision cannot be overstated. Edmund Kirby-Smith's impact on the Department of the Trans-Mississippi was immediate and lasted until the war's final days. The problems that plagued the department did not magically dissipate with Holmes's demotion. In truth, Kirby-Smith was a bit more successful in reorganizing the scattered commands that made up his new department. Despite this, he struggled to obtain his commanders' complete loyalty and cooperation, and get them to see his strategic vision. Kirby-Smith was also more successful than Holmes in securing partnerships with the various civilian state governments. Kirby-Smith worked exhaustively to feed and supply his new command, knowing he was taking on an extraordinary task, but he saw the opportunity as a chance for glory. Only after he had been in position for several months did he realize how enormous the challenge before him was. Writing to Joe Johnston in June 1863, Kirby-Smith lamented, "I have a herculean task before me on this side of the Mississippi. No army, no means; an empire in extent; no system, no order; all to be done from the beginning. I have entered upon my duties with misgivings, but believe the resources are here, and only require developing to make the department self-sustaining."[13]

Many in the South ceased calling the area the Trans-Mississippi. Instead, they now half-jokingly referred to it as Kirby-Smithdom, affirming Edmund Kirby-Smith's far-reaching impact and control over the region.[14]

Undoubtedly, one of the most significant impacts of Kirby-Smith's elevation to command was the long-running and bitter feud his transfer sparked with Maj. Gen. Richard Taylor. As we will discuss in relation to forthcoming decisions, the two men rarely saw eye to eye on anything. Throughout the

Red River Campaign, Taylor, who often believed he was a better commander than Kirby-Smith, defied his commander at crucial times during the campaign. This defiance impacted the direction of the operation on multiple levels. The argument between the two men concerning where to stand against Banks's army is a prime example. This bitterness was a hallmark of the Red River Campaign and a dark cloud that hung over Kirby-Smith's tenure of command of the Trans-Mississippi. In fairness, one must admit Taylor's personality rubbed more than a few people the wrong way, but his dislike and distrust of Edmund Kirby-Smith were legendary.[15]

Kirby-Smith's strategic policies also profoundly impacted the upcoming Red River Campaign. His insistence that Fort DeRussy on the Red was to be defended despite feedback that it was a forlorn hope is a prime example of this. Furthermore, Kirby-Smith's command style affected the coming campaign from a personnel perspective. He replaced Holmes with the equally problematic Maj. Gen. Sterling Price, influencing the campaign in Arkansas. Believing that Little Rock was too far from the region's center of gravity, Kirby-Smith made the city of Alexandria, Louisiana, his base of operations. He soon discovered Alexandria was also utterly impracticable as a base of command and subsequently moved his headquarters to Shreveport for the rest of the war. This action added to the growing list of reasons why the Union saw Shreveport as a viable operational objective, further impacting the direction of the coming campaign.[16]

In the face of all these challenges, Edmund Kirby-Smith somehow convinced his departmental commanders, who all believed they were better leaders, to cooperate and focus on throwing back the Federal invasion via the Red. Kirby-Smith was able to cobble together a combined force of around thirty-four thousand men from his entire department to meet the Union forces in Louisiana and Arkansas. Troops from the Texas, Arkansas, and Louisiana subdepartments participated in the most extensive operation west of the Mississippi. Kirby-Smith's outnumbered command eventually stopped the Union offensive designed to seize the Confederate Trans-Mississippi headquarters at Shreveport dead in its tracks, ultimately determining the campaign's outcome.[17]

Alternative Decision/Scenario

Had Davis retained Theophilus Holmes in command, we might have seen a different campaign altogether. It is safe to say that Holmes was a very different leader from Kirby-Smith, and he certainly did not have the same strategic vision as Kirby-Smith. Holmes would likely have retained his command in Little Rock instead of moving it to Shreveport. There is also evidence

Lieut. Gen. Theophilus H. Holmes, CSA, Commanding the Confederate Department of the Trans-Mississippi, Unknown, circa 1861–1865.

that he might not have been able to muster the same amount of cooperation from the scattered commands as Kirby-Smith could. We can only speculate how much the campaign might have been altered had Holmes stayed in control. Then again, Holmes's biographer Joseph G. Dawson succinctly states, "Holmes was a sincere Confederate patriot, but he often demonstrated his lack of leadership. . . . Holmes gained no credentials as a tactician, no victories as an operational commander and no favor as an administrator. . . . In the Trans-Mississippi, the Confederacy's status eroded during the months Holmes was in command."[18]

The Union Advances Up the Red River

Situation

Born in New York in 1815, Henry Wager Halleck was the son of Joseph Halleck, a veteran of the War of 1812. Entering West Point at twenty-one, Henry Halleck graduated third in the class of 1839. His classmates included five future Civil War generals—Edward Canby, Henry Hunt, James B. Ricketts, Edward Ord, and Isaac Stevens. In the prewar years, Halleck gave multiple lectures and authored several books on military professionalism and theory. His scholarly pursuits earned him the nickname "Old Brains." Later in his career, this moniker was used unflatteringly.

Shortly after the Civil War began, Halleck was given the rank of major general in the regular army in August 1861 and assigned to command the Department of the Missouri. During his time in the West, he began an uneasy relationship with Brig. Gen. Ulysses S. Grant. Halleck parlayed the Union's early success in the region into an opportunity to request overall command in the Western Theater. Impressed by Halleck's reputation as a military scholar and the recent victories in the West, President Lincoln summoned him to Washington to become general-in-chief of all the Union armies in July 1862.[19]

By the fall of 1863, many in the North presumed that the final chapters of the Civil War were finally within sight. The year began with the lingering memory of a stunning Confederate victory at Fredericksburg in December 1862, contrasted with a Confederate loss at Stones River. However, by that spring, the Confederacy saw its momentum rise as high as it ever would be. Southern hopes fed off a remarkable victory at Chancellorsville, but the bottom fell out of the cause by that summer and at Gettysburg, Vicksburg, and Port Hudson.

In the Western and Trans-Mississippi Theaters in 1863, the Union command was discussing what the next strategic move should be following the capitulation of Vicksburg and Port Hudson. While Ulysses S. Grant set his sights on Atlanta and Mobile, Halleck, acting on orders from Lincoln, still wanted an operation to advance into Texas. The general-in-chief pressed his commanders to develop a plan to these ends.

Maj. Gen. Henry W. Halleck,
John A. Scholten, circa 1860–1865,
Library of Congress Prints and
Photographs Division Washington,
DC 20540.

In the autumn of 1863, the Union's initial blueprint to support the administration's goal of conquering the Trans-Mississippi was to advance along a multipronged front. The Federals would operate in Arkansas toward Little Rock; west from Vicksburg toward Monroe, Louisiana; northwest from New Orleans into central Louisiana; and north at Sabine Pass on the Texas coast. This operation was designed to stretch Confederate resources in the Trans-Mississippi as far as possible in the impracticable task of simultaneously responding to all these advances. As a result, Union forces were expected to crush all significant pockets of resistance in the theater.[20]

Developments four hundred miles away along the banks of the Tennessee River quickly changed everything. Following a stunning defeat at Chickamauga in mid-September 1863, the Army of the Cumberland, commanded by Union major general William Rosecrans, fell back into Chattanooga. Confederate general Braxton Bragg capitalized on this dramatic victory by placing the Union army under siege, cutting off its supply lines. Forced to respond, Grant pulled units from other commands to avert another Union disaster should Chattanooga fall. Most Federal plans west of the Mississippi were consequently placed on hold. By November, Grant relieved Rosecrans, installing the aggressive Maj. Gen. George Henry Thomas in command of the Army of the Cumberland. Grant then led a successful counteroffensive that drove Bragg back thirty miles to Dalton, Georgia. As 1864 began, the specter of another Confederate defeat at the hands of U. S. Grant loomed. The Lincoln administration's gaze once again returned to Louisiana and Texas.[21]

On the verge of promotion to lieutenant general and assignment as general-in-chief, Grant contemplated a wholly unique perspective of future movements from his headquarters, now in Nashville. He wanted an advance on the Southern stronghold at Meridian, Mississippi, in preparation for the Atlanta Campaign. Meridian had a Confederate supply depot, and Grant wanted William Sherman to destroy it. Grant also desired Nathaniel Banks to operate against Mobile to support the inevitable Union advance on Atlanta in the spring, and Banks initially supported the Mobile operation. Thinking several moves ahead, Grant wanted every available unit in the area to support his preferred strategy, including men from the Department of the Gulf.[22]

Meanwhile, Henry Halleck, prodded by the president, continued to recommend that the Red River was the best path for advancing into western Louisiana and Texas. Nathaniel Banks had around thirty-five thousand to thirty-eight thousand men in his department to conduct any future campaign. However, he was hoping for reinforcements from other commands now that Chattanooga was secured.[23]

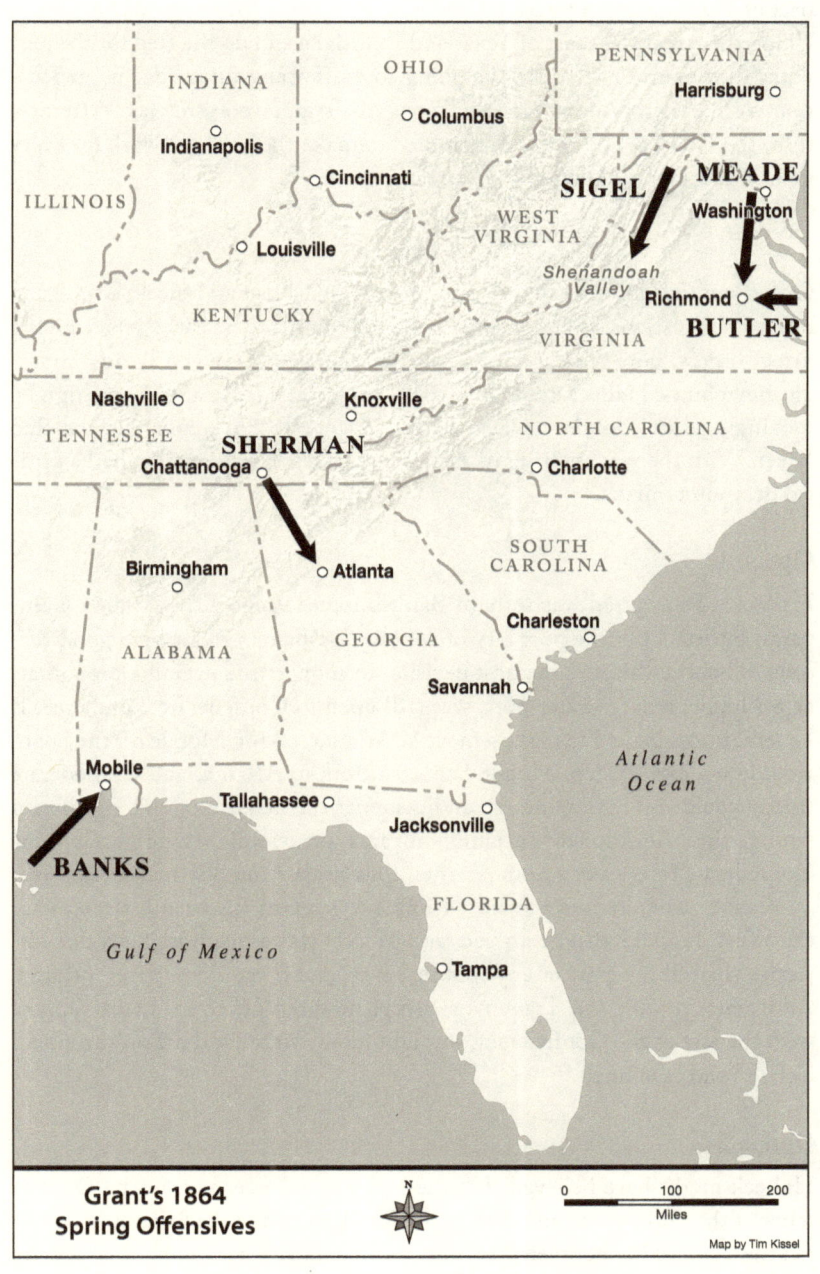

Behind Confederate lines, Dick Taylor, Edmund Kirby-Smith, and District of Texas commander Maj. Gen. John Bankhead Magruder had expected Union thrusts at the coast of Texas and Louisiana and up the Red for the past year. They planned to make the going rough for any future enemy expedition. While their resources in the Trans-Mississippi were stretched extremely thin, the Confederates were determined to make the Yankees work for every inch of territory, no matter their direction.

Options

One thousand miles away in Washington, DC, Henry Halleck, who often offered suggestions to and cajoled his field commanders rather than giving direct orders, now searched for a way to reconcile these conflicting strategic viewpoints. Halleck could have Banks support the Atlanta Campaign by moving against Mobile, or have Banks advance to Shreveport via the Red River. With the war entering its next phase, the general-in-chief had a critical decision to make.

Option 1

Halleck's first option was to have Banks's forces support the Atlanta Campaign by attacking the port city of Mobile, Alabama. There were good reasons to believe this was the best decision to support the overall Union strategy. Mobile, a deep-water port, was still open to Confederate commerce. If Federal forces looked to make a move at Atlanta, taking Mobile off the board would be a logical step. Mobile had a rail link to Atlanta, and Confederate troops could use it to reinforce and resupply the defense of this significant strongpoint. Additionally, a Union advance on Mobile would surely draw Confederate forces away from Atlanta, thus supporting Sherman's offensive.

Grant favored a move against Mobile to support his overall strategy for the West. It could also be argued that Mobile was a much higher value objective than Shreveport or any spot in Texas, and it should be given priority. Additionally, with the Trans-Mississippi now cut off from direct support with the rest of the Confederacy, it might likely wither and die on the vine if isolated and contained.[24]

Option 2

Halleck might have believed that the best use of forces within the Department of the Gulf was to advance up the Red River and take Shreveport. Politics and national policy were the most significant factors driving the idea of a campaign up the Red. Lincoln wanted Texas conquered, and he wanted it for several reasons. Not only did he believe the state was ripe for reconstruction, but the administration was also feeling pressure from French involvement in the Mexican government. The Lincoln administration believed the French installment of Ferdinand Maximilian I of Austria as a puppet emperor of Mexico signaled a prelude to European support of the Confederacy.[25]

Eastern Texas was a valuable resource for the Confederate commands in the Trans-Mississippi by this time. Communities like Marshall, Tyler, and Jefferson manufactured a variety of munitions and stockpiled arms and general supplies for the Southern war effort. A successful Union advance into Texas to destroy the facilities creating and storing these goods would significantly undermine the Southern war effort in the department.[26]

William T. Sherman was also one of the most vocal supporters of an excursion up the Red River. He supported such a move and lobbied Grant and Halleck to lead it. While we can argue that Sherman wanted to lead the campaign because of his long connection to the area, his voice had influence.[27]

Last, bonds backed by cotton financially supported the Confederate war effort. An open conduit between Texas and Mexico for the shipment of that cotton and the receipt of foreign weapons for Confederates meant that Texas, or at least its border with Mexico, had to be controlled as swiftly as possible to help extinguish the Confederates' progress on the battlefield.[28]

Decision

With the president's support, Halleck ordered Banks to begin planning for a campaign up the Red River toward Shreveport (Option 2). On January 8, 1864, Halleck, who was still general-in-chief, informed Grant that, while they all knew using Banks to move against Mobile probably made more sense militarily, an advance with Texas as the ultimate goal supported the administration's political and policy necessities.[29] On February 1, Halleck sent a message to Banks to move forward with the operation. In typical fashion, he also gave Banks the discretion not to do so if the risk was too significant. Halleck closed his message by saying, "Have you not overestimated the strength of the enemy west of the Mississippi River? All the information we can get makes the whole Confederate force under Magruder, Smith, and Price much less than ours under yourself and General Steele. Of course, you have better sources of information than we have here."[30] On February 11, the general-in-chief told Banks that it was up to him to determine a commencement date for the campaign, and that he was to communicate with Department of Arkansas commander Maj. Gen. Frederick Steele and Sherman for support and cooperation.

The Lincoln administration had three operational objectives for the Red

River Campaign. First, Banks was to destroy Confederate forces in Louisiana generally and Richard Taylor's command specifically. Second, he was to capture the state's logistically significant Confederate capital of Shreveport as a prelude to an invasion of eastern Texas. And last, Banks was empowered to seize as much Confederate cotton as he could lay his hands on.[31]

Results/Impact

The Red River Campaign, while something that Halleck and Lincoln wanted for some time, was not guaranteed. The results and impact of the decision to begin the campaign are noticeable. Halleck's verdict allowed Banks to move forward with his operation and the most critical decision that brought it about. Every decision made hereafter can be directly traced to the general-in-chief's choice. Halleck, Banks, and a reluctant Grant coordinated one of the largest combined operations yet seen in the Civil War. The campaign eventually involved the Department of the Gulf forces, including the Corps d'Afrique, some of the first Black troops to see combat for the Union.[32] The force also included three divisions from Sherman's army under the command of Brig. Gen. Andrew J. Smith, including the Mississippi Marine Brigade. In addition, the troops included three divisions from the Department of Arkansas commanded by Maj. Gen. Frederick Steele. This campaign consisted of a land force totaling approximately forty-two thousand to forty-five thousand Union men of all arms.

Moreover, Banks was to be supported by a river fleet of over one hundred vessels commanded by Rear Adm. David Dixon Porter. Porter's flotilla included ironclads, tinclads, river monitors, and other armed vessels mounting over two hundred guns. What seemed like an unstoppable force was about to descend on the patchwork Confederate commands now defending western Louisiana, Texas, and Arkansas.[33]

Alternative Decision/Scenario

Had Henry Halleck sided with Grant and convinced Lincoln that action against Mobile was the best decision, events would undoubtedly have been different. With no offensive launched against Tsaylor's army in Louisiana, history might not have recorded much from the department until the war's end, save Sterling Price's 1864 Missouri Expedition. With the Union holding the Mississippi, it was challenging for the Trans-Mississippi Confederacy to move any forces, ammunition, or supplies east of the Mississippi to support any other defensive efforts.

However, evidence suggests that Richard Taylor might have launched an operation at New Orleans, with no significant Federal presence in western

Smith's & Porter's expedition begins, Battles and Leaders of the Civil War, The Century Co., circa 1887–88, Vol. 4, p,345, New York City, New York, U.S.

Louisiana to contend with. Taylor was certainly keen to do so in 1863, and he might have seen a Union move at Mobile as an open invitation to do so again in 1864. However, General Taylor would likely have had a significantly smaller force than he mustered to defend against the combined Union Red River operation.[34]

We can only speculate about what other action might have been taken sans the Red River Campaign, whether it was a Confederate move against New Orleans or a purely defensive posture. However, the Battles of Mansfield and Pleasant Hill likely never would have occurred—or at least not as history now records them.

The Availability of A. J. Smith's Command

Situation

William Tecumseh Sherman was one of the more fascinating and controversial individuals the war produced. He has been described as impatient, irritable, depressed, petulant, headstrong, gruff, and ruthless in applying his particular brand of warfare. Sherman's failures were often just as spectacular as his successes. Despite this, the men he led often expressed enormous pride that they had served under his command.[35]

Sherman was born in 1820 in Lancaster, Ohio, to Charles Robert Sherman, a lawyer who was also a justice on the Ohio Supreme Court, and Mary Hoyt

Sherman. He was raised by a neighbor after his father's death. Attending the United States Military Academy at West Point, Sherman graduated in 1840, sixth in a class of forty-two. His graduating class included George H. Thomas, Richard S. Ewell, and Bushrod R. Johnson. After graduation, a young Sherman served in Florida, Georgia, South Carolina, and California. He resigned from the army in 1853, entering the private sector in California. In 1859, Sherman accepted the position as superintendent of the Louisiana State Seminary of Learning & Military Academy in Pineville. This institution later became Louisiana State University.[36]

Sherman had a remarkable journey during the Civil War. His first command was leading a brigade in the First Battle of Bull Run (July 1861). After that Union defeat, he was promoted to brigadier general, backdated to May, and was subsequently sent to the Department of the Cumberland. During his time in Kentucky, Sherman became increasingly cynical and depressed about the war and possibly suffered a nervous breakdown. He later admitted to having contemplated suicide.[37] By that December, Sherman had recovered and was detailed to the Department of the Mississippi until March 1862, when he was assigned to the Army of West Tennessee, leading the Fifth Division under U. S. Grant. At the Battle of Shiloh (April 1862), Sherman led this division in the bloody and hard-fought Union victory. He was promoted to major general after the engagement.

Maj. Gen. William Tecumseh Sherman, Mathew Brady, circa 1860–1865. National Archives, College Park, Maryland, 20740.

By the end of 1862, Grant had begun his campaign to capture Vicksburg, making Sherman a corps commander. Sherman's forces were defeated in December at the Battle of Chickasaw Bayou. In the spring of 1863, the bulk of Grant's forces were organized into three corps; Sherman commanded the Fifteenth Corps. When Vicksburg fell (July 1863), Sherman conducted a successful campaign to recapture the city of Jackson, Mississippi.

After the Battle of Chickamauga (September 1863), Union forces in the West were reorganized into the Military Division of the Mississippi under General Grant's command. Sherman then succeeded Grant as the head of the Army of the Tennessee. Sherman's forces were deployed to Tennessee, playing a significant role during the Union victory at Chattanooga (November 1863). Then, in February 1864, Sherman launched the Meridian Campaign as a prelude to the capture of Atlanta.[38]

As plans for the Red River Campaign began to take shape, one of the earliest strategic fundamentals decided that William T. Sherman would make part of his Army of the Tennessee available to support Banks. Ensuring that Banks had adequate numbers to succeed was paramount to Halleck and Banks. On February 16, 1864, Halleck and Grant exchanged several messages on the subject. Halleck indicated that part of Sherman's force would be available for the Red River Campaign, while Grant initially wanted Sherman to take charge if a part of his force was used. In fact, on March 2, 1864, Sherman traveled to New Orleans to confer with Banks about what such an operation might look like and whether he was to command, even though Banks technically outranked both Sherman and Grant at this particular moment.[39]

However, the Union effort faced several challenges in the West and Louisiana. First, Grant was not supportive of the Red River operation. He had divergent thoughts on Union strategy in the West, and taking Mobile was more important to him than capturing Shreveport. While he did not think the Red River operation was an excellent idea, Grant did not yet have the authority to overrule Halleck. Second, the Union high command was currently in a state of flux. By February 1864, everyone at the highest levels of the Union army knew that the bill to promote Grant to the rank of lieutenant general had been making its way through Congress since December 1863. The moment Lincoln signed this bill, Grant became the highest-ranking officer in the US Army, and it was very likely that he would then displace Halleck as general-in-chief. Would a promoted Grant use his authority to suspend the Red River operation? Only he knew the answer to that question. Last, the Union was planning to commence multiple operations once spring came. Having the manpower to cover all of these was no minor issue. Grant was likely concerned that the Red River operation might siphon much-needed troops, ammunition, and supplies from more critical operations in other theaters.[40]

In a message dated February 18, Grant ordered Sherman to supply men to support the Red River operation. However, Grant also told his lieutenant that he would likely lose these men from his command if he (Sherman) did not lead the campaign. Nevertheless, Halleck was unlikely to assign the position to Sherman, as Banks was the president's preferred choice. Determining that he was not interested in participating in the Red River Campaign if he had to answer to Banks, Sherman agreed to make forces available to support the operation.[41]

Options

To support the campaign in Louisiana, Sherman had two options. He could loan Banks the men he needed without restriction, or inform Banks that there was a time limit on their availability and hope Banks complied. With the fate of the operation possibly hanging in the balance, William T. Sherman had a critical decision to make.

Option 1

Sherman could allocate the needed forces without restrictions. Grant was not yet promoted, so he had no guarantee that Banks would agree to return them. Sherman and all the commanders in the West knew that Banks had a direct line to the president, and they had to tolerate this political general for the time being. Sherman might do as he was ordered and hope for the best. In his March 4 communication to Banks, he indicated his men should be returned by April 15. Incidentally, Sherman also told Frederick Steele that he believed Kirby-Smith would fall back to Texas once he saw three Union columns deciding on his position. Perhaps Sherman thought a swift Union victory was inevitable and no strict timeline was needed.[42]

Option 2

Sherman might insist on a time limit for the use of his men. He still had some pull within the army's hierarchy, and there seems to have been some consensus that come spring, Sherman would need these men back as he made his advance on Atlanta. In his February 16 communication, Halleck said as much to Grant, stating, "It was understood that as soon as Steele and Banks had effected a junction on that river, Sherman's army could all be withdrawn to operate east of the Mississippi."[43]

Decision

After several messages back and forth, Sherman agreed to provide a force to Banks (Option 2). He did so with the caveats that the troops not go beyond Shreveport, that they operate with Admiral Porter's fleet exclusively, and that they be returned thirty days after entering the Red, or by April 15.[44] This force consisted of the First and Third Divisions of the Sixteenth Corps and the Second Division of the Seventeenth Corps—these combined divisions under Brig. Gen. Andrew Jackson Smith totaled roughly ten thousand tough and experienced midwesterners. Smith was considered one of the best division commanders in Sherman's army, and his men had a reputation as hard and lean fighters. They would inject much-needed experience into the otherwise relatively untested forces of the Department of the Gulf.[45]

Results/Impact

This decision is interesting to discuss and debate because it is challenging to pinpoint the decision maker.

From the moment the notion of Sherman sending troops to support Banks was floated, conversations began concerning how many men would go and how long they would be absent from the Army of the Tennessee. All indications point to Lincoln's administration pushing for an advance up the Red, and the president made his wishes known to Halleck. In his February 16 message to Grant, Halleck mentioned a time limit on the force Sherman would send. Two days later, on February 18, Grant wrote to Sherman, "I can give no positive orders that you send no troops up Red River, but what I do want is their speedy return if they do go, and that the minimum number necessary be sent." Banks told Sherman on March 2 that Sherman should equip the force he was sending with enough supplies for a thirty-day operation, indicating he had some time limit in mind as well. However, Sherman seemed the most vocal and adamant about a limitation for using his troops. In his book *Through the Howling Wilderness*, a noted expert on the campaign, Dr. Gary Joiner, also points to Sherman as the decision-maker.[46]

Irrespective of the identity of the decision-maker, the choice's impact on the campaign was keenly felt. Banks made several critical decisions with this imposed deadline, as he feared losing these troops before Shreveport could be secured. After arriving in Alexandria, Louisiana, on March 24, Banks received a startling message from U. S. Grant. The new general-in-chief basically told Banks that he might have to abandon his expedition if he could not return the forces to Sherman by the date specified. Fearing his chance for glory was in jeopardy, Banks accelerated his heretofore-leisurely pace of advance. As a result of this decision, Banks was now making other decisions that he might not have made otherwise.

After reaching Grand Ecore on April 3, Banks, under a severe time crunch, moved his line of march away from the Red River to a road farther west. He believed advancing on a line closer to the river might needlessly delay his approach to Shreveport. This action altered the campaign's timeline and put it on a new course, another critical decision we will discuss later. Shifting the line of march also went a long way in determining the time and place for the future battles at Mansfield and Pleasant Hill. Had Banks been under less pressure to complete his operation sooner rather than later, he might have decided on an advance closer to the Red River. In that case, these key battles might never have happened. As it turns out, circumstances dictated that A.J. Smith and his command should remain with Banks until the end of the campaign. This self-imposed Union deadline was one of the most critical decisions made by either side, casting a die for the course of future events—one that was dramatically different than it had been before.[47] As will also be discussed in relation to a future decision, Andrew Jackson Smith's actions played a crucial role in the campaign, including the Union tactical victory at Pleasant Hill.

Alternative Decision/Scenario

Let us suppose for a moment that Sherman believed the men he was sending would not impact his upcoming campaign, or that Banks would be reluctant to return them. Without this deadline, Banks might conceivably have continued his slow and deliberate pace to Shreveport, and possibly closer to the Red and his naval support. While any number of alternative outcomes are possible, there is little doubt that with this alteration, the Battles of Mansfield and Pleasant Hill would not have happened as we remember. Furthermore, we might also speculate how the war might have been altered had Smith remained in the Trans-Mississippi for the balance of the conflict. Later, in 1864, Smith and his command featured prominently in the Battle of Tupelo in July and the Battle of Nashville in December.[48]

The Confederates Divert the Red River

Situation

Born in Augusta, Georgia, William Robertson Boggs descended from a Revolutionary War veteran, his maternal great-grandfather. Showing an interest in the military and engineering at an early age, Boggs entered West Point

The Red River near Alexandria, Louisiana, Author, Modern Image.

in 1849. Graduating fourth out of a class of fifty-two in 1853, he could count among his classmates men such as James B. McPherson, Philip H. Sheridan, John M. Schofield, and John Bell Hood. After graduation, Second Lieutenant Boggs served as a topographical engineer and then in the Ordnance Corps, completing assignments all over the republic, including the far-flung frontiers of Texas and Louisiana. Joining the Confederate army after Georgia seceded, Boggs rose steadily through the ranks, eventually assigned to Edmund Kirby-Smith's staff in August 1862. Promoted to brigadier general, he followed Kirby-Smith to the Trans-Mississippi, becoming his chief of staff. Knowing the thirty-five-year-old general's skill as an engineer, Kirby-Smith at once set Boggs to work improving the defensive fortifications and obstacles up and down the Red River.[49]

Boggs was among the most talented engineers the Confederacy ever produced. His fortifications along the Red and his understanding of the use of topography for defensive warfare provided a master class in military engineering. After the war, Boggs became a highly regarded professor of mechanics at the Virginia Polytechnic Institute, more commonly known today as Virginia Tech.[50]

However, as the weeks passed, William Boggs found himself increasingly amid the constant quarreling between his commander and Richard Taylor. Taylor and Kirby-Smith held vastly different philosophies on warfare and how best to thwart any Union advance up the Red River Valley. Kirby-Smith favored a solid defensive posture anchored by strong fixed fortifications. At

Brig. Gen. William Robertson Boggs, CSA—Unknown, circa 1861–1865, https://web.archive.org/web/20071108021535/http://www.generalsandbrevets.com/sgb/boggs.htm.

the same time, Taylor's highly mobile fighting style, likely influenced by Stonewall Jackson, was at odds with any notion of static defense.[51]

From the Union perspective, the Red River was one of the main factors determining when Federal forces could launch their campaign at Louisiana's Confederate capital of Shreveport. The Red often ran shallow and was not navigable up to Shreveport during the winter. But it typically rose several feet in March and April with the ubiquitous spring rains. This seasonality was essential to Union plans, as Adm. David Dixon Porter's deep-draft vessels needed additional clearance to navigate up the river and accompany the Union land forces to Shreveport.[52]

Even before Edmund Kirby-Smith arrived in the Trans-Mississippi, Confederate efforts to frustrate an expected Union thrust up the Red River had been underway since 1862. However, preparations escalated dramatically once Kirby-Smith and his staff reached Louisiana. The Confederates knew the Yankees had the resources to bring a massive flotilla to support any advance. This force could easily tip the scales in the upcoming campaign, as the Confederates had nothing to match it. In just over twelve months, Boggs oversaw the installation of more than a dozen forts, artillery positions, strongpoints, and river obstructions from Fort DeRussy below Alexandria all the way northwest to the outskirts of Shreveport. The Confederate defenders even sunk a large side-wheeler, the 880-ton *New Falls City*, in the river about a dozen miles downstream of Shreveport.

While all these defensive points proved challenging for the Union to overcome, Boggs had a truly inspired idea at a bend in the river just below Shreveport. In 1851, a somewhat disagreeable local planter named James Gilmer dug what came to be known as Tones Bayou. He planned to build a town below Shreveport and make it a competing shipping hub by diverting the flow of the Red into the bayou. Before the war, Louisiana state officials blocked this diversion, leaving the dam in place. Boggs, who knew the local history, realized that should the Tones Bayou dam be removed, as much as 75 percent of the Red River's flow could be redirected—like a plug pulled on a bathtub's drain.[53]

Options

While ingenious, the plan was not without downsides. And the Confederates had to ask themselves whether the project's results were worth the effort. Kirby-Smith could order Boggs to move forward with his plan, or he could rely on the existing defensive works to do the job. Advised by his talented chief of staff, the commander had a critical decision to make.

Option 1

Kirby-Smith and Boggs could implement the plan of diverting the Red, knowing it added to the layered defenses already in place. Those defenses were solid, but there was merit in the project. While Confederate forces were unsure of the exact number of vessels the Yankee navy would sortie against them, they undoubtedly believed it substantial. Based on this, any course that prevented that fleet from reaching Shreveport was justified. The results could be catastrophic if Union gunboats managed to reach this key city. Shreveport was not only the current seat of the displaced Confederate Louisiana state government, but also the main Confederate supply depot in the Trans-Mississippi. Draining the river to a limited flow might guarantee the city's safety from Adm. David Dixon Porter's Union flotilla.

Option 2

Kirby-Smith could decide that diverting the river had too many shortcomings to risk. While the Red River was a possible and likely avenue of invasion for the Federals, it also was an essential transportation tool for the Confederates. In 1864, this part of Louisiana had few "modern" roads, even by contemporary standards. West of the Mississippi, most roads in the state were little more

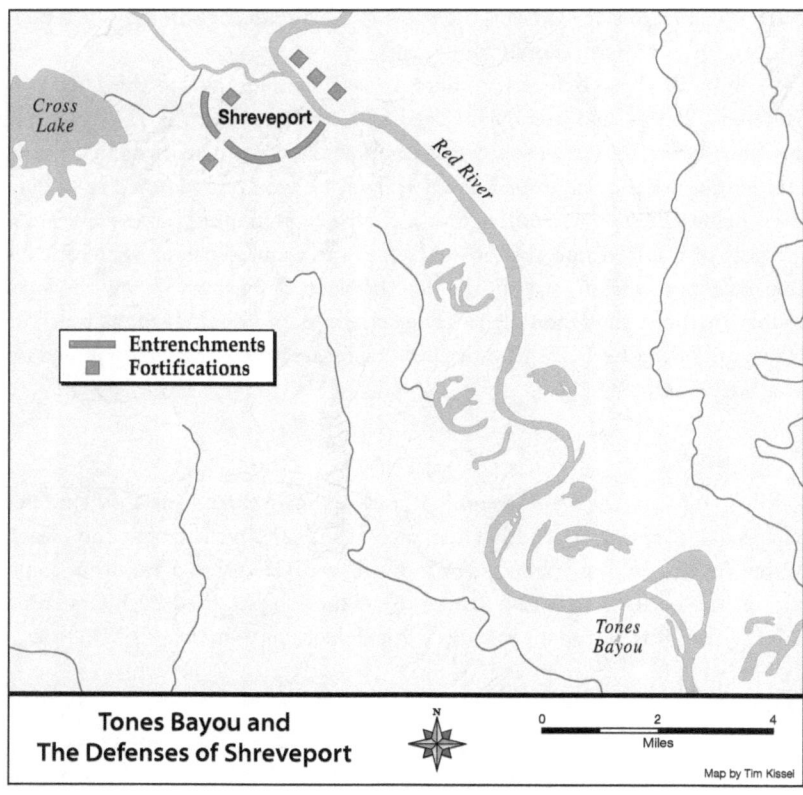

than dirt farm lanes that quickly transformed into bottomless muddy quagmires anytime it rained. Additionally, in the whole of the Trans-Mississippi, railroad mileage was virtually nonexistent, and no railroad connected Shreveport to any location southeast.

Before the war, the Red River was the most reliable means of transporting goods and people through the nearly three hundred miles of piney woods, bayous, and swampland in western Louisiana. Shutting down the river's flow just below Shreveport would severely limit the Confederates' ability to move troops and supplies up and down the river, just as it would the Yankees'. Kirby-Smith had to ask himself who might benefit most by restricting the navigation of the Red River, his army or Banks's.[54]

Decision

Kirby-Smith and Boggs were convinced the scheme was worth the risk and removed the dam that blocked the Red from flowing into Tones Bayou (Option 2). As the campaign began, the befuddled Union fleet waiting for the river to rise was astounded as, day after day, the level of the Red dropped to alarming levels.

Results/Impact

The results of the Boggs plan were far-reaching and decisive. While it is unclear how far the Union fleet might have advanced up the Red had the Confederates left the Tones Bayou dam intact, the action was essential to the campaign's outcome. The decision added to Union delays as the navy sat idle and waited for the river to rise. While other factors contributed, the shallow-running river prevented Porter and his fleet from advancing further than Loggy Bayou, about twenty miles below Shreveport. This meant Porter would never be able to move his fleet in a position to support any future attack on the city by Banks. Restricting the Union fleet also meant Porter's added firepower could not be brought to bear against any Confederate strongpoints, ensuring this massive fleet had little material impact on the campaign's outcome. The exceptions were the time, effort, and resources the Union army and navy spent dealing with multiple grounded vessels during the expedition. This action also confirmed that the Red River Campaign was to be primarily decided by infantry actions and not by overwhelming Union naval strength. Additionally, it took Porter several days to get his fleet turned around and safely back to Alexandria once Banks retreated. The forces then found they could go no further, exposing Porter's fleet to additional attacks from Confederate forces.[55]

Alternative Decision/Scenario

Had Boggs and Smith determined to keep the Tones Bayou dam in place, any number of alternatives could have been possible. With the ability to advance farther up the Red, Porter and his fleet might have reached as far as Shreveport, placing the city under siege. Even if Union gunboats were never able to attack Shreveport, just being in proximity of it might have altered the campaign. Assume that Banks had still advanced on the same road and fought a battle at Mansfield, but the Union fleet had advanced far enough to threaten the city. It would then be reasonable to assume Taylor might have detached a significant Confederate force to deal with Admiral Porter's flotilla. Would this, in turn, have affected the outcome of this critical battle?

USS *Eastport* Converted Ironclad, Unknown, circa 1863.

The Command of the Union Operation

Situation

When Union leadership began to plan for an operation up the Red River, conversations, ideas, and speculations on who its overall commander should and would be abounded. While the Red River Campaign was not the largest in terms of overall manpower that the Union conducted during the war, it covered a remote and vast geographic area. This presented unique obstacles to Federal command and control. Given the size and scope of the operation, it made sense to have a single individual in overall command.

Additionally, communication between the wildly dispersed Union departments in the Trans-Mississippi was unreliable on good days and almost impossible on bad ones. For example, messages often took days or even weeks to reach New Orleans from the War Department in Washington, DC. Communication between Steele's forces in Arkansas and Banks's forces in Louisiana was often more problematic and tenuous.

The proposed operation presented other unique challenges. On the Union side, the massive campaign required the coordination of forces from three separate departments and a schedule that necessitated units' simultaneous arrival at designated locations. The Red River expedition included troops from the Gulf, Arkansas, and Mississippi Departments, as well as the navy, which had its own internal communication challenges. Recent history demonstrated to the Federals that the larger the campaign, the greater the need for a single overall commander. The Vicksburg and Chattanooga operations were successes for the Union partially because one man (Grant) was in overall command, and because Grant, Sherman, and Porter had established solid working relationships by then.[56]

One influencing factor was that the Union command was in flux in early 1864. Grant's pending promotion to lieutenant general and likely supplanting of Halleck as general-in-chief put both men at a disadvantage. Grant did not yet have full authority to direct overall strategy, and Halleck was gradually becoming more hesitant to make changes that Grant might overturn. Additionally, Halleck was growing increasingly frustrated with a position he claimed to have never wanted in the first place. Additionally, believing Banks was the president's preferred choice, both men were disinclined to make a call that might displace him in favor of a more qualified general.

In a February 16 letter to Sherman, Halleck wrote, "I shall most cordially welcome him [Grant] to the command, glad to be relieved from so thankless and disagreeable a position. I took it against my will and shall be most happy to leave it as soon as another is designated to fill it."[57] The next day, Halleck wrote Grant a lengthy letter that seemed to be a preliminary handoff of duties. Halleck's communication that summarized all the current Union

U. S. Grant at his Cold Harbor, Va., Headquarters. United States, Egbert Guy Fowx, circa 1864. Library of Congress Prints and Photographs Division Washington, DC 20540.

operations ended with a statement that can be interpreted as relinquishing his authority: "As before remarked, I presume, under the authority of the President, the final decision of these questions will be referred to you."[58] U. S. Grant, who was never very keen about the proposed Red River operation, was even less enthusiastic about Banks's military skills. On February 18, he also wrote Sherman, asserting, "I have so little confidence in his [Banks's] ability to command that I would not want the responsibility of entrusting men with him, without positive orders to do so."[59]

Until the official word from the president and Congress on Grant's promotion came down, the command decision ultimately fell to Halleck.

Options

With the Red River Campaign now imminent, Halleck had four options. He could put Banks, Sherman, or some other general officer in command, or he could appoint no overall commander and hope for the best. With lives and the campaign's success possibly hanging in the balance, the general-in-chief faced a critical decision.

Option 1

General Halleck could decide that Nathaniel Banks was the best choice for the job, despite misgivings about his abilities. Banks was currently the highest-ranking general in the theater, and the commander-in-chief, Abraham Lincoln, personally selected him to lead this department. Though he lacked any military education, Banks had several West Point–trained officers around him. In an ideal scenario, he could rely on the input of these men to help make the campaign a success. This, of course, is the decision Banks favored. His desire for glory drove his belief that he was the best person for the job. Conversely, Halleck knew Banks's primary mission in Louisiana was political. Given this fact, he might have believed Banks's political activities were too distracting for a man responsible for coordinating such a large operation.

Notably, few regular army officers had faith in Banks's ability. Halleck and Grant privately expressed that they believed Banks incompetent and not suited for command. Porter was also not a fan of Banks. He doubtless got feedback from his adoptive brother David G. Farragut, a vocal critic of how the political general managed the Port Hudson affair. This was likely all the proof Porter needed to distrust Nathaniel Banks. Having Banks in command of or collaborating with officers who did not respect his abilities might set the stage for disaster.[60]

Option 2

Halleck could determine that William T. Sherman was the best choice. Sherman had become a close confidant of Henry Halleck and was one of the rising stars among the cadre of Union generals. He was aggressive and experienced in combined operations. From the moment this campaign was conceived, Sherman had expressed a desire to lead it. In 1859, he accepted a job as superintendent of the Louisiana State Seminary of Learning & Military Academy in Pineville, just across the river from Alexandria. As a result, he was intimately familiar with the challenges geography played in any such campaign up the Red.[61]

Then again, Grant had other plans for Sherman that did not include an extended campaign in Louisiana. Grant set his sights on the Confederate stronghold of Atlanta, Georgia, and what was left of Bragg's Army of Tennessee, now commanded by Joseph Johnston. Grant was unlikely to allow his best general to go floating up the Red in a campaign he believed was of no military value while there was more strategically vital work to be done in Georgia.[62]

Option 3

Halleck might conclude that looking to another officer made the most sense. While it would be a bit of a stretch, he could recommend that Banks place another officer in charge of the operation. In the early spring of 1864, Banks was deeply engaged in civilian politics. Louisiana was about to hold an election for a new governor, and Banks's job was to ensure the right man was elected. Given this distraction, Halleck might advise that another officer lead the campaign in his stead. A brief list of candidates might include Maj. Gen. William Franklin, Brig. Gen. Charles Stone, or Maj. Gen. Frederick Steele. In a February 18 communication to Sherman, even U. S. Grant expressed his hope that Banks would choose another man to head the operation, even suggesting Maj. Gen. John A. McClernand as a possible candidate.[63]

Option 4

Finally, Halleck could place no one man in charge of the operation and encourage all parties to cooperate toward a common goal. Given the current political climate, this might be a safe choice for Halleck. It would not create unnecessary drama or consternation, and it would allow each department to determine its best course of action. For example, in most combined army/navy operations, one branch was not given authority over the other; it was assumed that cooperation and the professionalism of the officers would prevail.

One hallmark of Halleck's tenure as general-in-chief was his tendency to suggest actions rather than issuing direct orders to his subordinates. This might have been a way for him to avoid blame should the actions lead to disaster. By avoiding the decision altogether, he could distance himself from responsibility. Halleck also had to consider another factor. Given the communication difficulties, it would be challenging for one man to exert authority over the entire Red River operation. Messages between Steele and Banks sometimes took over a week to arrive. This fact alone might convince Halleck that assigning an individual to the operation's command might be impracticable.

Last, more than a few senior Union officers believed the Confederates in western Louisiana were not up to the task before them. They erroneously speculated that once the two separate columns of Steele and Banks closed in on them, the Confederates in and around Shreveport would cut and run into Texas. If Halleck shared this belief, the need for an overall commander was diminished and less critical.[64]

Of course, the downside of such a decision is apparent. Halleck must have known how unpopular Banks was with regular army officers. The idea that they voluntarily cooperate with a man whose abilities they did not respect would seem to be an overly optimistic assessment on Halleck's part.

Decision

Halleck decided to place no one individual in charge (Option 4). Instead, he ordered each department commander to cooperate with the others. The most extensive campaign ever conducted west of the Mississippi would succeed or fail depending on the level of collaboration and communication of three independent commands. Incidentally, when Grant was promoted and made general-in-chief, he made no real effort to reverse Halleck's decision.

Results/Impact

The results of Halleck's decision were noticeable. As the campaign moved forward, it became a series of uncoordinated moves among the Union units taking part. Each commander had to act on faith that his counterparts were all working from the same plan. The Confederate army took full advantage of this lack of coordination, which negated the benefit of overwhelming Union manpower. Without a cohesive and specific strategy, the Confederates could respond to one Federal threat and then the other. As a result, Kirby-Smith was able to bring a more significant force to bear on Banks's army at Mansfield than he might have otherwise been able to. Subsequently, once Banks fell back after the clash at Pleasant Hill, Kirby-Smith relocated elements from that action north to deal with Steele's army. A lack of a single Union commander certainly contributed to this result.

Moreover, as Porter and A.J. Smith advanced up the Red River ahead of Banks's command, they made several decisions without informing Banks. Seizing Confederate cotton and burning private property are but two examples of this.[65]

Additionally, it is unclear what role Steele's forces were to play. Was his incursion from Arkansas designed to support Banks's advance and draw Confederate forces away, or was his mission to capture Shreveport? If Banks had been in charge of the entire operation, it is reasonable to assume he would have clarified his expectations to Steele. As he became bogged down in southern Arkansas, Steele eventually learned of the retreat of Banks's command on April 18, ten days after Banks and his forces had fallen back from Pleasant Hill.[66]

Alternative Decision/Scenario

Conversely, we might have seen a different campaign had Halleck placed Banks in overall command. Had Banks been able to issue direct orders to Porter and Steele, the campaign might have ended differently. Not enthusiastic about contributing to the offensive and even less so about working with Banks, Steele clearly dragged his feet. It is reasonable to assume that if he had had authority over Steele, Banks could have better controlled this

Mansfield State Historic Site, Mansfield, Louisiana, Author, Modern Image.

disjointed operation, possibly altering its outcome. Banks, in his appearance before the Joint Committee on the Conduct of the War, testified, "The difficulty regarding this expedition was that nobody assumed to give orders; each commander acted for himself."[67]

Banks Remains in New Orleans

Situation

Nathaniel P. Banks was, by definition, the most political of the political generals Lincoln promoted during the Civil War. That is to say, his skills as a politician far outweighed his talents as a commanding general. This goes a long way to explain why Lincoln selected Banks for this role in the first place. Banks knew this and was more than happy to accommodate and further the administration's political goals along with his own. If he had been exposed to Carl von Clausewitz's concept that war is politics by other means, Nathaniel Banks might likely have agreed. Familiar with the Prussian general's theories or not, Banks was determined to shape the politics of Louisiana by the force of his own will, even at the expense of military necessity.

Arriving in New Orleans on December 14, 1862, Banks spent much of 1863 cleaning up the mess his predecessor, Ben Butler, left for him in the Crescent

President Abraham Lincoln Seated, Gardner, A. & Brady's National Photographic Portrait Galleries circa 1862, Library of Congress Prints and Photographs Division Washington, DC 20540.

City. In addition to reorganizing the military forces in the Department of the Gulf, Banks labored to establish trust with the local citizenry by releasing political prisoners and tamping down on the corruption that was rampant in occupied New Orleans. These actions proved only marginally successful.

Banks did effectively implement President Lincoln's December 1863 Proclamation of Amnesty and Reconstruction. Lincoln's reconstruction plan for conquered Southern states was fundamental. As each Confederate state capitulated, the Union worked to hold local elections. The Federal officials charged with oversight, often in the military or backed up by it, always supported the pro-Union/pro-Lincoln candidates for key political positions. Additionally, if 10 percent of a particular state's citizens who voted in the 1860 election took a loyalty oath, and a new state constitution was adopted, that state could be readmitted to the Union. If this could be accomplished in Louisiana before the 1864 election, Lincoln could count another state's electoral votes all but in his pocket.[68]

By early March 1864, and after much delay, all the pieces on the Union side of the board were nearly in place, and the time had come to launch the campaign. Because of the time limit placed on the use of A.J. Smith's command and the War Department's insistence that the operation begin at once, Banks was under pressure to get moving. It was agreed that Banks and his command would meet Smith's force and Porter's fleet at Alexandria, Louisiana, about 165 air miles northwest of New Orleans, on March 17.

The Red River Campaign officially began on March 6, 1864, when Smith's command received orders to depart Vicksburg for the scheduled rendezvous with Banks at Alexandria. Smith and his force left four days later and were the first infantry to meet with Porter's fleet at the mouth of the Red. On March 12, the combined forces entered the Red River. As they advanced, an overarching sense of optimism and confidence accompanied the Union soldiers and sailors.[69]

Delayed by weather and poor communication, Banks's cavalry and the Union Thirteenth and Nineteenth Corps of the Department of the Gulf did not assemble at Brashear City (present-day Morgan City) near the mouth of the Atchafalaya River until March 7. These troops did not begin their advance until the following day. To reach Alexandria, their first objective, in nine days, these units had to march over 150 miles on narrow and rutted country roads through swampland and the unforgiving Cajun prairie. The whole of Banks's force would not arrive at the rendezvous point until March 26, twenty days after the official start of the campaign.[70]

For Porter and Smith, the initial moves of the campaign were efficiently carried off. The first objective was to capture Fort DeRussy near Marksville,

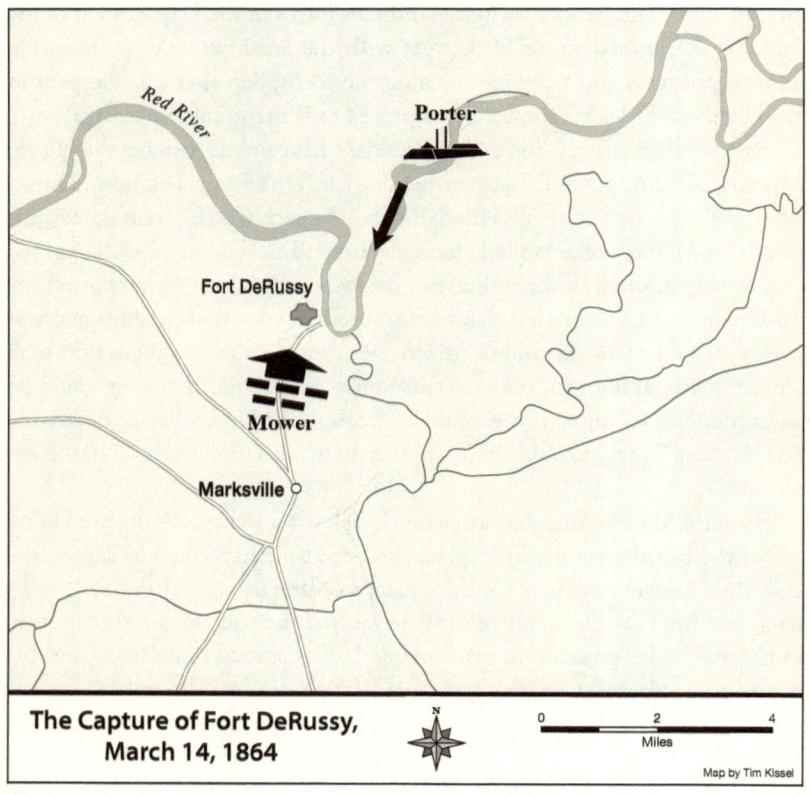

The Capture of Fort DeRussy, March 14, 1864

about thirty miles downstream of Alexandria. Confederate major general John G. Walker and his 3,800 Texas Greyhounds were able to contest the advance. However, Richard Taylor ordered his units to fall back. Taylor would pick the time and place to consolidate his forces and confront the Union advance. The three hundred Confederate defenders of DeRussy did not get the message and were subsequently captured. As the Yankees pushed forward, they cleared river obstacles, and Confederate pockets of resistance melted away. Fort DeRussy fell to Union forces on March 14, and Taylor subsequently abandoned Alexandria. And the city was occupied by Federal troops two days later, with barely a shot fired. After that, not much went right for Banks and the ill-fated campaign.[71]

Meanwhile, in New Orleans, Nathaniel Banks, who had spent the better part of a year preparing for this day, was as busy as ever. His staff was firing off messages and working diligently to have all the logistical elements in place. Banks, however, was distracted by other matters. George Michael Decker Hahn, whom he enthusiastically supported, won the governorship of Union-controlled Louisiana on February 22 with almost 60 percent of the vote. This crucial political victory was one to be savored. Hahn's inauguration scheduled for March 4 needed to be a spectacle equal to that victory if Banks had anything to say about it.[72]

Options

Politician Banks now collided and conflicted with General Banks. Banks could immediately join his forces, preparing to move against Shreveport, or he could stay in New Orleans to bask in his political achievements. Nathaniel Banks had a critical decision to make.

Option 1

Banks might conclude that remaining in New Orleans to celebrate his political victory was not the most crucial task of the moment. Lack of coordination within the loosely organized combined Union forces might create complications. If Banks realized this, he might determine that his presence in the field was a priority. The sheer scope of what he was undertaking could make him realize a skilled managerial and organizational hand was required for success. Additionally, one thing Banks should have learned in his tenure in Louisiana was that campaigning in the wilds of the state's interior was tremendously challenging on the best of days. Did it make sense to delegate this task to one of his lieutenants with so much riding on the outcome of the campaign? Last, Banks had actively lobbied Halleck to make him the operation's overall commander. Based on this fact, it would seem he placed some value on having the forces in the field competently led.

Option 2

Banks could determine that celebrating a political campaign whose planning and execution had taken several months was most important. From Banks's point of view, politics and the theater that accompanied it were critical to his mission. Thus, carrying out the president's reconstruction mandate was vital to reunifying the country. As a seasoned political figure, Banks knew pomp and circumstance were all part of the self-promotion successful political men savored. His staff and senior commanders were all experienced soldiers, and they could no doubt be trusted with the essentials of the opening moves of the campaign. Additionally, since Banks did not expect a significant battle with the enemy until his army reached Shreveport, he might reasonably assume a delayed departure would not adversely affect his military objectives.[73]

Decision

Banks decided to stay in New Orleans and revel in Hahn's victory, which was really his own victory (Option 2). The celebration was all the general had hoped for. On inauguration day, a banner behind the grandstand read, "Major General Banks, Hero of Port Hudson." A band of three hundred musicians played the "Anvil Chorus" while accompanied by fireworks, and a children's choir sang his praises. Banks estimated that fifty thousand people attended the event. Writing to Halleck, he proudly exclaimed, "I have never witnessed such a spectacle elsewhere."[74]

Banks, aboard his transport/command vessel *Black Hawk*, arrived in Alexandria on March 25 in a celebratory mood, two weeks after the campaign began. Tagging along with him was a cadre of reporters and cotton speculators. Almost instantly upon arrival, Banks's attention was diverted again as his forces marched toward Shreveport days later. At the end of March, he called for elections in Alexandria and Grand Ecore.[75]

Results/Impact

While it can be argued that Banks was merely fulfilling his mandate from the administration by ensuring the Union's political control of the area, the decision had a noticeable and far-reaching effect. When Banks arrived in Alexandria, he and the cotton speculators he had in tow were shocked to discover the Union navy and the Mississippi Marine Brigade had already grabbed all the cotton Richard Taylor's forces had not already burned. Banks had no authority over these units, so he could not order him to give it up. Aboard his flag vessel, also named *Black Hawk*, Porter became incensed when he learned Banks had given the same name to his command vessel. With Porter convinced this was a deliberate slight by the political general, tensions grew between the two men.

Moreover, the delays by Banks set the timeline for upcoming battles and provided Taylor and Kirby-Smith additional time to gather the scattered forces they would not have had otherwise. Banks's decision meant the size of the enemy force his army would eventually face, was significantly larger. For example, the bulk of Green's Texas cavalry left Hemphill, Texas, on April 4 and did not arrive at Mansfield until the seventh. The men of Green's Command not only played a significant role in postponing their Union counterparts on the seventh, but they were also crucial to the outcome of the battle fought the next day. This same battle fought a week earlier would have been missing a considerable number of Texas troopers in Green's Command, perhaps as many as 2,500 men. The delay also allowed Hamilton P. Bee's command from as far away as Matagorda Bay, Texas, to arrive in time to bolster Taylor's army. This time frame set for the campaign and upcoming engagements all but ensured that Banks's army would be stopped short of its goal, and that events would happen on the date history now records.[76]

Alternative Decision/Scenario

Had Banks forgone the political part of his assignment and focused solely on the military mission, the campaign might have ended differently. Even if Banks still moved his march away from the Red, had he done so a week earlier, he might have faced a different Confederate force. With the gift of time Banks's delays afforded them, Confederate commanders assembled a more significant force than they might have otherwise. Would an earlier timeline have tipped the scales in favor of the Union and enabled Federal forces to reach Shreveport? We can only speculate on what the Battle of Mansfield would have looked like if it had been fought one week sooner.

The Inauguration of George Michael Decker Hahn, - C.E.H. Bonwill, *Frank Leslie's Illustrated Newspaper*, v. 18, no. 444 (1864 April 2), pp. 24–25. Library of Congress Washington, DC 20540.

Banks Changes His Line of March

Situation

To support the campaign's objectives, Nathaniel Banks envisioned an advance up the Red River with Adm. David Dixon Porter's heavily armed and armored fleet at his side. The caliber of the Union navy's guns certainly favored the Federal forces. Having comparatively few heavy guns at their disposal, Kirby-Smith and Dick Taylor would be wholly outmatched by the superior firepower of the Union brown-water fleet, as it was often described. In fact, advancing at Shreveport via the Red River only made sense if the Federals could use the added firepower of Porter's fleet. Also, each of these elements, infantry and navy, depended on the other for support. The infantry guarded against enemy shore attacks and general harassment of the fleet. At the same time, the navy provided efficient transportation for troops and their supplies and brought large-caliber artillery to the operation that was impractical to transport overland. Moreover, as U. S. Grant learned in the Wilderness later that spring, fighting a battle in a densely wooded area with few roads could quickly negate any manpower advantage one army might have over another.

Given these factors, Banks's decision to detach from naval support stands out as the one that, in hindsight, significantly exposes his inability to grasp fundamental military acumen.

On April 3, after weeks of delay, Banks, Porter, and A.J. Smith had all their forces and vessels concentrated at Grand Ecore, a few miles northeast of Natchitoches and fifty miles upstream of Alexandria. Due to the shallowness of the river and the falls above the city, Porter could only get thirteen of his gunboats and thirty transport vessels above Alexandria. However, the Union's combined force was now within striking distance of Shreveport. Banks's and Smith's commands could count approximately twenty thousand infantry and cavalry and seventy-six artillery pieces in and around Natchitoches. Conversely, Richard Taylor, scrambling to gather every man he could lay his hands on, assembled a Confederate force that would eventually number just under nine thousand to meet them. With each passing day, the likelihood of a significant clash grew as the two forces gathered, and the distance between them closed.[77]

From the Union's perspective, circumstances altered the situation rather dramatically. The week before, in Alexandria, Banks received a startling communication from the new general-in-chief, Lieut. Gen. Ulysses S. Grant. Grant, who never considered the Red River expedition worthwhile, told Banks that he was to capture Shreveport as soon as possible. If Banks did not

Fortifications at Grand Ecore, Guarded by The First Missouri Battery, C. E. H. Bonwill, circa 1864, The Historic New Orleans Collection, Williams Research Center New Orleans, LA 70130.

complete this objective by the end of April, Grant indicated that he was to return Smith's force to Sherman regardless. Additionally, the general-in-chief ordered Banks to only garrison a captured Shreveport and return the bulk of his troops to New Orleans to support a move at Mobile. Last, Banks was not to advance into Texas.[78]

Banks was no doubt stunned by this communication, which suddenly altered the objectives and timeline for the campaign. His leisurely pace so far was abruptly working against him. This, combined with all the delays in the movement, added more pressure on the already struggling Union commander. In his *Through the Howling Wilderness*, historian Gary Joiner describes Banks as a man now "obsessed by time schedules and orders of march."[79]

This now brings us to one Wellington W. Withenbury. A self-described "steamboat-man," Withenbury had worked on the Red River for twenty-five years and was considered an expert river pilot. In the Red River Campaign narrative, Withenbury was something of an enigma. It is not entirely clear whether he was a Confederate spy, a "Union man," or simply a self-interested businessman eager to keep his personal stockpile of cotton safe from Confederates who wanted to burn it and Federals who wanted to confiscate it. Whatever his motivation, it can be definitively stated that he was an influential figure concerning one critical decision and possibly more.[80]

It was during his stay in Alexandria that Banks first encountered Withenbury. The river pilot had been advising Adm. Porter about the details of the Red River above and below Alexandria. Withenbury was an expert on the river's depth at specific locations and natural obstacles the fleet needed to

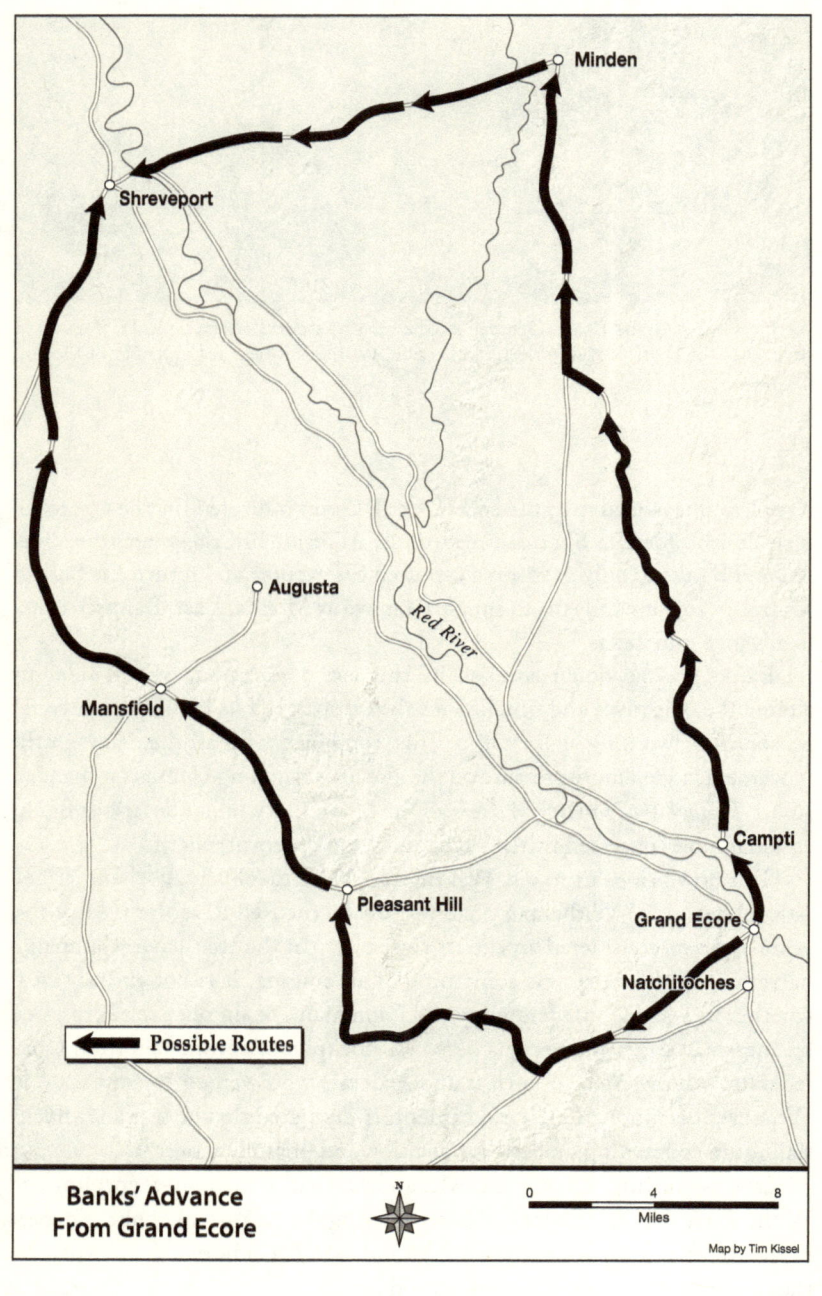

overcome. He now counseled Banks and his staff on the road system adjacent to the Red, including all possible avenues approaching Shreveport.

What happened next was a ruinous combination of sketchy maps, bad intelligence gathering, and Banks's limited ability to understand military maps and topography. Essentially, Banks could approach Shreveport in several ways. There were two potential routes on the eastern and western sides of the river. However, both veered away from the river at some point before connecting back to Shreveport. The "riverboat-man" informed Banks that the eastern approach had better roads, although it would likely add days to the march, as Union forces would have to maneuver around several lakes. In fact, two other roads ran right next to the Red River on either side, both beginning several miles above Grand Ecore. Evidence suggests that Withenbury omitted those details in his overview to Banks. Scholars of the campaign speculate that Withenbury persuaded the Union army to take a line of march away from the Red River to protect his cotton supply, or for some other unknown reason. Having few other reliable resources to consult, Banks drew on the implied expertise of the riverboat pilot.[81]

One other complication now influenced Banks's thought process. Due to the river's natural and man-made obstacles, as well as the generally low water level, Porter's river fleet was moving at a glacial pace. Moreover, natural falls or rapids above Alexandria prevented several of Porter's gunboats from navigating beyond it. Thus, the massive Union advantage in naval power diminished with each passing day.[82]

Options

Banks was suddenly under tremendous pressure to stay on the timeline. He could utilize the road network on the east side of the river or the one on the west or conduct cavalry reconnaissance to determine whether another route was possible. Without knowing what lay in store for him, Nathaniel Banks had a critical decision to make.

Option 1

Banks could decide that the eastern approach to Shreveport made better sense. According to Withenbury, this way contained the best road network. One possible path was an older road once used by the military. However, this route had several downsides to this route. First, it would take Banks far to the east and away from the river and Shreveport, adding days to his march. Second, if Banks chose this approach, the Union army would find itself on the wrong side of the river as it closed on Shreveport. Banks would have to cross back over the Red River before launching any attack on the city. Last, Banks and his staff were using old and incomplete maps. Many existing roads, especially on the eastern side, did not appear on them. Finally, this choice would also separate the Union army and navy for several days, complicating communications and eliminating the possibility of mutual support.[83]

Option 2

Banks could determine that the western approach to Shreveport was more practical. He had several good reasons to believe this was the best and most reasonable alternative. After this road went west for a few miles, it was almost a straight shot north to Shreveport, and this would save the Federals valuable time. As time became a factor, expediency was paramount in Banks's mind. Additionally, as he approached his intended objective from the western side of the river, Banks would not have the added challenge of figuring out how to cross the Red before attacking the city.

As with Option 1, this choice would also separate Banks from his naval support for some time. Banks was keenly aware of the issues the navy had navigating the Red. As the number of vessels Porter could sortie to support the infantry rapidly shrank and delays mounted, the advantage of having naval forces along ebbed.

Option 3

Nathaniel Banks could send out his calvary for reconnaissance before deciding on a route. Both Porter and William Franklin implored Banks to send out cavalry scouts and learn the nature of the roads for himself. As Union horsemen had been with the army since its arrival, it is stunning that no one thought of this before. On the other hand, a thorough reconnaissance would undoubtedly take time, and time was the one commodity Banks did not have an abundance of. Moreover, the deployment of Federal cavalry to scout would also potentially allow the enemy to choose where to fight; the Confederates could attack at any location in this howling wilderness. Albert Lee's cavalry at the Union vanguard led in large part to the Federals falling into the Confederate trap at Mansfield in less than a week.[84]

Decision

Banks decided that the western road network made the most sense (Option 2). As the clock was ticking, Banks still believed he would not face any significant Confederate resistance until he reached Shreveport. He ordered his forces on a line of march that took them miles away from the river on a narrow, heavily wooded road intersecting the towns of Pleasant Hill and Mansfield. As it happens, this was precisely what Richard Taylor was hoping for—he was waiting for Banks.

Results/Impact

The impact of Banks's decision would come to fruition in less than a week. Learning that Federal forces were advancing, Richard Taylor determined to meet them on the confined road south of Shreveport. Banks's decision put the Union column on the narrow, rutted Shreveport–Natchitoches Stage Line Road—a path surrounded by thick pine forests. Union forces could not effectively maneuver or deploy before, during, and after the Battle of Mansfield, ensuring Banks could not properly position his army. Banks's decision also eliminated the Union's advantage of naval support. Not only did his choice ensure that the Battles of Mansfield and Pleasant Hill occurred at the time and place we remember them, but it also cemented his future reputation as one of the most incompetent Union generals to command in the war. Upon seeing an optimistic message from General Banks predicting a quick and easy campaign, a somewhat cynical President Lincoln reportedly said, "I am sorry to see this tone of confidence; the next news we shall hear from there will be of a defeat."[85]

Alternative Decision/Scenario

Had Banks chosen differently, we might have seen a different campaign, and we certainly would not have seen a climactic clash at Mansfield and Pleasant Hill. If Banks had sent out cavalry reconnaissance, he might have learned of the roads paralleling the river. He might have decided to advance on Shreveport with whatever vessels Porter could push upriver. Taylor would have undoubtedly altered his plans and moved his command east to confront the Federals. Given this change, we might have seen a significant clash at any point along the Red River. This fighting might have involved at least a portion of Porter's fleet.

Steele Advances at Shreveport

Situation

Born in Delhi, New York, in 1819, Frederick Steele graduated from West Point in 1843, ranking thirtieth in a class of thirty-nine. His academy classmates included such notable names as Rufus Ingalls, William B. Franklin, and U. S. Grant. After graduation, Second Lieutenant Steele was posted to

The Red River at Grand Ecore, Louisiana, Author, Modern Image.

garrison duty in New York and Michigan, and he then served with distinction in the Mexican War. Before the Civil War, Steele was posted all over the frontier, eventually earning promotion to captain in the US Second Infantry.

Steele earned a reputation as a solid and steady infantry commander before the spring of 1864, quickly rising through the ranks. He commanded a battalion of Regulars (Second US) during the Battle of Wilson's Creek and was promoted to colonel of the Eighth Iowa in September 1861. Steele was made a brigadier general of US Volunteers in January 1862, heading the District of Southeast Missouri. Following the Battle of Pea Ridge, he took command of the First Division in the Army of the Southwest, leading this army briefly. In 1863, he was promoted to major general of volunteers. During the Vicksburg Campaign, Steele then commanded a division in the Fifteenth Corps in Sherman's army. Afterward, Steele received a brevet promotion to colonel in the regular army and was subsequently transferred to a command in Arkansas. There, his forces captured Confederate-held Little Rock in September, relentlessly pushing the Confederates south. On January 6, 1864, Steele was formally placed in command of the Department of Arkansas, designated the Seventh Corps.[86]

Part of the overall plan for the Red River Campaign was a coordinated Union advance with Steele's army moving south from Arkansas as Banks

Maj. Gen. Frederick Steele, U.S A, Unknown, circa 1860–1868. Library of Congress Prints and Photographs Division Washington, DC 20540.

moved north, putting Confederate forces at Shreveport at a significant disadvantage. A two-pronged move at northwestern Louisiana—i.e., Shreveport—would go a long way to ensure the effort's success by forcing Kirby-Smith and Dick Taylor to defend against two separate Union armies attacking from two directions. At the very least, an offensive drive by Steele from Little Rock might serve as a diversion, drawing Confederate forces away from Banks and his army approaching from the south.

However, like Grant, Frederick Steele was less than enthusiastic about the campaign from the outset. As soon as he learned that he was to support Banks's Red River operation in Louisiana, Steele began rationalizing the myriad of reasons why it was not feasible. While a professional soldier, he consistently dragged his feet, as he had no faith in Banks's ability as a commander. The matter was further complicated because Henry Halleck only suggested Steele's cooperation with Banks rather than simply ordering it. From February through March, communications that often took days to go from one command to another attempted to coordinate a date to launch the effort and persuade Steele to support it. He resisted for weeks until Grant summarily ordered him to do so on March 15.[87]

Steele's lack of enthusiasm for the Red River expedition was likewise grounded in the difficulties he foresaw in supporting such an operation,

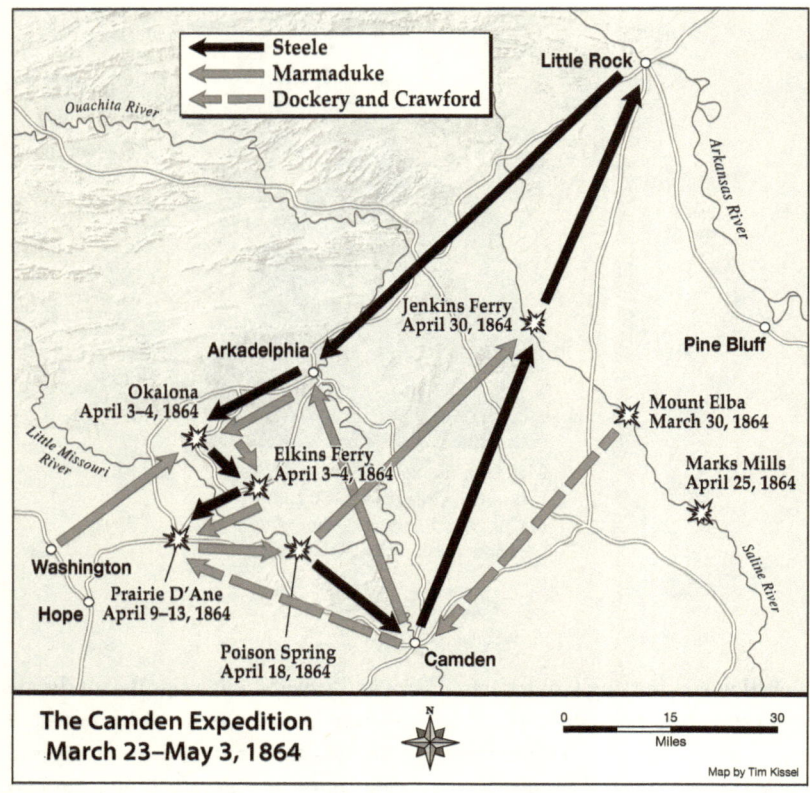

combined with the ongoing and multiple issues he faced managing his remote department. First and foremost, the road system in southwestern Arkansas and the entire state was no better than that in Louisiana. Unmaintained dirt roads quickly turned to impassable bogs during the rainy season, making marching any distance with efficiency or alacrity all but impossible.

Furthermore, operating in an area where the local population was openly hostile to the Union army presented any number of challenges for Steele and his command. Every citizen in this part of the state was a potential Southern sympathizer or an outright spy. Additionally, pockets of Confederate regular and partisan forces were very active throughout southwestern Arkansas. Just west beyond the frontier, hostile Native American tribes posed an ongoing threat. It was not unreasonable to assume one or all of these factions would take advantage of the Federals' diverted attention as they progressed toward Shreveport.[88]

Like every Trans-Mississippi commander, Steele also found his manpower resources stretched extremely thin. The aggregate of all Union forces in Arkansas was about twenty thousand men of all arms to cover an area of over fifty-three thousand square miles. Moreover, 60 percent of Steele's command was garrisoned at either Pine Bluff or far-off Fort Smith on the frontier.[89]

Finally, Steele had difficulty asserting authority over his new command. He and Brig. Gen. John Wynn Davidson were engaged in an ongoing dispute, and Steele was actively working on getting Davidson transferred from his department.[90]

Despite all these challenges, Steele eventually obeyed his orders and prepared to advance. He and his staff assembled a force of about ten thousand to eleven thousand men of all arms. In addition to Brig. Gen. Frederick Salomon's division of about 5,200 men from his Little Rock command, Steele expected 3,200 men from Brig. Gen. John Milton Thayer's Fort Smith garrison. Steele's troops would also include a cavalry division of around three thousand men commanded by Brig. Gen. Eugene Asa Carr. Steele set March 23 as the date he and his command were to depart from Little Rock.[91]

Here is where the lack of a singular overall commander dramatically affected the execution of the campaign. For Steele's advance to be practical, the Arkansas troops had to threaten Shreveport in a manner that supported Banks's advance from the south. With only orders to cooperate with Banks, it was up to Steele to determine precisely what that meant.

Steele and his staff reviewed their area maps to determine the best line of approach. Multiple routes were open to the Union force, and the most obvious and shortest path would lead directly south toward Monroe, Louisiana, and then west. However, the Union general would eventually take a course southwest to link up with Thayer's command coming south from Fort Smith.[92]

Steele had another critical factor to consider: his lines of communication and supply. Not knowing how long his forces would be in the field, he had to figure out how to keep his army adequately supplied with ammunition, food, and fodder. Shreveport was over 150 miles from Little Rock, and southern Arkansas was largely devoid of resources from which Steele's army could forage. Unlike Banks, Steele did not have the advantage of a large naval flotilla to support him.

Options

We may never know how aware Steele was of the impact of his actions or the way they drove the course of future events. The general could bring his needed supplies and ammunition with him or establish a supply line from Little Rock. With timing a factor, Frederick Steele had a critical decision to make.

Option 1

Steele's first option was to bring enough ammunition and supplies to keep his army fed and equipped for the campaign's duration. In any advance at Shreveport, Steele would have to figure out how to provide for his forces while maintaining a line of communication through hostile territory. Given the difficulty of maintaining that supply line, it might make sense for Steele to bring along all the provisions he might need. In doing so, he could protect his supply trains with his existing infantry and cavalry forces.

The downside to such a plan was that Steele could only guess how long his forces would be in the field and how much would be needed. Cutting himself off direct communication from his base meant things could get complicated if the campaign took longer than expected.

Option 2

Steele might determine that a secure supply line from Little Rock was necessary for his campaign to be successful. Not knowing how long his army was expected to conduct operations in southern Arkansas was a genuine consideration for Steele. If Confederate forces contested his advance, time and conditions could work against him. These factors alone might be enough for the Union commander to insist on a secure line of communication with his base.

Alternatively, maintaining a supply line of 150 miles or more was no small task. To ensure success, Steele would have to commit a large enough force to secure and protect it. The more men needed for such a detail, the fewer he could bring to clash with his Confederate opponents.

Decision

Frederick Steele decided to load his wagons and men to the hilt and bring the needed supplies with him (Option 1). On March 23, Steele's command left Little Rock, marching southwest. His troops arrived in Arkadelphia on the twenty-ninth. Six days earlier, Steele had ordered Brig. Gen. John Thayer, the commander of the Fort Smith garrison, to march his 3,200 men south to meet him seventy miles north of Shreveport.[93]

Encountering Confederate resistance and lousy weather, Steele and Thayer did not meet up until April 7, one day before Banks's and Taylor's armies collided at Mansfield. Steele was shocked to learn that Thayer's force had little or no supplies of their own. The Fort Smith garrison had been poorly supplied for weeks and expected their comrades from Little Rock to provide them with food and ammunition. Steele's command had been consuming supplies and ammunition, battling Sterling Price's Confederates while they waited for Thayer to arrive. That same day, Steele sent a message to Little Rock ordering a supply train containing thirty days of half rations for a force of fifteen thousand men. This was only the beginning of Steele's misfortunes and miscalculations.[94]

Results/Impact

The results of Steele's decision were impactful, to say the least. Due to Thayer's delays, the Confederate counteroffensive, and mismanagement of his supply lines, he never got closer than Washington, Arkansas, or eighty miles from Shreveport. Steele spent the better part of the next forty-three days fighting off Confederate attacks while desperately working out how to feed and supply his army. With each subsequent engagement, Steele's command fell back farther and farther from his objective, often losing men and valuable supplies in the process. And while his advance did manage to pull forces from Taylor's army in Louisiana, Banks had already fallen back to Grand Ecore by then. Steele's decision ensured his forces had no further impact on the campaign or putting Kirby-Smith's limited manpower to the test. In fact, due to the uncoordinated Union advances, Taylor and Kirby-Smith could deal with one Federal force and then the other.

Battlefield at Poison Springs, Arkansas, Author, Modern Image.

What came to be known as the Camden Expedition only added more disappointment to the long list of Union failures, hallmarking the overall campaign. On May 1, Steele's beaten, hungry, and bedraggled command was finally able to limp back to Little Rock, having achieved none of their operational objectives.[95]

Despite having to turn back to Little Rock, it was not all disaster for the Union forces in Arkansas. As we will discuss in the next chapter, Smith's advance did cause Kirby-Smith to look over his shoulder more than once, wondering what part of the Union advance, north or south, was more threatening.

Steele suffered a total of 2,750 casualties, or almost 28 percent of his forces, in his campaign in southwest Arkansas. More significant was his loss of equipment and animals. The total loss by the Department of Arkansas in this debacle was 635 wagons, 2,500 mules, and nine field pieces. The Confederates suffered 2,300 casualties and lost thirty-five wagons and two artillery pieces.[96]

Alternative Decision/Scenario

Had Steele planned better, we might have seen a different outcome. A better-prepared and more aggressive Steele could have drawn forces away from Banks's advance. Kirby-Smith pulled troops away from Taylor's army south of Shreveport to face Steele in Arkansas. These included portions of Maj. Gen. John G. Walker's Texas Division and Brig. Gen. John S. Marmaduke's cavalry. Both of these units were heavily engaged at Mansfield and Pleasant Hill. By threatening Shreveport before April 8, Steele might have put Kirby-Smith in a dilemma, forcing him to choose what part of the Union advance was more problematic. As a result, the outcome of these two battles might have altered.

CHAPTER 2

THE BATTLES OF MANSFIELD AND PLEASANT HILL

APRIL 6–9, 1864

The Battles of Mansfield and Pleasant Hill were two of the bloodiest battles fought west of the Mississippi. The clash at Mansfield had a combined 16 percent casualty rate of all forces engaged, higher than any other Trans-Mississippi engagement. For three straight days, Confederate forces under Richard Taylor and Union forces under Nathaniel Banks hammered away at one another in the piney woods of northwest Louisiana. By the time the sun set on April 9, 1864, the Union army had suffered one of the most humiliating reversals of the war, sustaining about four thousand casualties between the two battles. The stunning Confederate victory came at the cost of 2,626 casualties. Five critical decisions occurred during these days and those surrounding them.[1]

Banks's Order of March

Situation

In 1903, Pastor James Kendall Ewer, a former Massachusetts cavalryman who participated in the Red River Campaign, described the stretch of earth between Natchitoches and Shreveport, Louisiana, with the following passage:

"The road here winds off from the riverbank and traverses a barren wilderness. There is no good resting place for man or beast between Natchitoches and Shreveport. The enemy knew this and planned to trap the northern army in this 'howling wilderness.'"[2] By all accounts, this former trooper's depiction of the region was not an exaggeration.

The Shreveport–Natchitoches Stage Line Road that Nathaniel Banks selected for his march was barely a road, even by the most liberal definition of that word. Its extremely rutted and narrow red-dirt trace quickly transformed into mucilaginous clay at the first sign of precipitation. Fresh drinking water, readily available at the Red River, was scarce in this landscape except when it descended from the heavens in torrents. The ubiquitous rolling pastures and sugarcane and cotton fields along the banks of the Red River now gave way to endless stands of pine trees bordering the road. These pines were so impenetrable and thick that undergrowth was virtually nonexistent, apart from where it propagated in impassably dense thickets. Small communities like Mansfield and Pleasant Hill, literally hacked from the forest, were few and far between. The handful of cabins and homesteads the Yankees encountered on the march were largely vacant, their owners having fled the advancing blue tide. The local Black population, the only individuals remotely enthusiastic about seeing the Union army, likewise seemed to vanish from this harsh and hostile landscape, except for the very old and infirm.[3]

On April 6, 1864, a wildly overconfident Nathaniel Banks prepared to march his command through the very heart of this wilderness. An equally confident Richard Taylor had gathered an army of nine thousand determined Confederate defenders to meet them. The only question remaining was when and where that meeting was to take place. A cloud of dread shadowing the Federal army grew with every mile the soldiers marched.[4]

After weeks of fits and starts, the Union army and naval forces were ready for the final dash to Shreveport. Adm. David Dixon Porter was preparing for action a smaller subset of his vessels still able to navigate the shallowing river. The Union infantry, cavalry, and artillery planned to march the one hundred miles northwest from Natchitoches on the Shreveport–Natchitoches Stage Line Road, passing through the villages of Pleasant Hill and Mansfield. A soon-to-be-separated Banks and Porter arranged to meet at Springfield Landing, about ten miles below Shreveport, on or about April 10. They also agreed that Porter was to bring along the army transport vessels loaded with supplies for Banks's command.[5]

Until this point in the campaign, Confederate forces had offered only token resistance to Banks's operation. The Union commander and several of his lieutenants were absolutely convinced this trend would continue. They were

Admiral David Dixon Porter of U.S. Navy in Uniform, Gardner, A. & Brady's National Photographic Portrait Galleries circa 1862. Library of Congress Prints and Photographs Division Washington, DC 20540.

so confident that on April 4, Banks wrote his wife, "The enemy retreats before [us] & will not fight in a battle this side of Shreveport if then."[6]

As far as the Confederates were concerned, their delaying action was a military necessity. Richard Taylor ordered his men not to bring on a significant engagement until all available Confederate forces were concentrated and the time was right. As they were severely outmanned in the campaign's early days, Confederates were forced to simply skirmish with Banks's army and then disappear into the landscape. Taylor's Confederates fell back almost two hundred miles, parrying with the Union vanguard the whole way. An increasingly frustrated Taylor was spoiling for a fight, but he had to avoid a major battle before he was reinforced.[7]

As he prepared to depart Grand Ecore, manpower became an increasing concern for Banks. After conferring with his aides, Banks now counted only fifteen thousand to eighteen thousand men of all arms available to continue his operation. The one thousand men that made up the Mississippi Marine Brigade were summoned back to Vicksburg by Maj. Gen. John A. McClernand, and they were not part of the Union force going forward. Banks was also compelled to leave the 3,600 men of Brig. Gen. Cuvier Grover's Second Division of the Nineteenth Corps at Alexandria as an occupation force guarding

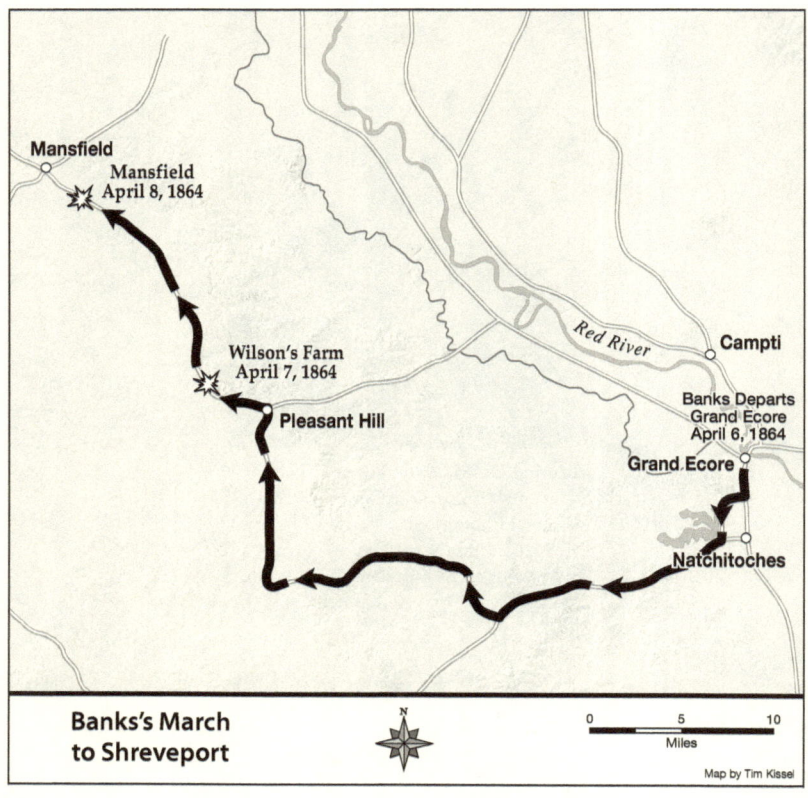

the supply depot and communications. Brig. Gen. Andrew J. Smith's command was likewise reduced to roughly 7,500 men, as Brig. Gen. Thomas Kilby Smith's division of the Seventeenth Corps was assigned to accompany Porter's fleet, supporting the navy's advance. Banks still outnumbered his opponent by almost two to one, but he could only guess at the number of Confederates that might be waiting for him at Shreveport.[8]

In addition, Banks was understandably concerned with how to supply this large and mobile force. As his line of march took him away from the river, his naval support, and his supply base for an unknown period of time, having the army bring a certain amount of supplies along was essential. Considering all relevant factors, the question remained as to the best and most efficient way to accomplish this.

Options

Banks could have his men carry all their needed supplies. Alternatively, he could bring along his wagon trains to keep his army fed and supplied with ammunition. As the campaign entered this next phase, Nathaniel Banks had a critical decision to make.

Option 1

Nathaniel Banks might determine that having his soldiers carry their necessary provisions made the most sense. Due to the difficulty the march presented, the Federals were sure to be extended in a lengthy column. Considering the narrowness of the road, the dense forest, and the fact that the entire force was compelled to use this road exclusively, Banks's army would be additionally drawn out with every wagon added. Also, as specific supply trains were often tied to individual brigades and divisions, it might be challenging to keep them close to the units they were intended to supply without creating undue gaps between the combat forces. Suppose the Union army encountered significant resistance on the march. In that case, moving units rapidly to support those at the front of the column might be problematic if a section of supply wagons occupied the road in between. Furthermore, if the Union column moved quickly through this wilderness, the men could easily carry enough food and ammunition to get them to the rendezvous with the navy in a few days. If Banks was confident Porter's fleet could resupply him on April 10, the need for excessive provisions diminished.

Option 2

Banks might conclude he needed his wagons to adequately supply his force. As noted, this part of Louisiana was almost completely denuded of food, fodder, and water. If Banks experienced any extended delay in his rendezvous with Porter, his army might go hungry. Additional supplies provided by well-stocked trains might just give Banks the cushion he needed should the unexpected happen.

Also, above Mansfield, the single-track road to Shreveport split into three separate routes. If Banks could get his forces past the town, he could divide his men equally on these roads, thereby shortening his columns. As a result, the added wagons might be less of an impediment. However, it is uncertain how much detail on the road system Banks possessed and whether it influenced his decision-making.

Additionally, having extra ammunition could be the deciding factor in combat. Why limit the men to what they could carry and risk defeat for lack of bullets and related supplies? Porter's fleet was having difficulty moving up the Red River, so relying on resupply that might never arrive might be particularly risky.

Last, every pound a soldier carried on his back added to the physical exertion of long-sustained marching. By having his trains along, Banks might ensure his men were less worn down from shouldering extra provisions.

Decision

Banks decided to bring his supply trains with him on the march (Option 2). Rather than use the bare minimum, he employed 1,000 wagons loaded with food, fodder, and ammunition—a staggering and unprecedented amount of supplies by any measure. Banks now had 56 wagons for every 1,000 men or approximately 2,000 tons of materiel. In comparison, by 1863, most of the major Union armies campaigned with just 30 supply wagons for every 1,000 men.[9]

This decision by Banks is challenging to unpack, as the commanding general seems to have had contradictory thoughts. Banks and many of his commanders firmly believed that the Confederates would offer little or no resistance and not make a stand below Shreveport. If the general sincerely believed this, why would he drag along all those extra wagons if he was not expecting a battle, and his army would have necessary materiel courtesy of the US Navy in a few days? Why would Banks needlessly extend his column with extra supplies he did not expect to need?

Ordered to assign an order of march, Nineteenth Corps commander William B. Franklin placed a large section of these wagons (approximately three hundred belonging to Brig. Gen. Albert L. Lee's cavalry) between the lead cavalry force and its supporting infantry.[10]

Results/Impact

Banks's decision was one of the most impactful of the Red River Campaign. It is uncontroversial to say that this choice likely determined the Battle of Mansfield's outcome and set the campaign's future direction.

Brig. Gen. Albert L. Lee's cavalry division was at the head of the column. Lee's men were followed by the cavalry supply train of three hundred wagons. Behind them were Brig. Gen. Thomas E. G. Ransom's two divisions (Cameron's and Landram's) of the Thirteenth Corps and one division (Emory's) of Maj. Gen. William B. Franklin's Nineteenth Corps. This command was followed by their train of seven hundred wagons. The two divisions of Brig. Gen. Andrew J. Smith's Sixteenth Corps brought up the rear. Due to the column's length, Smith's infantry could not depart Grand Ecore / Natchitoches until April 7. Col. William H. Dickey's brigade of the Corps d'Afrique was assigned to guard Franklin's main wagon train. Finally, Col. Oliver P. Gooding's cavalry brigade of Lee's division covered the rear and left flank of a column over twenty miles long. The thousand wagons added to Banks's order of march became the catalyst for a Union disaster.[11]

On April 7, to buy time for Taylor to gather his reinforcements, Confederate cavalry unleashed their most robust stand to date. About three miles north of Pleasant Hill, Brig. Gen. Thomas Green's Texas cavalry made an intense fight at Wilson's Farm, convincing his counterpart Albert Lee that a significant battle was imminent. Lee now requested infantry support. Franklin initially declined this request. When the appeal was escalated to Banks, he agreed, sending on a brigade from the Thirteenth Corps under division commander Col. William J. Landram. Col. Frank Emerson's First Brigade of the Fourth Division (1,200 men) moved ahead of the cavalry train to support Lee's cavalry.[12]

On April 8, Green continued his delaying action. After pushing Green's Confederate cavalry back several miles that morning, Lee's Union troopers reached a clearing at Sabine Crossroads, a few miles southeast of the town of Mansfield. Here, they found Taylor's army with its back to the forest, maintaining a strong formation and determined to fight. Ransom pushed another brigade under Col. Joseph W. Vance forward to support Lee. Tired of waiting for Banks to attack him, at 3:30 p.m. Taylor ordered his men forward. The Battle of Mansfield had begun.

Even before the action began, Lee sent for more reinforcements. Amazingly, Banks and Franklin dithered, still unconvinced that a significant battle was erupting. Behind Lee's three hundred wagons, the next-closest infantry support struggled to get men forward. Although he outnumbered his Confederate opponents, Banks labored with his generals to get units to the front and capitalize on his advantage as men, wagons, artillery, and caissons now jammed the narrow road. As a result, an outnumbered Taylor could take on the Union army a few brigades at a time.

As the Battle of Mansfield raged, determined Confederate assaults pushed the Federal lines back on themselves, and the Yankees began to retreat. With more pressure, the retreat soon became a rout. Panic erupted as infantry, artillery, and cavalry fleeing south became entangled with the wagons, men, and batteries struggling to get forward in a vain attempt to stem the Confederate tide. Only Confederate disorganization, the setting sun, and a final stand by units of Brig. Gen. William Emory's First Division of the Nineteenth Corps prevented Taylor's men from achieving a more decisive victory.[13] In addition to 2,235 battlefield casualties, Banks's army lost 20 pieces of artillery, 175 wagons, 11 ambulances, and over 1,000 horses and mules in the clash at Mansfield. Most of these were captured in the pandemonium along the Shreveport–Natchitoches Stage Line Road as frightened teamsters abandoned their teams, joining the fleeing infantry.[14]

Nathaniel Banks's critical decision to bring supply trains with the Federals enabled a new course for the campaign. As we will discuss, Richard Taylor capitalized on this choice by launching his attack at Mansfield, setting the stage for a decisive Confederate victory.

Beginning in late 1864 and continuing into 1865, the Joint Congressional Committee on the Conduct of the War held hearings on the disastrous Red River Campaign. Testifying before the committee, an aide on Banks's staff was asked what he attributed the disaster of April 8 to; he replied, "To the improper disposition of our forces. I think you will find that that is the general opinion of all the officers and men engaged in that campaign."[15]

Alternative Decision/Scenario

Let us suppose for a moment that Banks had concluded that additional wagonloads of supplies were unnecessary and a shorter column better suited his advance. As a result, a larger infantry contingent might have followed on the heels of Lee's cavalry. This fact alone might have enabled the Union commanders to bring more significant numbers to the battlefield quickly. While it is uncertain whether this additional manpower would have turned the tide of battle in favor of the Federal army, we might have seen a more robust stand by the Union and a more organized retreat from Mansfield.

A. J. Smith's men, accustomed to campaigning with limited supplies, should have set an example for their Department of the Gulf comrades. Marching lean with few provisions was par for the course in Sherman's army. Smith's "gorillas," as Banks's forces often referred to them, were somewhat incredulous at following such a massive supply train, certain it contained nothing but "paper collars and iron besteads for Banks's command."[16]

The Confederate Stand at Mansfield

Situation

In 1875, Joseph Palmer Blessington published *The Campaigns of Walker's Texas Division*, chronicling the history and exploits of this hard-fighting, hard-marching command. Blessington immigrated to the United States from Ireland in 1857, eventually moving to Texas in 1860. In March 1862, he enlisted as a private in the Sixteenth Texas Infantry. Organized at Hempstead, Texas, northwest of Houston, the Sixteenth became part of Scurry's Second Brigade of Walker's Texas Division. These Texans fought and marched at all

April 6–9, 1864

War in Louisiana—Battle of Mansfield, *Frank Leslie's Illustrated Newspaper*. H. Bonwell, circa 1864. Library of Congress Washington, DC 20540.

corners of the Trans-Mississippi for the next two years, including in the Red River Campaign. Wounded at the Battle of Pleasant Hill, Blessington was promoted to corporal by the war's end.

In his manuscript, Blessington described a pivotal moment in the campaign and a grim reality facing these Texans and every soldier, regardless of uniform, in the Red River Valley on April 8, 1864.

> The inhabitants of Mansfield appeared to be astonished when they beheld Walker's Division marching proudly back to meet the enemy, before whom they had so lately retreated. As the troops marched through the town, the sidewalks were thronged with ladies—misses and matrons—who threw their bright garlands at the feet of the brave Texas boys, beseeching them in God's name to drive back the enemy, and save their cherished homes; assuring us that they looked to us for protection. On hearing these patriotic words we felt that we were indeed "thrice armed," and, although greatly outnumbered, would in the end be victorious. Alas! how many a brave heart, which thrilled with patriotic emotion that morning, as we marched with flying banners through the town, was stilled in death before the last gleams of that day's sun rested upon the field of carnage! How many strong men, as they listened to the sweet voices of those maidens, and thought of their loved ones at home, ceased to think, or speak, or breathe, before that day had gone![17]

In early April 1864, as Confederate leadership discussed and debated what was to be done, two Union armies converged on Shreveport from two separate directions. On April 5, Lieut. Gen. Edmund Kirby-Smith in Shreveport sent a message to Maj. Gen. Richard Taylor in the field someplace south of the town of Mansfield. He wrote in part,

> At the last intelligence General Steele had not forced the passage of the Little Missouri. The distance between his column and that of Banks' is over 200 miles. It is far too great for us to concentrate on either column. Steele has, moreover, two lines of march after reaching Washington, upon one of which he must be committed before we can operate against him. The whole fate of this department will be staked upon the issue when we meet the enemy. The battle must be decisive, whether with Steele or Banks.

Three days later, on the morning of the Battle of Mansfield, Taylor sent a message back. He closed by stating, "I am not aware whether the enemy's whole force is in my front; if so, and he means to move on Shreveport, I consider this as favorable a point to engage him at as any other."[18]

No other exchange could have been more revealing of these two Confederate Generals' wildly contradicting command styles and how each man dealt with the uncertainty of war. Kirby-Smith, so concerned with making the wrong decision, hesitates to make any decision. While Taylor, somewhat uncertain of what is coming at him, commits to an aggressive course of action, knowing full well the consequences if he is wrong. These two generals' decisions would soon ignite one of the most significant battles west of the Mississippi.

The slow but steady concentration of thousands of armed men on both sides increased the likelihood of a significant battle. By the evening of April 7, 1864, all the previous decisions coalesced in an engagement in a two-hundred-acre clearing southeast of this small Louisiana town.[19]

The Confederate commanders in Louisiana had anticipated a Union thrust up the Red River as early as the summer of 1863. In fact, seven days after the fall of Port Hudson on the Mississippi, Richard Taylor wrote to Maj. Gen. John B. Magruder in Texas, asserting, "If the enemy means to overrun and occupy Louisiana, it is within his power to do so. The rise in the Mississippi and Red and Atchafalaya Rivers will enable them to throw their gunboats and transports into the very heart of Western Louisiana."[20] This belief was bolstered by the multiple invasion attempts the Federals launched in 1863 at the coasts of Texas and Louisiana. However, in February 1864, Taylor's and

April 6–9, 1864

Maj. Gen. John G. Walker, CSA, Commander of Walker's Texas Division, H. R. Marks, circa 1866–1869, DeGolyer Library, SMU.

Kirby-Smith's suspicions that the Red River Valley was destined for a Union invasion were further reinforced when they learned that Nathaniel Banks had pulled troops from his foothold in Matagorda, Texas. In addition, the generals received reports from Confederate spies in New Orleans of Union troops massing. This could only mean Banks intended to use these forces for a campaign up the Red River.[21]

Kirby-Smith also began amassing an army from his widely scattered commands to answer this new Federal threat. In March 1864, he ordered the various Trans-Mississippi subdepartments to send every available man to either join Richard Taylor in northwestern Louisiana or travel directly to his garrison in Shreveport. This proved to be far easier said than done.[22]

Maj. Gen John B. Magruder was ordered to send Brig. Gen. Thomas J. Green's cavalry corps from Texas to Alexandria. The conspicuously named Brig. Gen. Camille Armand Jules Marie, Prince de Polignac, marched his brigade from Trinity, Texas. It was combined with the brigade of Col. Henry Gray under the command of Brig. Gen. Jean-Jacques-Alfred-Alexandre "Alfred" Mouton. The men of Maj. Gen. John G. Walker's Texas Division (a.k.a. the Greyhounds), relieved from the backbreaking work of reinforcing Fort DeRussy, had been checking the Union advance since the fall of that position. They, too, were summoned to fall back and join the gathering Confederate commands. Furthermore, Taylor had an unknown number of "reserves," as he referred to them. Experts on the campaign speculate that these men were unexchanged Confederate soldiers paroled after Vicksburg surrendered. The best estimates are that by the morning of April 8, Richard Taylor had assembled a force of between 8,800 and 9,000 men of all arms.[23]

Kirby-Smith also ordered Maj. Gen. Sterling Price in Arkansas and Brig. Gen. Samuel B. Maxey in the Indian Territory to send all available reinforcements from their departments to Shreveport by the quickest possible route.[24]

Having done what he could to address his manpower situation, Kirby-Smith turned his attention to other matters. The Confederate general desperately needed arms, ammunition, and supplies for his ever-growing army. Several units, like some of Green's troopers from Texas, arrived in Louisiana without weapons. Communicating with Magruder in Texas, Kirby-Smith sent an urgent request for rifles, indicating he had four thousand unarmed men.[25]

Kirby-Smith also had competing strategic priorities to deal with. Learning of Frederick Steele's departure from Little Rock on March 2, Kirby-Smith was concerned that Steele's column from the north might be a more imminent threat than Banks advancing from the south. Even though Banks's army was closer, Kirby-Smith now began to hesitate, looking over both shoulders. The Confederate commander initially decided that Confederate troops would first concentrate on Banks's army moving up from New Orleans. Once that force was defeated, the Confederates would move north to take on Steele's command. However, Kirby-Smith suddenly changed his mind, believing Steele's command might pose the most immediate danger.[26]

The quarrel between Edmund Kirby-Smith and Richard Taylor that had slowly simmered for months suddenly heated to a boil. Kirby-Smith wanted to concentrate all available Trans-Mississippi forces at Shreveport and make a stand against the Federal troops near the town. He believed that such a posture would enable Confederate forces to move reinforcements quickly from one sector to another via interior lines. With a concentration at Shreveport, Kirby-Smith could attack one Union column or the other depending on which most threatening. Taylor, given his penchant for aggressiveness, clearly had other ideas. The Louisianian favored a more bellicose stand. He wanted all reinforcements in the Trans-Mississippi sent to him so that he could strike Banks's army head-on as soon as it was practical and ideally below Mansfield. Once that force was eliminated, the unified Confederate commands could turn their attention to Steele. Convinced he was right, Taylor expressed his feelings to Kirby-Smith at every opportunity.[27]

During March and April, the two generals exchanged numerous and often contentious communications. They clashed over everything, including reinforcements, defensive strategies, and the lack of cooperation from other Trans-Mississippi departments.[28] An increasingly frustrated Taylor wrote to Kirby-Smith's headquarters on April 4:

April 6–9, 1864

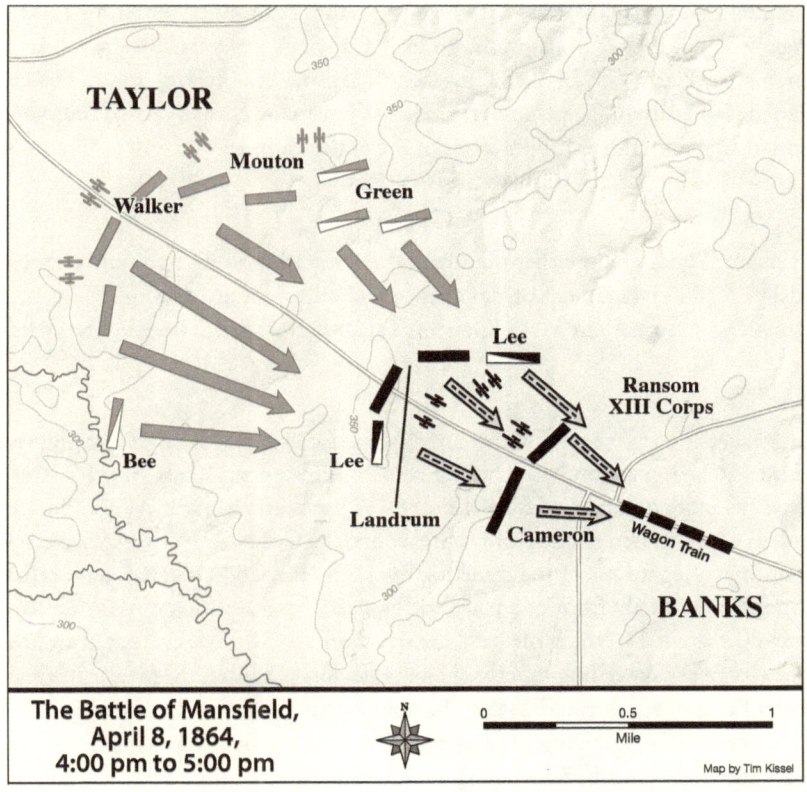

The Battle of Mansfield, April 8, 1864, 4:00 pm to 5:00 pm

Map by Tim Kissel

Steele's advance has been long expected by me (refer to several dispatches on the subject), and his movements have been connected with those of the column in my front; hence my extreme anxiety to fight the latter before it gained too much territory. Like the man who has admitted the robber into his bed-chamber instead of resisting him at the door, our defense will be embarrassed by the cries of wives and children. Action, prompt, vigorous action, is required. While we are deliberating the enemy is marching. King James lost three kingdoms for a mass. We may lose three States without a battle.[29]

The next day, Kirby-Smith left for Mansfield to smooth his best commander's ruffled feathers and to consult on overall strategy. Having massed his forces near Mansfield, Taylor was becoming more convinced the whole of Banks's army was within one day's march of his position. He thus requested permission to attack Banks. Kirby-Smith, rather than simply ordering Taylor, merely suggested that all might be lost if Taylor's army was destroyed in a premature clash with Banks. Kirby-Smith returned to Shreveport on April 7, satisfied the situation was understood.[30] What followed was one of the more interesting and impactful decisions of the entire campaign.

Options

Richard Taylor could either obey orders from Kirby-Smith and not bring on a significant engagement or defiantly stand and fight at Mansfield. The aggressive and impatient Major General Taylor had a critical decision to make.

Option 1

If persuaded to agree with Kirby-Smith's assessment, Taylor might continue to fight a delaying action while falling back to Shreveport. Kirby-Smith's strategy was more of a passive stance, but it was not without merit. With all their forces concentrated at one point, Shreveport, the Confederates possessed interior lines. Regardless of the direction of attack, the Confederates could move troops more easily from one place to the next, concentrating strength at the most threatened sector. Miles of defensive works had been constructed around the city in the preceding months. Having his forces behind these fortifications meant Kirby-Smith could negate the manpower advantage the Federals had.

Adequately supplying his scattered forces in the field was a genuine concern for Kirby-Smith. Shreveport had a decent food supply, and stationing all troops in and around the city would simplify the quartermaster's job.[31]

Option 2

Taylor might decide that now was the time to make a stand despite the commanding general's warnings to the contrary. From the moment Union forces entered the Red River, Richard Taylor had been itching to strike a blow. As a student of Stonewall Jackson's tactics in the Shenandoah Valley, he believed aggressiveness gave the often-smaller Confederate armies the edge against their more powerful Union foes. Taylor also thought giving more ground to the enemy was counterintuitive, and akin to "the man who has admitted the robber into his bed-chamber instead of resisting him at the door." This hard-hitting, uncompromising general wanted to fight Banks at the front door, and retreating to Shreveport never made sense to him.

Moreover, Taylor knew that above Mansfield, the single-track road the Federals were advancing on split into three separate lanes, all terminating at Shreveport. Should Union forces get past Mansfield, Banks could divide his army, making a successful defensive stand on the part of the Confederates much more difficult.[32]

However, as confident as he was, Taylor had to consider the possibility that his commander might be correct. If the Union army somehow managed to roll over Taylor's much smaller Confederate force, the consequences for the Trans-Mississippi might be dire indeed. All that said, even if Banks defeated Taylor's force, the Federal army would still be bloodied and weakened.

Decision

Seeing his opportunity slipping away, Dick Taylor decided to stand and fight (Option 2). He likely chose to offer battle at Mansfield even before Kirby-Smith's visit. Perhaps needing a way to justify this decision, late in the evening of April 7, Taylor sent a message to Kirby-Smith that read in part, "I respectfully ask to know if it accords with the views of the lieutenant-general commanding that I should hazard a general engagement at this point, and request an immediate answer, that I may receive it before daylight to-morrow morning."[33]

It has been speculated that Taylor sent this message at the last moment and by the slowest possible means, ensuring he would not receive a response before the fighting erupted. Kirby-Smith replied, still urging his lieutenant not to bring on a general engagement.[34] On the evening of April 8, after the battle was over, Taylor wrote Kirby-Smith again, boasting, "We fought the Thirteenth Army Corps all day and late in the evening met the Nineteenth Army Corps; repulsed and drove them back. We have captured about 2,000 prisoners, 20 pieces of artillery, 200 wagons, and thousands of small-arms."[35]

Richard Taylor spent almost the whole of April 8 waiting for Banks to foolishly and impulsively attack his army. Growing tired of the Union general's unwillingness to throw his army at his lines, at 3:30 p.m., Taylor, riding among Mouton's Command, ordered the Louisianians and Texans forward. Turning to Brigadier General Polignac, Taylor shouted over the growing din of battle, "Little Frenchman, I am going to fight Banks here if he has a million men."[36]

Results/Impact

Taylor's decision had a far-reaching and immediate impact on the Red River Campaign. By standing at Mansfield, Taylor not only ensured a battle south of the town would occur, but he also secured an undisputed victory that guaranteed all subsequent actions in the campaign happened as we remember them. Richard Taylor's choice ignited the Battles of Mansfield and Pleasant

Hill and led directly to Banks's army's retreat to the mouth of the Red River. The ensuing battles at Blair's Landing, Monett's Ferry, Mansura, and Yellow Bayou, fought as Banks continued to fall back, are all directly linked to this single decision.

One famous and perhaps dubious account tells of a courier from Kirby-Smith bearing a message informing Taylor not to fight, but to fall back to Shreveport. The messenger found the general just as Mouton's Division was driving the Federal line back. "Too late, sir," a defiant Taylor exclaimed, "the battle is won."[37]

Alternative Decision/Scenario

Suppose for a moment Taylor was persuaded by Kirby-Smith and fell back into the defenses of Shreveport. With this alternative decision, any number of scenarios are possible. Banks might have placed the city under siege or launched assaults at the entrenched Confederates. Without the battles south of Shreveport, Kirby-Smith might have sent more men than he did to attack Steele's command. It is impossible to state that the campaign's outcome would have differed had a significant battle occurred near Shreveport.

Rebel attack on Gen. Lee's wagon train at Mansfield, *Frank Leslie's Illustrated Newspaper*, C. E. H. Bonwill, circa 1864, Library of Congress Washington, DC 20540.

However, given the pressure Banks was under and his questionable military prowess, it is reasonable to assume that disaster might have easily befallen the Union at another time and place, just closer to Shreveport. As Napoleon Bonaparte opined, "The logical conclusion to defense is defeat." Thus any siege of Shreveport would probably have ended similarly to that of Vicksburg.

Banks Retreats to Pleasant Hill

Situation

Lieut. Col. Richard Bache (Biddle) Irwin was only twenty-four years old at the time of the Battle of Mansfield. Born in Pennsylvania, he was a direct descendant of Founding Father Benjamin Franklin. Irwin was working as a clerk in the War Department in 1861 when he left his job and volunteered to fight for the Union once the news of the fall of Fort Sumter reached the nation's capital. Rising through the ranks, he eventually earned a position as assistant adjutant general for the Nineteenth Army Corps, serving on William B. Franklin's staff. After the war, Irwin became a writer for the *New York Tribune* and authored several works on the war and his personal experiences as a young officer. In 1892, the same year Irwin passed away, his titled *History of the Nineteenth Army Corps* was published.[38]

A witness to the Union catastrophe on April 8, Irwin gave the following thoughts on the mood of the Union army after the Battle of Mansfield:

> So great a change had these few hours wrought that the same sun rose upon an army marching full of confidence that within two days Shreveport would be in its grasp, and set upon the same army defeated, brought to bay, its campaign ruined, saved only by a triumph of valor and discipline on the part of a single division and of skill on the part of its intrepid commander from complete destruction at the hands of an enemy inferior in everything and outnumbered almost as two to one.[39]

As darkness slowly embraced the carnage and devastation at Sabine Crossroads, the Union army faced a crushing defeat and a critical decision.

In the saddle all afternoon and evening on April 8, Nathaniel Banks moved from point to point shouting orders, rallying his men, and doing all he could to stem the deluge of retreating men, wagons, horses, and artillery. Despite his personal courage and appeals for them to stop, his troops deserted the field. A soldier in the Thirty-Eighth Massachusetts described the chaos: "The teams were abandoned by the drivers; the traces cut and the animals

Maj. Gen. William B. Franklin,
USA Mathew Brady, circa 1860–1865.
Library of Congress Prints and
Photographs Division Washington,
DC 20540.

ridden off by the frightened men. Bare-headed riders rode with agony in their faces, and for at least ten minutes it seemed as if all were going to destruction together."[40]

Banks's army suffered 240 men killed, 671 wounded, and 1,508 missing in the confrontation at Mansfield, a casualty rate of 20 percent of those engaged.[41] Four Union artillery batteries (22 guns) were essentially obliterated as the artillery men were overrun and forced to abandon their guns. Nineteenth Corps commander William B. Franklin broke an arm, had a bullet glance off his leg, and had two horses shot from underneath him during the melee. In addition, the Thirteenth Corps Division of Brig. Gen. Robert A. Cameron endured nearly 50 percent casualties in the desperate attempt to stop Taylor's assaults. Brig. Gen. Thomas E. G. Ransom, commander of the Thirteenth Corps, was wounded and had to be carried from the field. In Col. William Landram's Fourth Division of the Thirteenth Corps, brigade commander Col. Frank Emerson was wounded and captured, and brigade commander Col. Joseph W. Vance was killed.[42]

It was not all bad news for Banks and his commanders that day. As the sun was setting, three of Brig. Gen. William H. Emory's brigades made a determined stand three miles south of the initial Federal position at Mansfield near a small waterway called Chapman's Bayou. After letting the retreating

Northern men pass through their lines, Emory's soldiers stood firm against renewed Confederate assaults before falling back from this position in good order. Banks also had a strong contingent of reinforcements. Thirteen miles southeast at Pleasant Hill, the uncommitted 7,500 men of Brig. Gen. A. J. Smith's command paused to rest, having marched twenty-one miles that day from Grand Ecore. Encamped just south of town, Smith had almost as many men in his command as Taylor had in his entire army.[43]

The Confederate assault on the eighth also lost momentum due to the setting sun and many Confederates' looting of the abandoned wagons loaded with Union supplies. In 1862, while fighting in the Shenandoah Valley, Nathaniel Banks earned the unfortunate nickname of "Commissary Banks" for his tendency to lose large amounts of supplies and arms in clashes with Jackson's army. The miserable results of April 8, 1864, did nothing to undo this label.[44]

On the Confederate side, the battle's results were far better than Richard Taylor could have reasonably expected despite the losses to his meager force. Taylor reported that his army suffered one thousand men killed and wounded in the assault. Brig. Gen. Alexander Mouton's Second Division suffered grievously during the fight. Mouton was mortally wounded, reportedly shot several times in the back. All the field officers in Col. Henry Gray's First Brigade of Mouton's Command were either killed or wounded, save Gray himself. In the very eye of the storm, the Crescent Consolidated Louisiana Regiment saw nearly two hundred men, all of its field officers, and seven color-bearers killed. It has been estimated that Gray's Brigade of Mouton's Division sustained a casualty rate of 40 percent of those engaged.[45]

Despite the death of one of his favorite division commanders, Taylor was undoubtedly pleased with the results. His men had stopped Banks's army dead in its tracks and pushed them back several miles south, capturing dozens of wagons full of supplies and hundreds of horses and mules in the process.[46]

Told by his commanding officer that the risk of a general engagement with Union forces outside Shreveport was too high, Taylor must have felt vindicated by the day's outcome. He sent off several messages to Kirby-Smith in Shreveport, extolling a largely one-sided victory while vowing to press his advantage by pursuing Banks to finish him off.[47] Taylor repeated this self-satisfied tone in his memoir while disparaging his Union opponent: "With a much smaller force on the field, we invariably outnumbered the enemy at the fighting point; and foreseeing the possibility of this, I was justified in my confidence of success. The defeat of the federal army was largely due to the ignorance and arrogance of its commander, General Banks, who attributed my long retreat to his own wonderful strategy."[48]

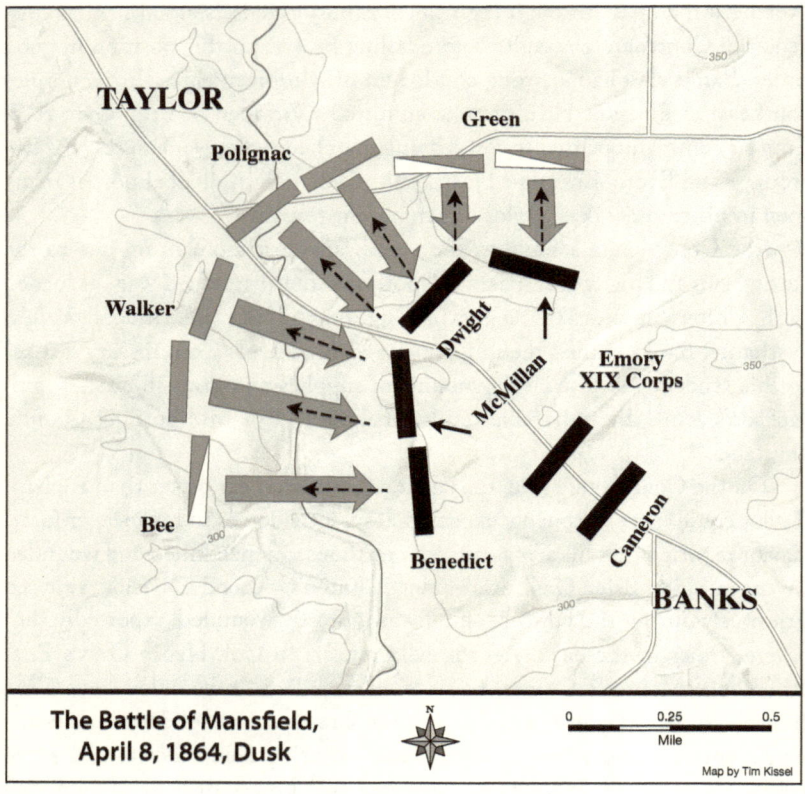

South of Mansfield, Nathaniel Banks was working feverishly to salvage his campaign, which was now at risk of coming entirely off the rails.

Options

Banks had four options to choose from. He could order a renewed advance, order a full retreat, stand his ground where he was, or pick a new location to make a stand. With the campaign's success hanging in the balance, Nathaniel Banks had a critical decision to make.

Option 1

Banks might determine that continuing his advance was the best option. Despite the defeat at Mansfield, Banks still outnumbered his opponent, although he likely did not know this. And while it might be difficult, renewing his advance was still an option. Nathaniel Banks had invested a great deal of time and resources in getting his campaign to this point, and it would be a shame to end it without achieving any of his operational objectives. He was now as close to Shreveport as he would likely ever be, and if he retreated now, Richard Taylor would be disinclined to give him a repeat opportunity.

Conversely, Banks was far from the most aggressive officer in the Union army. Renewing the advance in the face of such a devastating defeat might be hard for this political general to imagine. The loss of supplies and men, coupled with the disorder from the rout, certainly had the potential to damage Banks's political career. Still, a victory just might see all previous sins forgiven. U. S. Grant had the same experience; his lack of success before taking Vicksburg was forgotten when that key city fell in July 1863.

Option 2

Banks might decide it made tactical sense to order a full retreat back to Grand Ecore. The Federal forces had suffered a significant defeat. It is safe to say that the general's army was vulnerable and was still at risk of being overrun by the Confederate troops. If Banks could withdraw his army back to the Red River, the additional firepower of Porter's fleet might offer the Union men extra protection. Considering the current circumstances and the losses sustained, the most prudent choice might be to play it safe by retreating to the river.

Moreover, the issue of Banks's supplies and wagons on the narrow Shreveport–Natchitoches Stage Line Road was now compounded by the chaos of the hasty retreat. The general would find it difficult to renew his advance in any circumstances. Adding in the bedlam of a fleeing army might make the task all but impossible.

Option 3

Nathaniel Banks might conclude that standing at Chapman's Bayou was the best solution. On the evening of April 8, Brig. Gen. William H. Emory's First Division of the Nineteenth Corps had made a solid stand at sunset. And despite getting pushed beyond Chapman's Bayou—or Pleasant Grove, as it is sometimes referred to—Emory's men had helped stop the Confederate momentum. If Banks reinforced this position with Smith's command, he might have the opportunity to hit back at his aggressive Confederate opponent.

Option 4

General Banks might choose a more advantageous location to make his stand, like Pleasant Hill. Banks now had a reserve force of 7,500 uncommitted soldiers (five brigades) at Pleasant Hill under Brig. Gen. Andrew J. Smith. This was almost 80 percent of the men Taylor had mustered against Federal forces at Mansfield. If Banks could fall back to that position, the added manpower and experience of Smith's command might just provide a meaningful advantage over the Confederates. Additionally, Smith's command had marched all day on the eighth to reach Pleasant Hill. Asking them to march the extra distance to join the rest of the army at Chapman's Bayou might be too much even for Smith's veterans.

Decision

After a council of war with his lieutenants, Banks decided to mass his entire force at the line at Chapman's Bayou and directed Smith to bring his command forward (Option 3). However, after further discussion, Union leadership decided Smith's men needed rest, and the position at Chapman's Bayou did not have an adequate water supply. Banks subsequently ordered the army to fall back to Pleasant Hill, joining A. J. Smith's hardened and determined veterans (Option 4). Between 10:00 p.m. and midnight, the remnants of Banks's beaten army began to retreat. Taylor's exhausted men rested on their arms and listened to wagons, men, and horses withdrawing to the southeast.[49] Lieut. Col. Richard B. Irwin recounted Banks's decision this way: "Clearly the next thing, whatever might be the next after, was to concentrate and reform on the first fair ground in the rear. Such were Banks's orders. Accordingly at midnight Emory marched in orderly retreat, with all his material intact, and at eight o'clock the next morning, the 9th of April, went into bivouac at Pleasant Hill, where A. J. Smith was found near his resting-place of the night before."[50]

Results/Impact

Thanks to the decision by Nathaniel Banks, the die for the next phase of the campaign was cast. The Federals fell back, and Dick Taylor, determined to retain his initiative, pursued them with every available man. The most apparent result of Banks's decision was that it ensured that the next battle of the campaign occurred at the small village of Pleasant Hill the following day. Now the momentum of the campaign shifted noticeably. For weeks, a Union army inching its way forward suddenly found itself going in the opposite direction. This first step backward portended many more to follow for the political general from Massachusetts.

April 6–9, 1864

Alternative Decision/Scenario

Had Banks stayed with his original plan, we would have seen a different course of events than the one we now remember. If he could somehow have gotten A. J. Smith's exhausted command to join him, Banks might still have stopped Taylor at Chapman's Bayou. A concentrated Union force at this point might have been too much even for Taylor to overcome. Depending on what moves Taylor employed, the Confederates could possibly have outflanked Banks and cut off his lines. A renewed clash at Chapman's might have been a more significant event. We now recall the Union stand here as an extension of the original fight at Mansfield. A battle here the next day would have changed the campaign's history for all time.

Churchill Fails to Find the Union Flank

Situation

By the time of the Battle of Pleasant Hill, Brig. Gen. Thomas James Churchill had certainly seen his fair share of fighting and the insides of enemy prison camps.

Born in Kentucky in 1824, Churchill studied law before joining the First Kentucky Cavalry Regiment, serving under Zachary Taylor, the father of Richard Taylor, in the war with Mexico. While on a reconnaissance mission in January 1847, Lieutenant Churchill was captured by Mexican cavalry, and he spent the next several months as a prisoner of war. Finishing the rest of

War in Louisiana—The Battle of Pleasant Hill, *Frank Leslie's Illustrated Newspaper.* H. Bonwell, circa 1864. Library of Congress Washington, DC 20540.

the conflict with a bad case of yellow fever, Churchill returned to the United States once the war ended.

The Kentuckian then relocated to Little Rock, Arkansas, to marry and raise a family. At the start of the Civil War, Thomas Churchill left his job as postmaster general of Little Rock to organize the First Arkansas Mounted Rifles, who ironically often fought dismounted. Colonel Churchill led this regiment at the Battle of Wilson's Creek in August 1861, having two horses shot from underneath him. His First Arkansas Mounted Rifles then participated in the Confederate disaster at Pea Ridge in March 1862. Promoted to brigadier later that same month, Churchill led a division under Kirby-Smith at the Battle of Richmond, Kentucky, in August 1862. By December 1862, Churchill commanded the Confederate garrison at Fort Hindman, Arkansas. At the Battle of Arkansas Post (January 1862) downstream of Pine Bluff, Union army and naval forces moved up the Arkansas River while assaulting the Confederates. Vastly outnumbered, Churchill surrendered the garrison to Maj. Gen. John A. McClernand and once again found himself a prisoner of war. Detained at Camp Chase in Ohio and released three months later, Thomas James Churchill returned to Arkansas in December 1863 to command a division, eventually reporting to Sterling Price when the latter took command of Arkansas troops in March 1864.[51]

When Kirby-Smith ordered Sterling Price to send reinforcements from his command to Shreveport, Churchill was selected to lead a detachment of

Brig. Gen. Thomas James Churchill, CSA, Unknown, circa 1862, https://web.archive.org/web/20071108042626/http://www.generalsandbrevets.com/sgc/churchill.htm.

two small divisions. One division included Arkansas units under Brig. Gen. James Camp Tappan, and the other consisted of Missouri regiments under Brig. Gen. Mosby Monroe Parsons. Churchill's Command numbered approximately 4,300 men of all arms. Leaving Camp Sumter in Arkansas on March 20, these soldiers tramped the seventy miles to Shreveport, arriving on the twenty-fourth.[52]

Remaining in Shreveport until April 3, Churchill's small division marched forty-five miles in thirty-six hours to reach the battlefield at Mansfield, reporting to Taylor sometime between 4:00 p.m. and 6:00 p.m. on April 8. Richard Taylor placed Churchill in reserve as the struggle at Mansfield was winding down. Later that evening, Taylor ordered Churchill to have his men prepare two days' worth of rations and be ready to advance. At 3:00 a.m. on April 9, Churchill's Command began the march toward Pleasant Hill on a road littered with Union prisoners, stragglers, small arms, and burning wagons—all evidence of the Federal army's hasty retreat.[53]

Taylor was now attempting to determine Banks's next move. On the one hand, the Federals might just fall back to the Red River to link up with Porter's fleet via Grand Ecore. Or Banks might attempt to open communication with Porter via Blair's Landing on the Red, due east of Pleasant Hill—a road connected Blair's Landing to the town. To respond to this contingency, Taylor sent part of Green's cavalry to occupy this road near the Bayou Pierre Crossing. Taylor also mistakenly believed that A. J. Smith's entire force was with Porter's fleet. In fact, as Taylor would soon discover, just one division was with Porter, while the balance of Smith's command was at Pleasant Hill.

Determined to hold on to the initiative, the aggressive Taylor ordered an advance. Following the rest of Green's cavalry, the head of Churchill's column reached a point west of Pleasant Hill sometime after 9:00 a.m. The rest of Taylor's command followed. In a reverse of the events of the day before, the Confederates were stunned to find the Union army was not retreating but in line of battle, waiting for them.[54]

At the time of the battle, the village of Pleasant Hill, Louisiana, consisted of perhaps a dozen buildings, including shops, a hotel, and a small college. Pleasant Hill was all that one might expect from a small rural town in the nineteenth century. It was a quiet, unassuming, idyllic place carved from the surrounding woods, situated on an open plateau about a mile from end to end. Dick Taylor spent the next several hours positioning his forces as they arrived while allowing his men time to rest. His lines on the west end of the clearing stretched north to south and were anchored in the wood line. Left to right were the commands of Green, Polignac, Walker, and Churchill. With the arrival of Churchill's Command, Taylor now had a force of about 12,500 men facing a Union force of just shy of 12,000 men.[55]

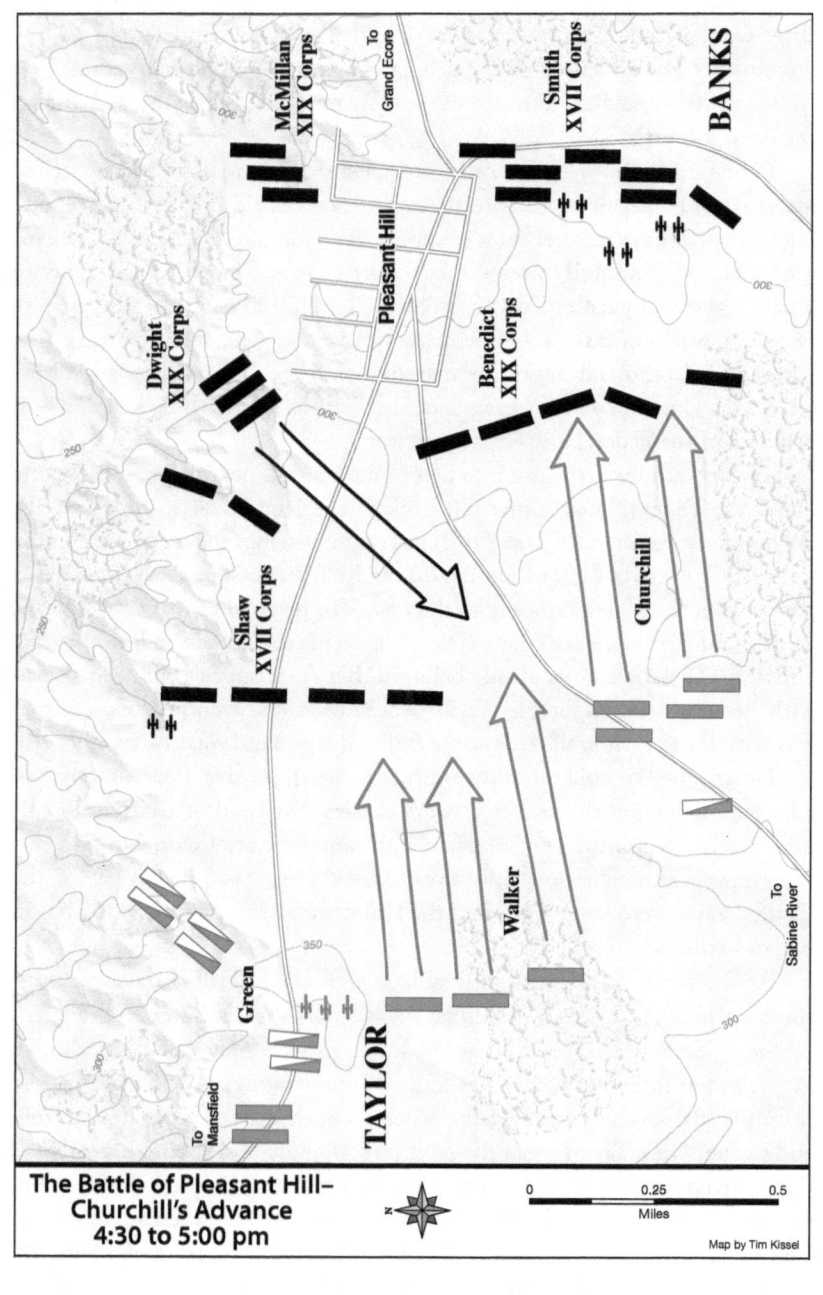

Having fallen back from Mansfield, Banks and his generals stationed their troops in and around the village, making use of the terrain and the surrounding defilade. Following the shape of the plateau, the irregular Union line stretched for about a mile. On the right was the brigade of Brig. Gen. William Dwight of the Nineteenth Corps, with Col. William T. Shaw's brigade of the Sixteenth Corps just to his left. Brig. Gen. James W. McMillan's brigade from the Nineteenth was in reserve behind them. The men of Col. Lewis Benedict's brigade, also of the Nineteenth, positioned themselves on a line paralleling the Shreveport–Natchitoches Stage Line Road with the rest of Smith's command behind them. Just before noon, Nathaniel Banks rode to the front for a look, hearing nothing but skirmishing fire. As he now had his men more or less where he wanted them, the general returned to his headquarters for lunch, convinced no battle would take place that day.[56]

The Battle of Pleasant Hill began at 3:00 p.m. when Richard Taylor gave the order to advance. His battle plan was reasonably straightforward. Churchill was to march south and east through the woods and get on the left flank of the Federals. Once this attack commenced, the rest of the Confederate force, starting with Walker, would advance en echelon, driving the Yankees from the field. A local man familiar with the roads was sent with Churchill as a guide. About ninety minutes later, Churchill's Command emerged from the woods. The Confederates from Arkansas and Missouri quickly discovered that they were, in fact, not on the flank of A. J. Smith's veteran Union line, but facing its very center.[57]

Options

It is not entirely clear whether Churchill was misled by flawed directions from his guide or by his miscalculation. However, Churchill threw the blame squarely at his local guide in his after-action report. With the rest of the Confederate army waiting for the sounds of his attack to go forward, the brigadier general could now either advance or fall back. Either choice would be a critical decision.[58]

Option 1

Churchill's first option was to advance regardless of the position of his brigades. This meant moving directly toward the Union lines, creating a real challenge for the men of his command. Per Taylor's orders, the rest of the army was to advance once they heard the sounds of Churchill's attack. Time was running out; it was now close to 5:00 p.m., and only a few hours of daylight remained. Any further delays on Churchill's part would likely decrease the odds of victory, as Civil War–era armies rarely fought once the sun went down, for obvious reasons.

Option 2

Churchill could fall back and reposition his force to get around the Union flank as initially intended. The whole purpose of the end around march was to disrupt the Union lines by attacking them on the flank, where they were the most vulnerable. If Churchill sent his men directly at the Yankee line, the Confederates might suffer casualties too grievous to overcome. By this time in the war, most commanders had witnessed the toll frontal assaults took on the attacking infantry, and the smart ones worked to avoid it. Whether he knew it then is debatable, but Churchill was facing the battle-tested veterans of A. J. Smith's command, and caution was called for. Given this fact, it might make sense to reposition his force.

However, additional maneuvering on Churchill's part would take time, and time was running out for Richard Taylor and his plans. Selecting this option would no doubt delay the start of the battle until later in the day or possibly the next morning.

Decision

Realizing he was out of position, Churchill decided to advance (Option 1) and adjust his alignment simultaneously. In his after-action report, the general from Arkansas described his choice: "After advancing a few hundred yards in line of battle I discovered that I was not far enough to the right and ordered the command to move by the right flank until I had passed the whole of General Parsons' division to the right of the road. The line of battle was again advanced, and pressing forward we immediately and hotly engaged the enemy along the entire line."[59] Realizing he needed to position his men better, Churchill made a slight change, placing most of his command south of the Sabine River Road. His new position was not entirely on the Union flank, but it would have to do.

Results/Impact

Despite the mistake, Churchill moved forward. Very soon after, the entire Confederate army was engaged. After an hour of fighting, the Union lines began to collapse under the weight of Taylor's attacks. Battling through one Federal brigade and then the next, Churchill's Command advanced some seven hundred yards, taking almost five hundred prisoners and capturing several enemy batteries. All seemed to be going Taylor's way until Churchill's advance suddenly exposed his own flank to the Union brigade of Col. William F. Lynch. Seeing his chance, A. J. Smith ordered his whole command forward (our next critical decision). Churchill was forced to fall back in confusion—the entire Confederate assault ground to a halt. Again, as on the day before, darkness prevented Union forces from inflicting additional damage on the fleeing Confederates.[60]

In his memoir, Taylor described a meeting with Churchill after the clash at Pleasant Hill: "Churchill came to report the result of his attack and seemed much depressed. I gave such consolation as I could, and directed him to move his command to the mill stream, seven miles to the rear, where he could find his trains and water. A worthy, gallant gentleman, General Churchill, but not fortunate in war."[61]

Churchill's advance on the Union line had an unmistakable impact on the campaign. What seemed to be another Confederate victory suddenly turned into a defeat or, at the very least, a tie. Beaten and exhausted, Taylor's command was forced to fall back, affording Nathaniel Banks the opportunity to reclaim the campaign's initiative. If Banks acted decisively, he could erase the stain of the previous day's debacle and continue with his operation. The only question remaining was whether Banks had the strength and courage to do so.

Alternative Decision/Scenario

Had Churchill taken the time to move his force farther to the right to be wholly on Smith's flank, many alternatives might have been possible. The attack launched an hour later might have allowed Taylor the advantage he needed to collapse the Union position. It seemed to participants on both sides that just before Churchill was forced to fall back, the Confederates were on the verge of another victory. A different decision by Churchill might have resulted in another success for Richard Taylor.[62]

A. J. Smith Counterattacks

Situation

A. J. Smith's nickname was "Whiskey," although it is unclear whether this was because he regularly imbibed that spirit or because of his reputation as a hard-bitten, curt, and bold combat commander. What is indisputable is that this diminutive, bespectacled Union general was respected by his superiors, extremely popular with his men, and one of the best general officers the war produced on either side.[63]

Pleasant Hill Battlefield Park, Louisiana, Modern Image, Author.

Named for the famous general and president, Andrew Jackson Smith was born in rural Bucks County, Pennsylvania, in 1815 to a father who fought in the Revolutionary War and the War of 1812. A. J. Smith graduated from West Point in 1838, thirty-sixth out of a class of forty-five. His noteworthy classmates included P. G. T. Beauregard, William Hardee, Henry Sibley, and Irvin McDowell. Before the war, Smith served in the West as an officer in the First Dragoons. He began the Civil War as a colonel in the Second California Cavalry, and in March 1862, he was promoted to brigadier. Smith was Henry Halleck's chief of cavalry during the latter's advance on Corinth, Mississippi, in the spring of 1862. By January 1863, Smith was made a division commander in the Thirteenth Corps, Army of the Tennessee. At the Battle of Arkansas Post that same month, the Army of the Tennessee forced the surrender of a much smaller Confederate force. Leading the Confederate garrison at Arkansas Post was Brig. Gen. Thomas James Churchill. Coincidentally, fifteen months later, Churchill's new command was driven from the field at Pleasant Hill by a well-timed critical decision by none other than Andrew Jackson Smith.[64]

The men under Smith's command had a reputation as some of the best marchers and hardest fighters in Sherman's army. Often called "gorillas" by their comrades, Smith's men wore the nickname as a badge of honor. One claim to fame the Pennsylvanian could make was that he was perhaps the only Union general who defeated Nathan Bedford Forrest in battle. Forrest was wounded fighting Smith's command at the Battle of Tupelo in July 1864.[65]

By the first week of April 1864, Andrew Jackson Smith had been a part of the Red River Campaign since its opening days. Being exposed to Banks's decision-making and command style for almost a month had begun to wear on the gruff, old-school army general. No one knows how much of his negativity toward Banks was "baked in" as opposed to how much came from direct exposure during the campaign. Either way, by the time the sun set on April 9, Smith had lost all respect for this political general from Massachusetts.

Until now, the few Union successes during the Red River Campaign were almost all credited to Smith's command. On March 14, Smith's men captured Fort DeRussy, its three hundred Confederate defenders, and eight heavy guns. Among the first troops to advance on Alexandria, Smith and his men helped to drive Richard Taylor and his command from the city on March 20. On March 21, a smaller force under Brig. Gen. Joseph A. Mower of Smith's command surprised and captured nearly 250 Louisiana Confederates and a four-gun artillery battery at Henderson's Hill, near present-day Boyce, Louisiana, almost without firing a shot.[66]

Now at the tail end of the Union column advancing to Shreveport, Smith and his 7,500 men let their camp near Grand Ecore on the morning of April 8,

Brig. Gen. Andrew Jackson Smith, USA, Unknown, circa, 1861–1865, Library of Congress Washington, DC 20540.

arriving near Pleasant Hill after a twenty-one-mile march. Hearing the sounds of battle emanating from Mansfield, Smith sent for instructions from Banks. After some debate among the generals at Mansfield, Smith was told to wait at Pleasant Hill, and the rest of the army would fall back and join him.

Allowing his men to rest in the early morning hours of April 9, Smith then moved into position south of the town, forming a line that crossed the road to Mansfield. Elements of the Thirteenth and Nineteenth Corps fell into line to his right. Solders in Banks's army now rested on their arms waiting for Taylor's Confederates.[67]

Richard Taylor's plan at Pleasant Hill was to have Churchill's Command attack the Union left flank. As Churchill was rolling up the Federal line, Taylor would throw the balance of his force at the Yankee line. At 4:30 p.m., Taylor ordered his artillery to open fire. Shortly after Churchill's attack could be heard from his right, Taylor called for an echelon attack.[68]

At the far left of the Union line was the brigade of Col. William F. Lynch of Smith's command. The brigade of Col. Lewis Benedict, First Division, Nineteenth Corps, was in front and slightly to his right. Lynch had also sent his Fifty-Eighth Illinois Regiment half a mile in front. The Illinois men took shelter behind a makeshift breastwork.

Churchill's attack drove the irregular Union line back on itself, and Green's Texas cavalry and the Frenchman Polignac leading a brigade of Texas infantry did the same on his right. But Churchill failed to position his command far enough to the right, exposing his own flank as he advanced. Lynch's brigade was now collapsing Brig. Gen. John Bullock Clark Jr.'s Confederate brigade at the far right of Churchill's line. The old army brigadier Andrew Jackson Smith witnessed the desperate struggle unfolding before him.[69]

Options

Smith, sensing an opportunity, could either hold his ground or advance. The forty-eight-year-old veteran of more than a dozen battles had a critical decision to make.

Option 1

Smith's first option was to hold his line and let the Confederates come at him. The general was an experienced commander who had seen the results of reckless charges firsthand. While he had an appetite for aggressiveness, having his men stand their ground while pouring a relentless fire into the advancing enemy was often tactically prudent.

From December 26 to December 29, 1862, Smith had personally witnessed the challenge of sending men into well-defended positions. On the last day of

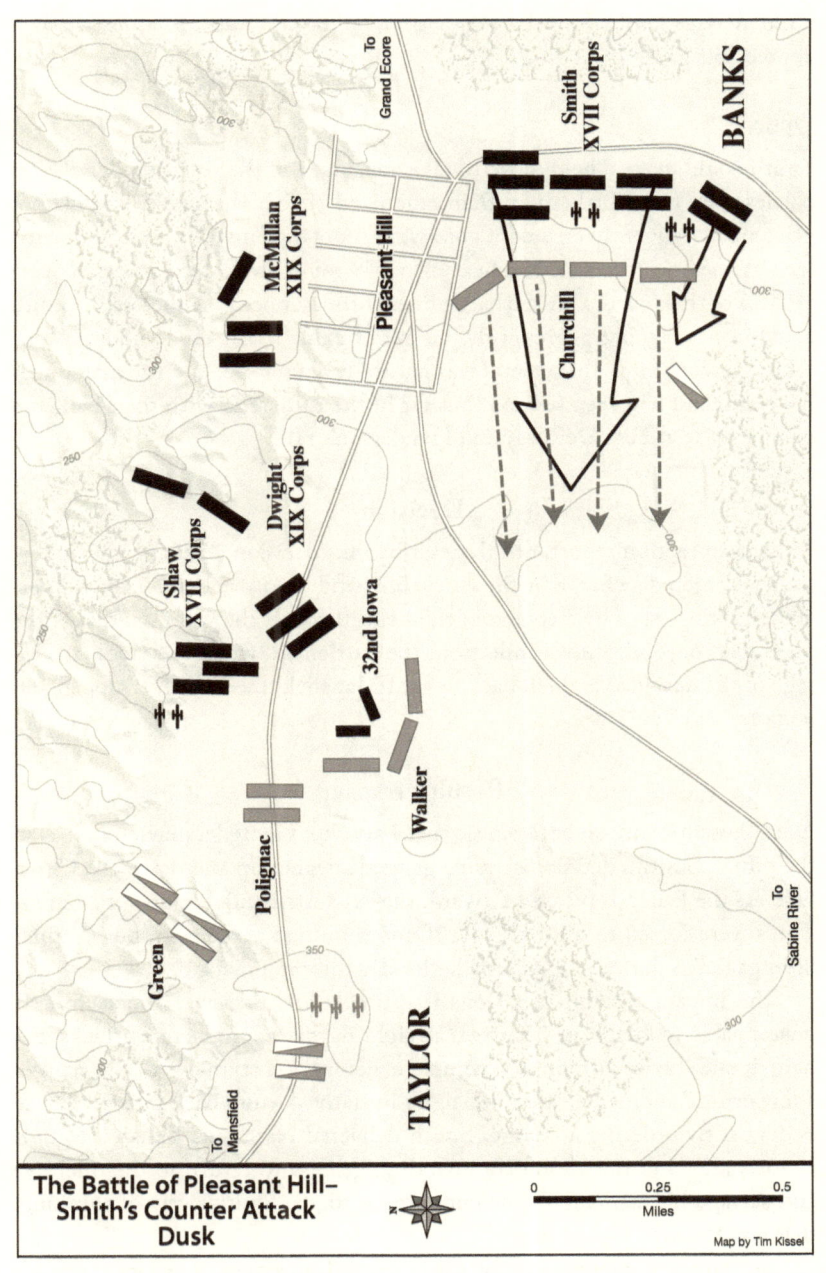

the Battle of Chickasaw Bayou, forces Smith commanded participated in the Union loss. William T. Sherman threw waves of Union men at entrenched Confederates led by John C. Pemberton, suffering 1,800 casualties with no appreciable gains.[70]

Option 2

Smith could make a bold move to take advantage of the situation. Civil War battles were often little more than organized chaos. The smoke and clamor of combat frequently created a confusing morass of men, horses, and artillery. Attacking forces in the heat of battle routinely lost cohesion or were victims of their success as the battle lines shifted or became undone. If Smith acted decisively and aggressively, he might exploit that exact situation unfolding before him. The general was naturally aggressive, and the men under his command had seen success thus far in the campaign with their bellicose combat style at Fort DeRussy and Henderson's Hill.

Decision

In his after-action report, Smith described his decision: "Seizing the opportunity I ordered a charge by the whole line, and we drove them back, desperately fighting, step by step across the field, through the wood, and into the open field beyond, fully a mile from the battlefield, when they took advantage of the darkness and fell back toward Mansfield thoroughly whipped and demoralized."[71]

Results/Impact

Even though many on both sides sensed another Confederate victory was in the offing, Smith's decision set off a general advance up and down the Union line. As the Federals pressed forward, the exhausted and fought-out Confederates were forced to fall back. As if under mutual agreement, both armies disengaged as darkness again made the slaughter impractical.

The impact of Smith's actions was timely and decisive. The seemingly unstoppable momentum from two straight days of Confederate attacks was halted, and Taylor's vision of a complete victory was stymied. In the span of a few critical moments, the campaign's initiative swung back in favor of the Federals. By ordering a charge, Smith delivered Nathaniel Banks a tactical victory, allowing the Union commanding general to return to the offensive and salvage his campaign if he chose to do so. To Smith's way of thinking, that was the next logical move.[72]

Becoming more indignant by the hour, Smith went on to record the result of his choice in his report: "The opinion of Major-General Banks as to the action of the command and its results may be gathered from his own words to me on the field just after the final charge, when, riding up to me, he remarked, shaking me by the hand, 'God bless you, general; you have saved the army.'"[73]

Alternative Decision/Scenario

It is impossible to determine what might have happened had Smith had his men stand in line and not advance as they did. Another Federal defeat was certainly a possible outcome of such a decision. Those who study the campaign often agree that the Union position at Pleasant Hill was so poorly thought out that defeat should have been a foregone conclusion. A different choice by Smith would have gone a long way in making the Union defeat at Pleasant Hill a reality, thereby altering the history of the campaign we now know.

In his testimony before the Joint Committee on the Conduct of the War, William B. Franklin declared, "The position at Pleasant Hill was weak, and had the enemy attacked us in rear as well as in front we would have probably had a disaster."[74] In his *Red River Campaign: Politics & Cotton in the Civil War*, noted expert on the campaign Ludwell H. Johnson, reinforces this notion, writing, "A glance at a map showing Federal troop dispositions as they were at the beginning of the action makes the Union success seem all the more remarkable. A worse placement of troops for defensive operations could scarcely be envisioned."[75]

Repulse of the Rebels at The Battle of Pleasant Hill, *Harpers Weekly*, Vol 8, May 7, 1864, p. 297, New York City, New York, U.S.

CHAPTER 3

THE AFTERMATH

APRIL 9–APRIL 30, 1864

Harvey C. Medford, with his father in tow, made the five-hundred-mile trip from Alabama to Angelina County, Texas, in 1852 to make a new home. Northeast of Houston, Angelina County boasted an 1860 population of 4,200 people. A schoolteacher before the war, the thirty-year-old Medford joined the Eleventh Texas Infantry in February 1862. He served all over the Trans-Mississippi during the war, eventually earning a position on the staff of Confederate brigadier general James Patrick Major, who led a division in Brig. Gen. Thomas Green's Confederate cavalry command during the Red River Campaign.[1]

In the late evening of April 9, 1864, after the clash at Pleasant Hill had ended, Medford, still on the field of battle, recorded the following contemplations in his diary: "Have passed camp after camp of prisoners, taken in the fight this evening. I do feel so heavy at heart tonight; my pensive soul is heavy and my eyes weep, fearing that our loss is greater than that of the enemy. This fierce encounter has been dreadful on both sides. I wish I knew the true state of the affair. It is low twelve, and so ends this eventful day."[2]

Two critical decisions occurred after the Battles of Mansfield and Pleasant Hill.

Banks Withdraws to the Red River

Situation

Brig. Gen. Thomas Kilby Smith led a division of the Union Seventeenth Corps under the command of Brig. Gen. Andrew J. Smith during the Red River Campaign. On February 4, 1865, Smith testified before the Joint Congressional Committee on the Conduct of the War, which was investigating the disastrous Union performance during the Red River Campaign.

During his testimony, the following exchange took place between Kilby Smith and a member of the committee:

> Question: Do you know whether or not General A. J. Smith, during the time he was with General Banks, considered himself to be in all respects under the command of General Banks?
>
> Answer: His rank precluded his occupying any other position. I know General A. J. Smith was adverse in opinion to that entertained by General Banks because I heard him on more than one occasion express himself very freely, without approaching to mutiny or sedition. He, of course, expressed himself freely to his brother officers. He felt as many of the rest of us felt, that our command was to a considerable extent being wasted. An anxiety on the part of General Banks's staff seemed to be felt to avoid a fight; (whenever a fight was had, General A. J. Smith was brisk for bringing it on;) and yet there was no time when we did not feel ourselves entirely competent to handle the enemy.
>
> Question: Was it or not, the opinion of General A. J. Smith that our army should have advanced after the Battle of Pleasant Hill?
>
> Answer: It was, most decidedly; to such an extent was that opinion entertained by him that he proposed, and was anxious, to march to Shreveport with our command, feeling entirely competent to go to Shreveport and do all the devilment that was necessary and return.[3]

This testimony perfectly demonstrates how and why Andrew Jackson Smith and a growing number of commanders in Banks's army had become extraordinarily disillusioned with their commanding general by the end of the Battle of Pleasant Hill. Even if Kilby Smith was somewhat restrained in his description of A. J. Smith's actual demeanor. A wave of distrust and disillusionment had begun to permeate Nathaniel Banks's command.

On April 9, 1864, as the sun descended slowly below the western pines, the guns fell silent, the acrid smoke dissipated, and the tattered battle flags

Brig. Gen. Thomas Kilby Smith
USA, Unknown, circa 1898.

were rolled and put away. By unspoken mutual agreement, the two armies disengaged. Duplicating a scene played out on countless battlefields across the war-torn nation since the summer of 1861, the deafening clamor of battle was replaced by the pitiful and agonizing cries of scores of grievously wounded men. Some of these poor, suffering souls begged for water, while others spoke to the Almighty or unseen loved ones in inaudible or muted tones. After three days of combat, Reb and Yank paused the killing, taking a long, exhausted communal breath.

Richard Taylor's army had battled Banks's command for almost three straight days, beginning with Brig. Gen. Thomas Green's April 7 attack on Albert Lee's Union troopers at Wilson's Farm. The action continued with the assault at Mansfield the next day, and the final attack at Pleasant Hill the day after that. While the more than 2,600 combined casualties suffered by the Confederate army were undoubtedly a grim reality facing its commanders, the damage to Taylor's officer corps was even more devastating. In Brig. Gen. Alfred Mouton's division alone, five brigade and regimental commanders were killed, including Mouton himself.[4]

Dick Taylor was not the least bit dissuaded by his losses. The uncompromising Confederate general was determined to keep pressure on the enemy. Committed to driving Banks and his invading army out of Louisiana and into the Gulf of Mexico if necessary, Taylor would allow no amount of casualties or damage to his command to get in the way of this objective. Convinced that the Union forces were staggered and whipped, he wrote, "The enemy's campaign for conquest was defeated by an inferior force, and it was doubtful if his army and fleet could escape destruction." Taylor continued, "Banks, with the remains of his beaten army, was before us and the fleet of Porter, with barely enough water to float upon. We had to strike vigorously to capture or destroy both."[5]

Despite his desire to strike Banks again, Taylor did recognize he and his men were close to exhaustion. As the darkened battlefield grew quiet, the Confederate general finally gave in to his weariness, lying down for a well-earned rest. Tomorrow would be soon enough to crush what was left of the Yankee army and navy.[6]

Deliberations and assessments were now taking place on the Union end of the battlefield. In a repeat of the night before near Mansfield, Nathaniel Banks was busily consulting with his staff and senior generals as to his army's next move. Despite a weak defensive alignment, Union forces not only stopped the main Confederate assault at Pleasant Hill, but also, thanks to A. J.

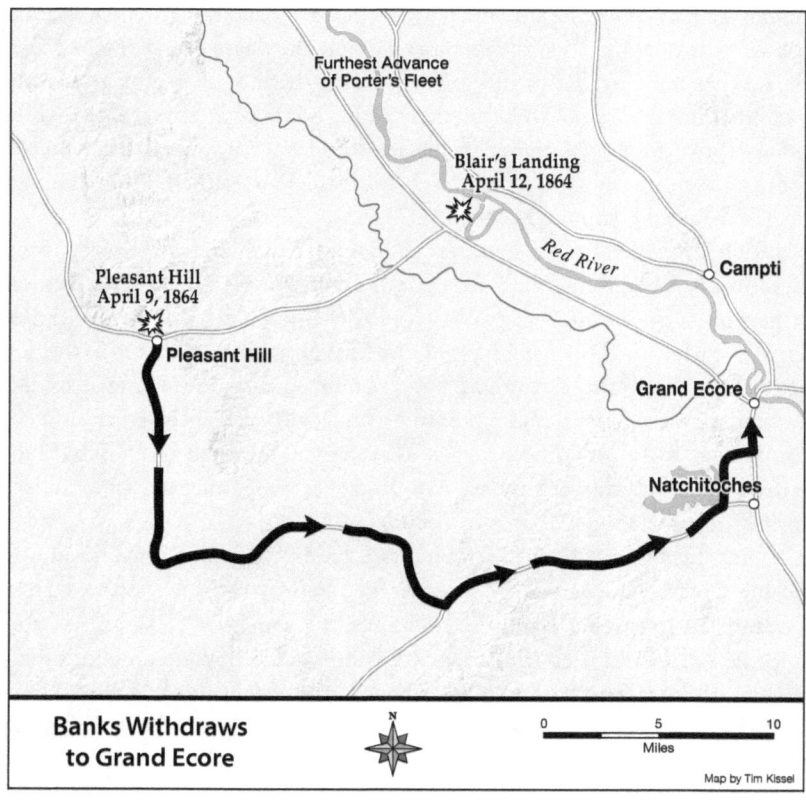

Smith, the Yankees drove the Confederates back to where they started at the outset of the battle. Just as it was after Mansfield, Banks's commanders reached no consensus on the next strategic action. The difference was that tonight's council of war came after a Union victory, and not a humiliating defeat and desperate retreat. Even though Banks could claim tactical victory, it is safe to say that Richard Taylor's aggressive moves had somewhat unnerved his Union counterpart. Banks likely anticipated further enemy assaults on his position when dawn came.[7]

Since April 7, Banks's command had suffered just over 4,000 combined casualties, including 529 killed, 1,444 wounded, and approximately 2,051 men missing. Many of the missing, over 60 percent, were men captured during the calamitous retreat from Mansfield.[8] Banks and Taylor both believed they were outnumbered by as much as two to one. In reality, subtracting the casualties suffered during the day's contest, each army had roughly ten thousand to twelve thousand men to renew the fight the next day. The main difference was that Taylor's army was reaching the end of its endurance, while Banks's forces were not nearly so worn down.[9]

Despite these losses, the Union army still had a strong force at hand. Banks also had a 5,600-man reserve available to him—the 3,600 men of Brig. Gen. Cuvier Grover's Second Division of the Nineteenth Corps were at Alexandria, and the 2,000 men of Brig. Gen. Thomas Kilby Smith's division of the Seventeenth Corps were with Porter's flotilla. The challenge here was that Banks was not precisely sure where Porter and Kilby Smith were, and Grover's command was almost seventy miles away.[10]

Last, while the humiliating rout at Mansfield shook the morale of the Union army, the outcome of the clash at Pleasant Hill undoubtedly bolstered Federals' confidence. Union lines had been stretched, bent, and cracked but not broken. The two armies ended the day very near to their positions before the battle had begun.

Options

Haunted by the prospect of additional combat come the morning and unsettled by an unusually aggressive opponent, Nathaniel Banks vacillated. The New Englander could stand and fight in his current position, fall back, or advance. With time, manpower, and logistics as influencing factors, the Federal commander had one more critical decision to make.

Option 1

Banks could determine that standing at his current position at Pleasant Hill was his best alternative. There were good reasons for the Union to remain in place and fight. First, the army was here, and Banks would only need to reinforce his location and adjust his lines to make the position stronger. It should be evident to Banks by now that Taylor was predisposed to strike again, and a solid defensive line would give the advantage to the Federals in any renewed attack the following day.

On the other hand, standing at Pleasant Hill meant there was no foolproof way to anchor either end of the Union line, and Banks's flanks would be exposed. Taylor had tried to get on the Federal flank the day before and would likely try again, given the opportunity. He and his men were familiar with the countryside and the limited road network. The Union army would be highly vulnerable if Taylor managed to get between Banks and his naval support on the Red River. This is precisely the scenario a shaken William B. Franklin feared.[11]

Option 2

Nathaniel Banks might reason that falling back to Grand Ecore or some other point near the Red River made the most sense. Banks and his command were vulnerable in the wilderness of central Louisiana. As the Confederates were more familiar with the terrain, they could use that knowledge to flank the Federals on either side. Falling back to the Red River meant that Banks would have secure communications, a solid point to anchor his lines on, and the added firepower of the powerful Union naval guns. Indeed, a position near the river would only add to Federal advantages. Banks might then have time to contemplate his next move, knowing his army was relatively safe. The number of Union killed and wounded surely affected Nathaniel Banks's decision-making. A position closer to the Red River would provide his men time to rest, recuperate, and reorganize, and afford their commander time to consider his remaining options.

Banks also had to consider Porter and his fleet. At that moment, the commanding general was unsure where Porter's flotilla was located, and he did not know whether the ships were in a position to support a continued campaign. If Porter could not turn his vessels around to join Banks, he risked getting cut off if the Confederates managed to block the river.

Conversely, a retrograde movement to the banks of the Red River would give up all the advantages gained so far. These advantages had been purchased with the lives of hundreds of Union soldiers.

Option 3

Banks might decide that continuing to advance toward Shreveport was his best option. While weakened, the Federals still had a manpower advantage over their Confederate foes, and Banks still had a powerful force at his disposal. And while he did not fully realize it, his Confederate opponents were approaching their physical limits. Moreover, Kirby-Smith was at that moment contemplating pulling men from Taylor's Command to counter Frederick Steele's operation in Arkansas. However, it is certain Banks did not know this fact.

Several generals in Banks's command expressed a desire to advance and continue the operation. The tough and aggressive A. J. Smith undoubtedly favored continuing to move north. Sure that this would be the next logical move, he advanced his Third Brigade of the Third Division over two miles on the same road the Confederates had used to fall back from the field at Pleasant Hill.[12]

If Banks took a more defensive posture, realizing Union objectives for the campaign might become a forlorn hope. If the general did not advance now, there was no guarantee that he would gather the mental courage to try again from farther downstream.

Decision

After conferring with his generals, Banks initially decided to continue the advance toward Shreveport (Option 3). Still, after consulting with Franklin, Emory, and Dwight of the Nineteenth Corps, he was convinced to fall back to Grand Ecore. Sometime around midnight on April 10, Banks ordered a full retreat to the safety of the Red River (Option 2).[13]

When quizzed by the investigating committee about why he favored a retreat rather than a stand at Pleasant Hill, William B. Franklin gave an exhaustive list of logistical and tactical reasons for his position. Still, he also volunteered the following unflattering assessment of his commander: "Besides, from what I had seen of General Banks's ability to command in the field, I was certain that an operation dependent upon plenty of troops, rather than upon skill in handling them, was the only one which would have a probability of success in his hands, and that, therefore, when we next met the enemy, we ought to have all the strength available to us."[14]

A. J. Smith was furious with the decision. Not only did he wish to continue to Shreveport, but he also protested that a retrograde movement to Grand Ecore meant Smith would have to leave his dead and wounded on the field and Kilby Smith's command on the Red River would risk being cut off. Banks was unmoved by Smith's protests.

One perhaps apocryphal version of what happened next was relayed by two officers on A. J. Smith's staff. The incensed General Smith asked William B. Franklin to place Banks under arrest and take command in his place. He assured Franklin that such a move had the full support of all the Sixteenth and Seventeenth Corps officers. A stunned Franklin refused to go along with the scheme, stating, "Smith, that is mutiny." This apparently extinguished Smith's fury, ending any further discussions on the subject.[15]

Results/Impact

The most apparent result of the Union army's withdrawal from Pleasant Hill was that Nathaniel Banks turned a tactical victory into a strategic defeat with a single stroke. The decision also ended the possibility of any further combat at Pleasant Hill. And last, Banks's decision set the stage for the campaign's next phase. For the next six weeks, at places like Blair's Landing, Monett's Ferry, Cane River, David's Ferry, and Yellow Bayou, Union and Confederate forces engaged in a running gun battle. The combat stretched over one hundred miles as the Federal army gradually fell back from one position to the next, Taylor and his meager force hounding them the whole way.

As we will learn with respect to our next decision, Banks's choice also helped convince Kirby-Smith that the Union threat to his south had disappeared. Thus, it would be safe to pull forces from Taylor's army and march them north to stop Frederick Steele advancing from Little Rock. In addition, the withdrawal from Pleasant Hill helped prevent any possibility of Union forces becoming outflanked as the Confederates moved east to the Red River.

Alternative Decision/Scenario

Had Banks decided to stand and fight at his current position at Pleasant Hill, any number of alternate scenarios might have been possible. Given his proclivity for aggressiveness, Richard Taylor could have thrown another attack at the Union lines. Or the Confederate commander might have simply moved around Banks's flank to get between him and the Union fleet on the Red River. Conversely, Richard Taylor could have paused to rethink his strategy. At that moment, Taylor and Kirby-Smith were engaged in a heated discussion on the commanding general's desire to pull forces from Taylor's Command to respond to the emerging Union threat in Arkansas—our next critical decision. Given a drastic reduction of his manpower, it is not clear whether Taylor would still have favored a renewed assault at Pleasant Hill.

April 9–April 30, 1864

The Battle at Blair's Landing, Battles and Leaders of the Civil War, The Century Co., circa 1887–88, Vol. 4, p. 364, New York City, New York, U.S.

Kirby-Smith Moves Forces to Arkansas

Situation

Late in 1864, Kirby-Smith and the Davis administration exchanged several messages that often took weeks to travel from one point to another. This correspondence primarily revolved around the administration's desire for Kirby-Smith to send troops east of the Mississippi to support John Bell Hood's rapidly disintegrating army and Kirby-Smith's reasons why this was impossible.

In a message written on Christmas Eve 1864, the Confederate president rebuked his Trans-Mississippi commander generally while criticizing Kirby-Smith's decision-making during the late Red River Campaign specifically. Davis wrote in part,

> It is to be regretted that the withdrawal of so large a portion of the army of the enemy, heretofore employed in the Trans-Mississippi Department, and their concentration against our forces on this side of the Mississippi River with such unfortunate results to us, was not either promptly met by the forwarding of re-enforcements from you, or that in the Trans-Mississippi Department such vigorous measures did not rapidly follow your victories in April as would have prevented the enemy from sending troops to re-enforce his armies elsewhere, and perhaps would have created an effectual diversion.[16]

Facing a storm of condemnation and second-guessing from above and below, Edmund Kirby-Smith persevered, having few other realistic options.

It is safe to say that Edmund Kirby-Smith had one of the most thankless jobs in the whole of the Confederacy. Indeed, by the winter of 1864–65, every command in the Confederacy suffered from shortages in manpower, arms, supplies, and logistical support. Moreover, every commander in the South faced some form of internal strife and a severe deterioration of morale by this time in the war. Each frayed corner of the Confederacy was slowly and steadily coming apart at the seams. All that said, the difficulties faced by Gen. Edmund Kirby-Smith were compounded by Union control of Mississippi that isolated his command, as well as a relentless stream of criticism from Richmond.

Despite the Confederate setback at Pleasant Hill, by the evening of April 9, Richard Taylor was convinced he had stopped the Federal momentum north. In fact, Taylor believed his only mistake at Pleasant Hill was not leading Churchill's attack himself. Putting a positive spin on the outcome, he later referred to the fight on the ninth as "emphatically the soldier's victory." However, at that exact moment, unbeknownst to the Confederate commander, Banks had decided to withdraw back to Gand Ecore, giving Taylor the strategic victory.

Regardless of his own casualties and his army approaching a point of complete exhaustion, Taylor was determined to operate from the same playbook as before. That book told him that continued pressure on Nathaniel Banks's infantry and David Dixon Porter's Union flotilla would shatter the Union resolve and push the enemy back down the Red River.

Now that the fighting was over, most of Taylor's worn-out army fell back some six miles from the battlefield. The exception was two brigades of cavalry that Taylor had posted on the Blair Landing Road earlier that day; these remained in position to block any Federal movement to the river and to prevent a linkup with the Union navy.[17]

Richard Taylor had been everywhere in the past several days—firing off communications to Shreveport, directing operations in the field, personally placing units in line of battle, and ensuring the wounded had the best care he could provide. He had not stopped for nearly a week, and he had barely slept. Having made the needed arrangements for his army and finding himself overcome by exhaustion, Taylor finally lay down to sleep. Much to his disappointment, this respite was not to last. A renewed debate on Confederate strategy soon interrupted the general's much-needed slumber.

Forcing the fog from his brain, Taylor saw a familiar figure standing over him: Edmund Kirby-Smith. For the second time in three days, the commanding general was compelled to travel from Shreveport to Taylor's head-

President Jefferson Davis, Confederate States of America. Mathew B. Brady, circa 1861, Library of Congress Prints and Photographs Division Washington, DC 20540.

quarters in the field. Kirby-Smith was here to consult with his lieutenant and to convince him of a change in strategy.[18]

Having ridden all day to reach Taylor, a frustrated Kirby-Smith sought to rein in his irrepressible general. Kirby-Smith and Taylor, as was routine, had very different thoughts on what the subsequent actions should be. Taylor wanted to continue the attacks and crush the Union army and navy—leaving Sterling Price in Arkansas to check Steele's advance with whatever forces he had. He argued that if Banks and Porter were forced to fall back downstream, Steele would have no choice but to retreat back to Little Rock. In Taylor's mind, the best way to accomplish this was to direct all available Confederate strength at Banks and Porter. Taylor also pointed out that Union general Steele was still over one hundred miles from Shreveport, posing no immediate threat to the Confederate capital.

Conversely, Kirby-Smith believed Taylor's army was worn down, paralyzed, and disorganized from continuous marching and fighting. Moreover, with Steele's command moving south, Kirby-Smith was also concerned that the Union general in Arkansas now posed a more significant danger. Kirby-Smith therefore wanted all the department's resources brought to bear against this threat from the north.[19]

Kirby-Smith's perspective of the past few days was fundamentally different from that of his chief lieutenant in Louisiana. Despite his orders to

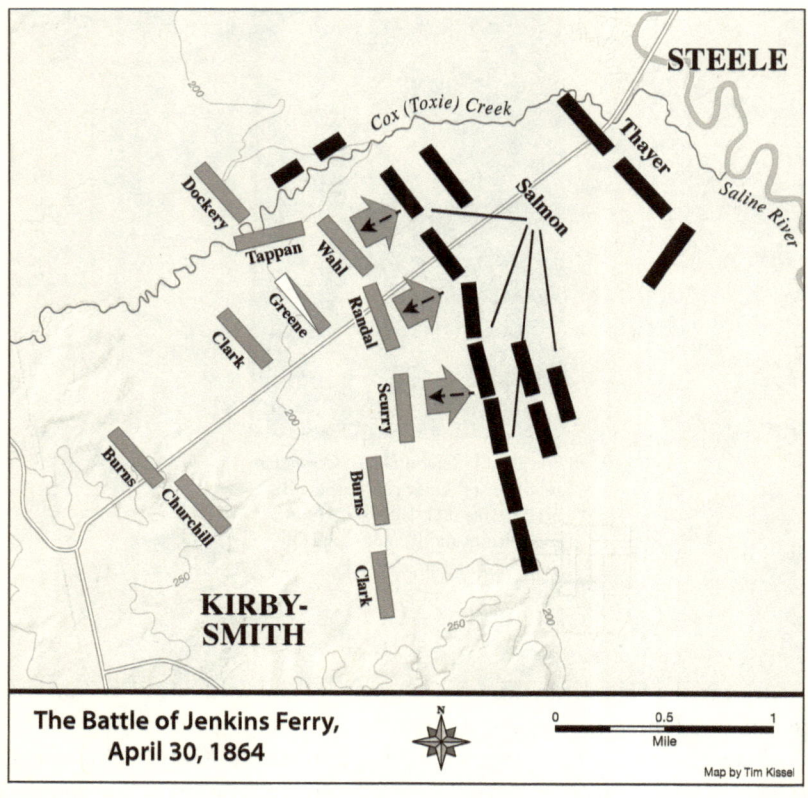

The Battle of Jenkins Ferry,
April 30, 1864

Taylor not to fight with the Federals below Shreveport, the Union army had been stopped. He certainly understood the significance of the outcomes of the last several days, realizing that Taylor and his army had performed well despite their disadvantages. But Kirby-Smith could not help continuing to throw his gaze to the north, and to the growing threat that was Frederick Steele's Union force. The Confederate commander only saw potential disaster in Arkansas, real or imagined.[20]

Meanwhile, in Arkansas, Maj. Gen. Frederick Steele and his Union command had reached Arkadelphia on March 26. He paused here for several days, waiting for Brig. Gen. John Milton Thayer's 3,600 men from the Fort Smith garrison to join him. By April 3 and 4, tired of waiting, Steele threw a bridge across the Little Missouri River and moved his army toward Washington, Arkansas. Steele had battled Brig. Gen. John S. Marmaduke's Confederates at Mount Elba and Elkin's Ferry, but the Confederate attacks had only slowed his advance.

Thayer and Steele finally connected on April 7, five miles south of Elkin's Ferry and about one hundred miles north of Shreveport. Steele now had over ten thousand men with which to continue his operation. The inability to supply this army became Steele's Achilles' heel. Brig. Gen. John S. Marmaduke had perhaps 3,600 mounted Confederates to oppose the Yankees. However, promised reinforcements were on the way.[21]

Back in Louisiana, on the other side of the battlefield at Pleasant Hill, the Union army was on the move. By this time in the evening, Nathaniel Banks had determined to give up his victory and fall back. The telltale sounds of an army in motion were now becoming evident to the Confederates in Taylor's army. Stragglers soon confirmed to Edmund Kirby-Smith and Richard Taylor that Banks was in full retreat.[22]

Options

Though the debate between Kirby-Smith and Richard Taylor was a bit calmer this evening, the two men still disagreed. Kirby-Smith could either leave Taylor's improvised army intact or send part of it to Arkansas to support Sterling Price. The beleaguered commander of the Trans-Mississippi had a critical decision to make.

Option 1

Kirby-Smith's first option was to keep the army he had assembled in Louisiana intact. If Taylor could persuade him that Nathaniel Banks's army and David Dixon Porter's fleet still posed the most significant threat to Shreveport, keeping as many of his reinforcements with Taylor as possible made sense. Most Trans-Mississippi forces were already here and ready to continue the fight. Moving men over a hundred miles away to Arkansas would undoubtedly take time and add to the physical toll the campaign had already taken on Confederate troops. Leaving the Confederates where they were would undoubtedly be the most straightforward plan to execute.

On the other hand, Kirby-Smith seemed to have growing doubts about the skills of his general in Arkansas, and this decision would leave Sterling Price alone to deal with Steele's advance.[23]

Option 2

Kirby-Smith might determine that his best option was pulling forces from Taylor to reinforce Sterling Price. Steele's army advancing from Little Rock was now below the Little Missouri River, approaching Prairie D'Ane near modern-day Prescott. Sterling Price's forces had fallen back following a fight lasting several days. With his supply issues worsening, Steele began to move southeast toward Camden, Arkansas.

Without fully understanding that supply problems were affecting the Union army in Arkansas and that Steele's operation was likely doomed to fail, Kirby-Smith considered his forces in the state vulnerable. He was unsure that Price and Marmaduke were in any position to stop Steele. If Kirby-Smith really believed that Banks was in full retreat, it is somewhat reasonable that he now saw Steele as the most severe threat.[24]

Decision

In the end, Kirby-Smith was unpersuaded by Taylor's arguments. In his *Battles and Leaders* article on the Red River Campaign, Kirby-Smith cited a captured communication also influencing his decision: "An intercepted dispatch from General Sherman to General A. J. Smith, directing the immediate return of his force to Vicksburg, removed the last doubt in my mind that Banks would withdraw to Alexandria as rapidly as possible."[25] On April 14, 1864, Edmund Kirby-Smith ordered the divisions of Walker, Churchill, and Parson to march north to reinforce Maj. Gen. Sterling Price's command in Arkansas (Option 2). Hoping to keep some control over these units, Taylor offered to command them. Kirby-Smith refused, taking command himself while keeping this quarrelsome general in Louisiana. Roughly speaking, about five thousand men were detached from Taylor's force for the campaign's duration.[26]

Results/Impact

This decision impacted the campaign in several significant ways. First, it reduced the number of men available to Taylor by roughly half. A determined Richard Taylor was now forced to try and destroy Banks's command with a fraction of the men he had before. For the next several weeks, he tried unsuccessfully to land a decisive blow on Banks's army. While Taylor's men were undoubtedly willing, most of the Federals escaped across the Atchafalaya River.

Second, the choice drove a further wedge between Kirby-Smith and Richard Taylor. Smith gave Taylor a brevet promotion to lieutenant general as a reward for his recent performance, leaving him in charge at Shreveport while Kirby-Smith marched reinforcements to Arkansas. Taylor was anything but grateful. On April 19, he rejoined what remained of his army, facing

Banks's command at Grand Ecore.[27] Increasingly incensed, Taylor spent the last months of his tenure in the Trans-Mississippi battling his commanding officer more than he did the enemy. On June 5, 1864, Taylor demanded to be relieved of duty, no longer wanting to serve under Edmund Kirby-Smith.[28]

Frederick Steele had been getting intelligence regarding Banks's defeat and subsequent retreat, and by April 22, the rumors were confirmed. In an almost constant state of combat for a week, Steele's army was hemorrhaging men, supplies, arms, wagons, and mules. Learning of Kirby-Smith's approach all but sealed his fate. The final battle at Jenkins Ferry on April 30 was a strategic victory for Steele, as he was able to hold off Kirby-Smith and Sterling Price's combined forces. But in the end, the Federals were forced to fall back to Little Rock.[29]

Edmund Kirby-Smith convinced himself that his actions saved Shreveport and the Trans-Mississippi, and he later affirmed this belief his after-action report:

> I have written thus at length in advance of my report, delayed by being unable to get the reports of my subordinate commanders, because I learn that my policy and plans have been much discussed at Richmond, and that it has been charged that but for my errors much more important results would have been achieved. In this connection I have only to remark that I have honestly done what appeared to me

Admiral Porter's Flotilla on the Red River, *Harpers Weekly*, circa April 30, 1864, p. 277.

to be right and proper. I claim that my combinations have resulted in great successes, and beg to doubt whether more could have been accomplished under a different system of operations.[30]

Alternative Decision/Scenario

Had Kirby-Smith decided to leave these divisions or most of them with Taylor, we might have seen a different outcome to the Red River Campaign. In all likelihood, Banks and Porter would have pursued the same course as before. But if Taylor had a more significant force at his disposal, would the Battle of Yellow Bayou have ended differently?

With twice the men as we know he had at the battle, Taylor might have overrun the Union defenders and trapped the escaping Union army at the banks of a flooding Atchafalaya.

Who knows what different outcome might have resulted had Kirby-Smith made another decision? Would the course of the Red River Campaign have differed from what we now know?[31]

CHAPTER 4

CONCLUSIONS AND CONSEQUENCES

"Come on boys, you have got your chance at last!" the forty-three-year-old lawyer and newspaper editor from Clinton, Texas, called to the men of his brigade. "Come on!"[1] Struggling to be heard over the growing tumult of battle, Brig. Gen. William R. Scurry urged his command forward into an ever-increasing storm of musketry, shot, and shell. His brigade, part of John Walker's Texas Division, had heard similar cries from similar battlefields at almost every point of the Trans-Mississippi. From Milliken's Bend on the Mississippi to Fort DeRussy on the Red River, from Bayou Bourbeux to Mansfield, Louisiana, the men of Walker's Division enjoyed a reputation in battle matched only by their ability to undertake long and arduous marches. For this reason, these hard-fighting and highly mobile troops were dubbed the *Greyhounds*.[2]

The late afternoon of April 9, 1864, was pivotal in the Red River Campaign. As the battle at Pleasant Hill crested, Walker's Greyhounds held the center of the Confederate line. Churchill's Arkansas and Missouri troops were on their right, and Mouton's Division, now led by the French Prince de Polignac, was on their left, with Green's Texas cavalry to the left of him.

At 5:00 p.m., Scurry's Third Brigade was ordered to advance, supporting Churchill's attack. Union General A. J. Smith's men had gotten on Churchill's flank. Smith, seeing his chance, called the entire blue line forward. The Texans likewise pushed forward, colliding with Col. William T. Shaw's Second Brigade, also of Smith's command. At the extreme left of Shaw's blue line, the men of the 32nd Iowa could hear the Confederate officers shouting orders as the Texans advanced. "Dress up on the right! Steady on the center! Steady! Steady boys! Keep cool! Keep cool!" The officers of Shaw's command replied in kind, "Let them come," they cried, "let them empty their guns, and then shoot low; Never shoot above the belt!"[3] With Scurry's men now joined by Walker's two remaining brigades, the center of the battle line exploded into a bewildering, smoking morass of Union and Confederate forces alike. Eventually forced to fall back, Scurry's Brigade suffered devastating casualties, including 247 men captured.[4]

One regiment in Scurry's Brigade, the Seventeenth Texas Volunteer Infantry, was in the very thick of the afternoon's fight. The Seventeenth was characteristic of many regiments from the Lone Star State. Seventy-eight percent of the men who made up its ranks made a living in agriculture—they included everyone from planters and small subsistence farmers to hired laborers. From a wealth perspective, many could aptly be described as men of modest means. More than 50 percent of the Seventeenth's soldiers were under age twenty-five at the time of their enlistment. These men were recruited from central and eastern Texas counties, and their original commander was former West Pointer and Texas Military Institute superintendent Robert T. P. Allen.[5]

Capt. Elijah Parsons Petty commanded Company F of the Seventeenth. Like Scurry, Petty was a lawyer before the war. Originally from Tennessee, he moved his family to the small town of Bastrop, Texas, just east of Austin, in 1851. Leaving his young family behind, Petty joined the Seventeenth Texas in 1862. A loving husband and father, he wrote to his wife and children whenever he had a moment to put pen or pencil to paper. His letters home told of long, weary marches, the drudgery of a Confederate soldier's everyday life, the numerous engagements he fought in, and the men he served with.[6]

On the field at Pleasant Hill, the rifle and artillery fire now consuming the Seventeenth made the very air come alive. In his customary position at the head of his company, Captain Petty fell after being fatally struck in the chest by a grapeshot round that passed entirely through his body. In excruciating pain, Petty begged his men not to move him.

Knowing he would likely be captured, a member of Company F volunteered to stay with the captain, comforting him and giving him water as the rest of the regiment fell back. Petty was eventually borne to a Union hospital at the home of Mrs. Maria Childers of Pleasant Hill. In addition to a makeshift hospital, Mrs. Childers's home was the headquarters to Union general Nathaniel P. Banks. Petty died of his grievous wound within a few hours of his arrival. After the Union army retreated, vacating the town, a detail from

Conclusions and Consequences

the Seventeenth Texas discovered Petty's body among the dead outside the improvised hospital. The soldiers buried their captain in the Childers's yard.[7]

Elijah Petty was a typical nineteenth-century Texan. Chasing the promise of a new and better life, scores of Americans of all stripes and from all corners of the nation made the long and difficult journey to Texas long before it became a state, and even before it won its independence from Mexico. From 1861 to 1865, ninety thousand Texans went to war, countless among them fighting for their adopted state. Many of them, like Captain Petty, never returned home. The lawyer, father, and husband was thirty-four years old at the time of his death.[8]

In time, life in Pleasant Hill slowly returned to normal. The Childers family kept up Petty's grave for over twenty years. When curious visitors to the home asked about the simple plot in the corner of the yard, Mrs. Childers's descendants dutifully and solemnly recalled that terrible April day so long ago. They described a desperate and deadly battle that had raged just beyond their front door and the dozens of dreadfully wounded men cared for at their home. And they told the tale of the gallant young Captain Petty from Texas, a stranger far from his home and family who gave his life helping to defend their state.[9]

Years later, Elijah Petty's son placed a marker at the site where his father fell. For decades, this single simple memorial was the only thing honoring the fallen at the battlefield of Pleasant Hill.[10]

Step by step and mile by mile, the Union army ignominiously withdrew down the Red River. The great and glorious campaign begun with such

Capt. Elijah Parsons Petty, CSA, Seventeenth Texas Infantry, Unknown.

promise, optimism, and fanfare had disintegrated into a fighting retreat stretching for almost a hundred miles. For the next month, Nathaniel Banks methodically fell back to the mouth of the Red River as Richard Taylor and his ever-shrinking army pressed him the whole way. Even though almost all his infantrymen were essentially detached from his command and sent to Arkansas, a single-minded Dick Taylor never entertained any other possible course save the complete destruction of the Federal invaders in Louisiana.

Now south of Loggy Bayou, on April 10, Union admiral David Dixon Porter was advised by Federal cavalry of the Union reversals at Mansfield and Pleasant Hill and the planned retreat to Grand Ecore. His escort from the Seventeenth Corps under Kilby Smith was likewise ordered to join the rest of the infantry at this rendezvous point. Seeing no practical alternative, Porter ordered his six gunboats and twenty transport vessels to reverse course and fall back to the town as well.[11]

On the twelfth, the same day Banks's command arrived at Grand Ecore, Brig. Gen. Thomas Green, 2,500 Texas Confederate cavalry, and a four-gun battery attempted to trap Porter's fleet at Blair's Landing, about fifteen miles upriver of the town. The ships Green and his troopers found were the rear of the flotilla, which had already begun its retreat downriver.

After a two-and-a-half-hour struggle, three Union vessels, *Osage*, *Lexington*, and *Black Hawk*, managed to drive off Green's men and escape. There were perhaps one hundred combined casualties in this engagement, but among those killed was Thomas Green, decapitated by a Union canister round fired from the river monitor *Osage*.[12]

After enduring almost constant Confederate harassment, the battered Union fleet steamed into Grand Ecore on April 13. Rushing to meet with Banks, a stunned Porter learned that the commanding general insisted that he had won both the Battles of Mansfield and Pleasant Hill, only conducting this retrograde movement due to a lack of fresh water. According to Banks, Porter "unequivocally expressed" that neither the army nor the navy should attempt any new advance up the Red River. A disgusted Porter later remarked, "There is a futile attempt to make a victory out of this, but two or three such victories would cost us our existence."[13]

On April 21, as the navy was working to get all its vessels downstream, a reinforced Banks began to march his tired and hungry men toward Alexandria on the strip of land between the Red and Cane Rivers. With only five thousand men, Taylor raced to trap Banks at Monett's Ferry, where the Cane River flows into the Red. After a two-day running fight, the Union army slipped the Confederate snare, and on April 25, Banks's command limped into Alexandria and dug in.[14]

In the meantime, Banks's army began to unravel from the inside out. The general was working to shift blame for the disastrous campaign to anyone and anything but himself—including Frederick Steele in Arkansas and the Red River. Banks fired his chief of staff, Brig. Gen. Charles P. Store, and relieved his cavalry commander, Brig. Gen. Albert E. Lee. Banks's message of April 2 declaring his intention to chase Edmund Kirby-Smith into Texas found its way to U. S. Grant, along with detailed reports of the disasters at Mansfield and Pleasant Hill. A furious Grant wanted Banks removed from command immediately, but Lincoln declined for purely political reasons. Once again, Nathaniel Banks's most vital asset was the political capital he offered the Lincoln administration.

The morale in Banks's army, which had been rapidly deteriorating since April 8, sank to new levels. The rank-and-file soldiers began singing marching ditties that openly mocked Banks, knowing the general was within earshot. They also started referring to the commanding general as Mr. Banks, acknowledging the Massachusetts politician's glaring lack of military competence.[15]

Federal forces licked their wounds at Alexandria for the next three weeks under almost daily attacks and harassment from Taylor's Confederates. Meanwhile, Porter struggled to get his fleet over the falls above the city as the level of the Red River continued to drop. Admiral Porter was forced to destroy a badly damaged *Eastport*, the most powerful warship in his flotilla, adding to his misfortunes. Faced with the prospect of leaving Porter's fleet to the mercy of Confederate forces or destroying it, Banks and Porter okayed an unlikely plan. Union colonel Joseph Bailey, a former lumberman from Wisconsin, proposed damming the river to enable the Federal fleet to navigate the obstruction. Bailey's Dam, as it was called, worked as advertised, and Porter's fleet continued downstream. Colonel Bailey was awarded the Medal of Honor for saving the Federal navy, making him one of only a few Union men to leave the campaign with an enhanced reputation.[16]

With Porter's fleet free to follow, Banks and his army withdrew south and east from Alexandria on May 13, setting the town ablaze as they departed. Five days later, Richard Taylor's newly appointed cavalry commander John Wharton, who replaced Hamilton P. Bee, made one last attempt to trap and destroy the Union army at Yellow Bayou near Simmesport, Louisiana, some fifty miles northwest of Baton Rouge. In an all-day struggle on May 18, 4,500 Union men held off 5,000 Confederates, allowing the rest of the Federal army to escape over the Atchafalaya River.[17]

That same day, Maj. Gen. Edward R. S. Canby, waiting for Nathaniel Banks at Simmesport, informed the former bobbin boy that he had been relieved of his command. After almost three long months, the Red River

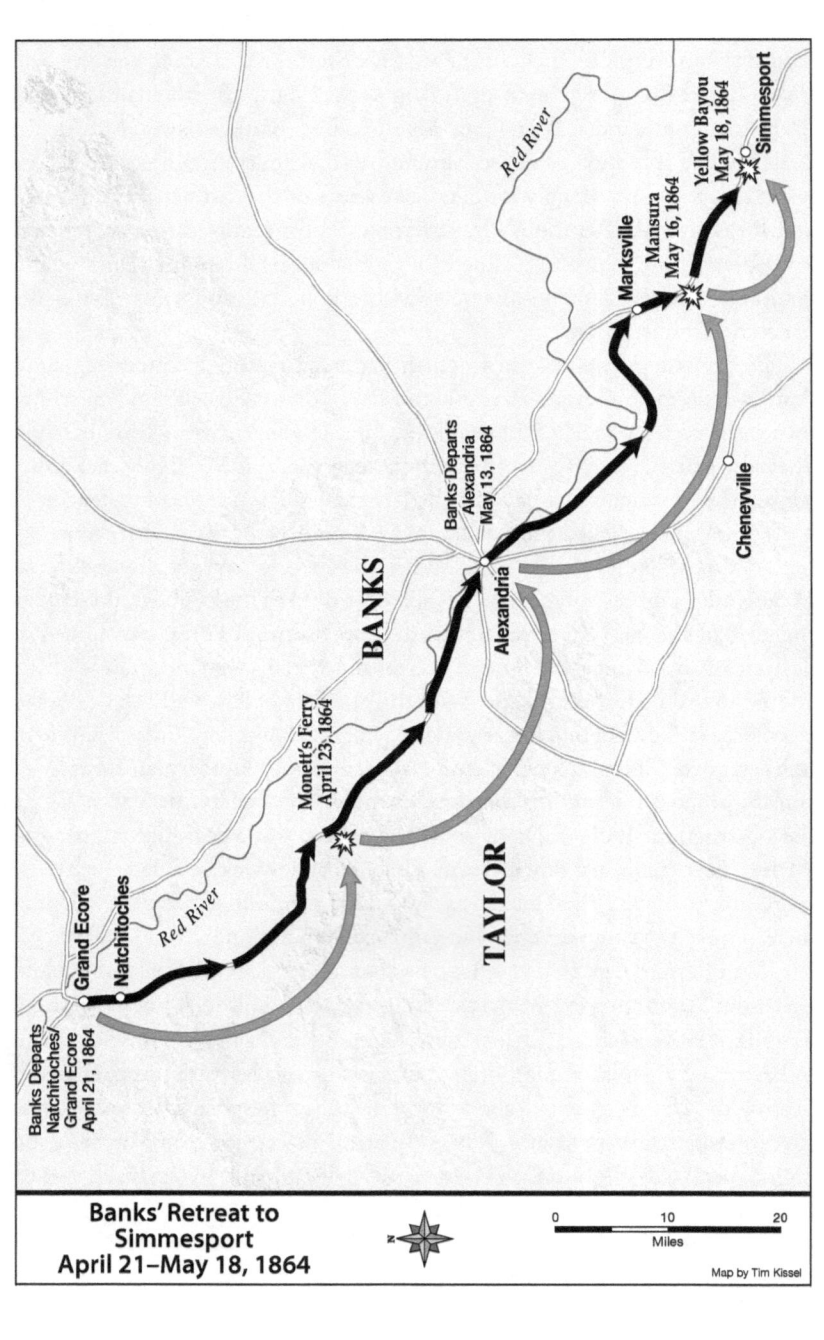

Campaign finally and mercifully concluded. A defeated Union army finished the operation at practically the same point from which it started, having achieved none of its operational objectives. Shreveport, east Texas, and most of western Louisiana would remain under Confederate control until the war's end.[18]

Banks, A.J. Smith, and Steele's combined Union armies had marched hundreds of miles during seven weeks of campaigning, fighting nearly two dozen separate engagements. In aggregate, these commands suffered over 8,000 casualties. They also lost 57 field guns, 822 wagons, and 3,700 horses and mules. David Dixon Porter's flotilla lost 9 vessels during the operation. By contrast, the combined Confederate forces, who probably marched even more miles, sustained 6,500 casualties and lost perhaps 26 fieldpieces, 50 wagons, approximately 700 horses and mules, and 3 vessels.[19]

Nathaniel Banks remained in Louisiana for a time, working to educate freedmen and freedwomen and shaping political affairs on behalf of the Lincoln administration. Banks was then ordered to Washington after the election of 1864. In December 1864, the Joint Committee on the Conduct of the War began hearings on the disastrous Red River Campaign that ran for four months. The committee was undoubtedly looking for a scapegoat, but Banks, with his questionable decision-making during the campaign, made its job an easy one. The committee leveled blame for the failure on several shoulders, but Nathaniel Banks received the lion's share of the responsibility.

After Abraham Lincoln's assassination in April 1865, Banks lost his most vital ally in Washington. Stripped of his military rank, the former general eventually returned to formal politics, serving his home state of Massachusetts in the US Congress from 1865 to 1873, in the Massachusetts State Senate from 1875 to 1879, and in the US Congress again in 1888. Nathaniel Prentiss Banks died in the town where he was born, Waltham, Massachusetts, on September 1, 1894. The judgments of history fixed his legacy as one of the worst Union generals to serve during the Civil War.[20]

On April 8, 1864, Richard Taylor was promoted to lieutenant general. However, this did nothing to quell his animosity toward Kirby-Smith, whom he blamed for the Confederates' failure to destroy the Federal army and navy during the campaign On June 5, having resisted the urge for weeks, Taylor wrote to Kirby-Smith, stating, "The same regard for duty which led me to throw myself between you and popular indignation and quietly take the blame of your errors, compels me to tell you the truth, however objectionable to you. The grave errors you have committed in the recent campaign may be repeated if the unhappy consequences are not kept before you. After the desire to serve my country, I have none more ardent than to be relieved from longer serving under your command."²¹

Richard Taylor's wish was granted. On June 11, Kirby-Smith removed him from command. After a short respite, Taylor was sent to command the Department of Alabama, Mississippi, and East Louisiana and then briefly given command of the Army of Tennessee. On May 4, 1865, he surrendered his department, the last major Confederate force east of the Mississippi, to Union general Edward Canby at Citronelle, Alabama.

The Civil War destroyed Taylor's home and devastated his fortune. The former general relocated his family to New Orleans at the war's end, remaining there until the death of his wife in 1875. Moving to Winchester, Virginia, Taylor spent his remaining years fighting as hard for Federal leniency toward the former Confederate states as he did in battle during the war. He also worked on his memoir, *Destruction and Reconstruction: Personal Experiences of*

Confederates attack Union Gunboats on the Red River, *Harpers Weekly*, circa May 14, 1864, cover.

the Late War. Richard Taylor died on April 12, 1879, and his memoir was published the same year. The work is regarded as one of the era's best and most accurate personal accounts of the war.[22]

* * *

For decades, Iowa residents often repeated the myth that their state's name was the Dakota word meaning "beautiful land." In fact, the word is an Anglicization of the Native American word Kiowa, roughly translated as "this is the place." Over the years, Iowa's former and more congenial derivation gained popularity for obvious reasons.[23]

Born of the Louisiana Purchase, Iowa became the twenty-ninth state of the Union in 1846. Despite some Confederate sympathies in some southern and eastern parts of this Trans-Mississippi state, Iowa was a free state siding with Lincoln and the Union in 1861. With an 1860 population of 674,913, the Hawkeye State contributed over seventy-two thousand men to the Northern war effort. Almost half (47 percent) of the men of military age residing in Iowa at the outbreak of the war signed up to fight for the Union.

These volunteers were mustered into forty-eight infantry regiments, four cavalry regiments, and three artillery batteries. When it was over, thirteen thousand Iowans had given their lives fighting for the Union cause. Serving primarily in the Western and Trans-Mississippi Theaters, Iowans fought at Forts Henry and Donelson, Shiloh, Vicksburg, and Atlanta, as well as in Sherman's March to the Sea, along the Texas Gulf Coast, and during the Red River Campaign.[24]

One regiment that served during the Red River Campaign was the Thirty-Second Iowa Volunteer Infantry. The Thirty-Second was mustered at Camp Franklin near Dubuque in August 1862, and Col. John Scott of Story County was made the regiment's commander. By March 1864, the Thirty-Second Iowa was part of Shaw's Second Brigade in Mower's Third Division, Seventeenth Corps, Army of the Tennessee under the command of Brig. Gen. Andrew J. Smith. By the late spring of 1864, these Iowans had battled Richard Taylor's army up and down the Red River for three months, moving from Fort DeRussy to Pleasant Hill to Simmesport. The Thirty-Second had its bloodiest fight on April 9, 1864, on the field at Pleasant Hill, Louisiana. At the center of the Union line, the Thirty-Second was almost surrounded by three brigades of Walker's Texans. Holding the line with 415 men, the Thirty-Second suffered 210 casualties before A. J. Smith's counterattack forced the Texans to fall back.[25]

After the Red River Campaign was over, Sgt. J. Mitchell Boyd of Company F of the Thirty-Second relayed his impressions of the operation while

Ironclad USS *Essex* at Baton Rouge, Louisiana, McPherson & Oliver, photographer, circa 1862, Library of Congress. Washington, DC 20540.

recalling his search for a comrade who fell at the campaign's final battle, Yellow Bayou.

> Much of the "inner history" of this campaign, doubtless, never has been written; never will be, and now, never can be. How much of its failure was due to jealousy and envy among our own Generals? Who can tell?
>
> There is much unwritten history in this and some other campaigns which if truthfully written up, would make more interesting reading than very much that is written; and would place a goodly number of prominent Generals and other officers in a very different light before the world from that in which they now stand.
>
> The troops marched across the peninsula and camped at Morganza's Bend. On the 22nd., while the fleet was lying at Morganza's Bend, I bunted over the transports Cheautau, Sioux City and Des Moines in search of John Myers, who was killed in the battle of the 18th. Some of the boys who were near him thought he was not dead when the regiment changed its position, and hence might have been brought into the Des Moines, then our hospital boat, by the ambulance corps. I was granted the privilege of searching the boat to see if I could recognize my man, but what a sight! There was scarcely a spot from the boiler to the hurricane deck where a man could be laid, but was occupied

by the wounded. Men lay there who were wounded in almost every conceivable way. I noticed one with both arms off, another with both legs gone—blown off, I think, by a shell—and a few were fearfully mangled.

These were only a small part—those of Mower's division. Afterwards on searching the records of the ambulance corps on Mower's headquarters boat, I found this:—"J. Myers, Co. F. 32d Iowa, killed." How brief, and what it tells: Killed on the field of battle; and fills an unmarked grave![26]

APPENDIX I
DRIVING TOUR OF THE CRITICAL DECISIONS OF THE 1864 RED RIVER CAMPAIGN

This portion of the book is a guide to the critical decisions of the Red River Campaign. As this operation encompassed such a large geographical area, this tour may take some time to complete. A reliable vehicle and a navigation device or smartphone are essential to locate each stop. I also recommend using a compass or a compass mobile app to better orient yourself at each of the various tour stops. Part of this tour will involve some light hiking, so plan accordingly.

The tour begins in New Orleans and has stops in Louisiana and Arkansas. Depending on the time spent at each destination, the journey could take up to three days. If you decide to visit each stop, you will cover a total distance of over five hundred miles.

The final decision, "Steele Advances at Shreveport," may be reviewed at Jenkins Ferry Battleground State Park in Arkansas or any other suitable location. As this stop is much farther north than the rest of them, some readers may wish to avoid traveling the extra distance.

You may also enter or leave the tour anytime that suits you. Some stops do not have an actual address and are located in very rural areas. I will provide more detailed directions in those cases. As the locations are often some distance from one another, in some instances, I am providing directions from the closest town or landmark.

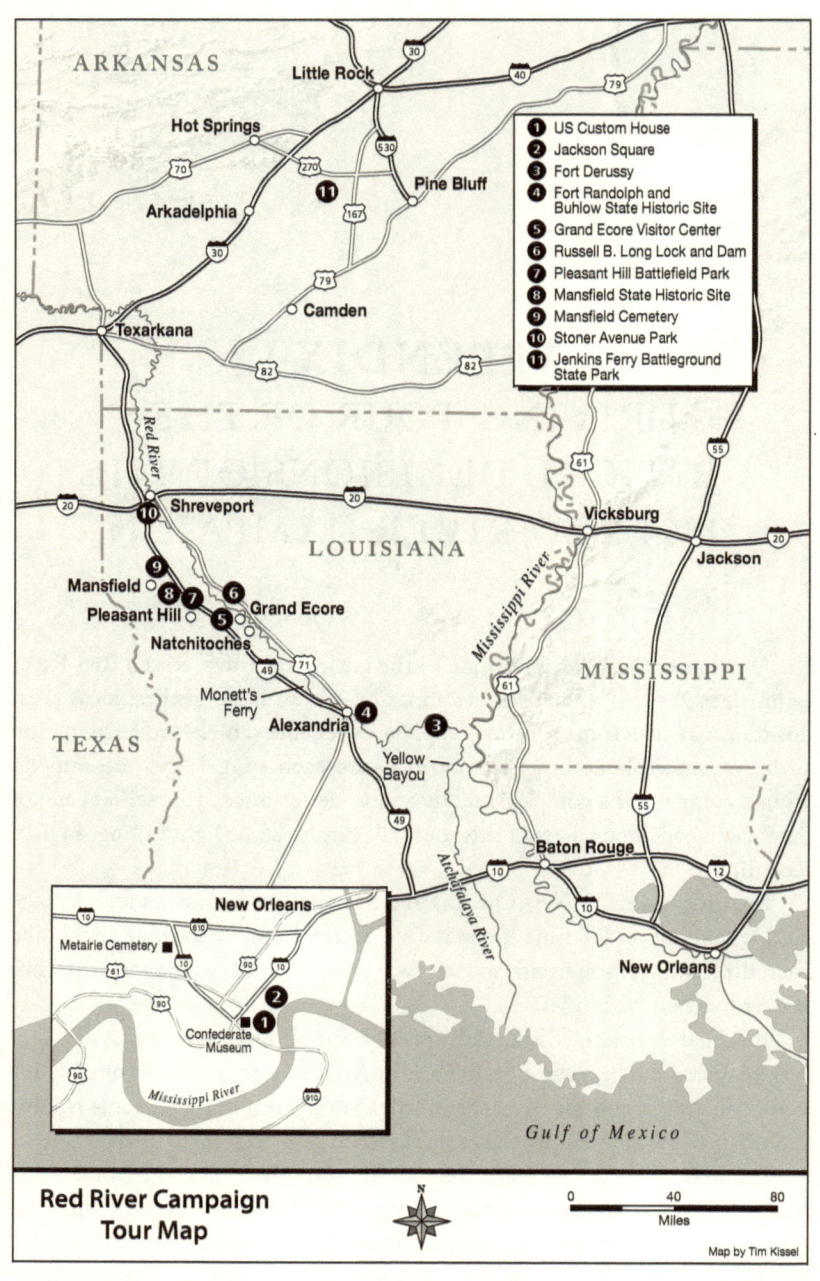

Driving Tour of the Critical Decisions of the 1864 Red River Campaign

Each stop includes an address, if one exists, and GPS coordinates—for example, 423 Canal Street, New Orleans, LA 70130 (29.95218088535499, -90.06628123728831).

Each decision will be recapped, just not necessarily in order or in reference to the exact location where the decision occurred. Last, this tour is not a detailed blow-by-blow account of the Red River Campaign; it is a tour that aligns with the critical decisions covered in this book. Understanding the operation events is essential to comprehending this work and the campaign tour.

Recognizing how location frequently influences decision-makers is essential to the critical decision process. Knowing what these individuals saw or could not see often provides context that may not otherwise be apparent. Before starting the tour, I recommend reviewing a map of the area to enhance your understanding of the ground to be covered.

Notable changes in the past 150 years have impacted the ground this trip will cover. Yet the terrain is unaltered enough to provide a sense of the challenges the armies faced. While we will be traveling on modern roads and visiting modern cities and towns, the area's rural nature means that some locations retain the essence of their appearance in 1864. Also, due to the natural shifting courses of the rivers in this country, some sites will only be near the historical location.

Stop 1—US Custom House, New Orleans, Louisiana

423 Canal Street, New Orleans, LA 70130 (29.951813, -90.066581)

Decision—The Union Advances Up the Red River
Decision—The Command of the Union Operation

We begin our tour at the United States Custom House in New Orleans, Louisiana. You can reach this location via a variety of routes. Canal Street is a busy thoroughfare, so you may need to park a block or more away and walk to the site.

If you face the main entrance on the southwest side of the building with Canal Street at your back, you are facing northeast. Jackson Square is just under 0.5 miles away in that same direction. The Mississippi River is 0.25 mile to your right. Baton Rouge is to your left, about 75.0 miles away. Roughly 95.0 miles beyond that is the city of Alexandria, and 280.0 miles beyond that is Shreveport.

In 1845, the US Congress appropriated $500 to prepare plans for a custom house in New Orleans. Antebellum New Orleans was one of the busiest international ports in the nation. Construction that started a few years later was

United States Custom House - New Orleans, Louisiana, Modern Image, Author.

suspended at the outbreak of the Civil War. When the fighting began, the unfinished building was initially used to manufacture gun carriages for the Confederacy. When the Federals occupied the city in the spring of 1862, the US Custom House was used as Union army headquarters and later a Federal prison. Department of the Gulf commander Nathaniel Banks likely operated in this building from time to time during his tenure in the Cresent City. Experiencing several renovations over the years, the location is currently listed in the National Register of Historic Places.[1]

Henry W. Halleck made both subsequent decisions in Washington, DC, but this is a great site at which to review them and begin our tour.

Decision—The Union Advances Up the Red River

By the end of 1863, Union leadership began to believe that the final chapters of the Civil War were possibly within sight. By the spring of 1863, the Confederacy drew hope from a remarkable victory at Chancellorsville, only to be brought back to earth that summer by devastating losses at Gettysburg in the East, and at Vicksburg and Port Hudson along the Mississippi.

Abraham Lincoln and Jefferson Davis understood Vicksburg's importance in the war's outcome. Lincoln told David Dixon Porter, "Let us get Vicksburg and all that country is ours. The war can never be brought to a close until that key is in our pocket."[2] Davis described the Mississippi city as "the nailhead that holds the South's two halves together."[3] Hearing that Vicksburg had finally surrendered, Lincoln famously declared, "The Father of the Waters again goes unvexed to the Sea."[14] Both men were more correct than they knew.

As 1863 turned into 1864, the Union command pondered the next strategic moves following the "unvexing" of the Mississippi. Ulysses S. Grant set his sights on Atlanta and Mobile, while Halleck, acting on orders from Lincoln, wanted an operation to advance into northwestern Louisiana and Texas. The administration had wanted a Federal military presence in Texas for the better part of a year.

In a letter to Grant in January, General-in-Chief Henry Wager Halleck explained the administration's position and priorities for the Department of the Gulf.

Communication from Halleck to Grant, January 8, 1864

In regard to General Banks' campaign against Texas, it is proper to remark that it was undertaken less for military reasons than as a matter of State policy. As a military measure simply, it perhaps presented less advantages than a movement on Mobile and the Alabama River, so as to threaten the enemy's interior lines and effect a diversion in favor of our armies at Chattanooga and in East Tennessee. But, however this may have been, it was deemed necessary as a matter of political or State policy, connected with our foreign relations, and especially with France and Mexico, that our troops should occupy and hold at least a portion of Texas. The President so ordered, for reasons satisfactory to himself and his cabinet, and it was, therefore, unnecessary for us to inquire whether or not the troops could have been employed elsewhere with greater military advantage.

I allude to this matter here, as it may have an important influence on your projected operations during the present winter.

Keeping in mind the fact that General Banks' operations in Texas, either on the gulf coast or by the Louisiana frontier, must be continued during the winter, it is to be considered whether it will not be better to direct our efforts for the present to the entire breaking up of the rebel forces west of the Mississippi River, rather than to divide them by also operating against Mobile and Alabama. If the forces of Smith, Price, and Magruder could be so scattered or broken as to enable Steele and Banks to occupy Red River as a line of defense, a part of their armies would probably become available for operations elsewhere.

> General Banks reports his present force as inadequate for the defense of his position and for operations in the interior, and General Steele is of opinion that he cannot advance beyond the Arkansas or Saline, unless he can be certain of co-operation and supplies on Red River.
>
> Under these circumstances it is worth considering whether such forces as Sherman can move down the Mississippi River should not co-operate with the armies of Steele and Banks on the west side.[5]

On the verge of promotion to lieutenant general and assignment as general-in-chief, Grant had a different perspective. Grant wanted to move on to the Southern stronghold at Meridian, Mississippi, in preparation for the Atlanta Campaign. Meridian had a Confederate supply depot, and Grant wanted William Sherman to destroy it. Grant also desired Nathaniel Banks to operate against Mobile to support the inevitable Union advance on Atlanta in the spring, and Banks initially supported the Mobile operation. Thinking several moves ahead, Grant wanted every available unit in the area to support his preferred strategy, including men from the Department of the Gulf.[6]

Grant made his feelings known in the following correspondence with William T Sherman.

Communication from Grant to Sherman, February 18, 1864

Inclosed I send you copy of dispatches between General Halleck and myself relative to a movement up Red River on your return from your present expedition. Whilst I look upon such an expedition as is proposed as of the greatest importance, I regret that any force has to be taken from east of the Mississippi for it.

Your troops will want rest for the purpose of preparing for a spring campaign, and all the veterans should be got off on furlough at the very earliest moment. This latter I would direct even if you have to spare troops to go up Red River.

Unless you go in command of the proposed expedition, I fear any troops you may send with it will be entirely lost from further service in this command. This, however, is not the reason for my suggestion that you be sent; your acquaintance with the country, and otherwise fitness were the reasons. I can give no positive orders that you send no troops up Red River, but what I do want is

> their speedy return if they do go, and that the minimum number necessary be sent. I have never heard a word from Steele since his department has been placed in the military division. Do not know what he proposes nor the means he has for executing.
>
> The time necessary for communicating between here and Vicksburg being so great, you will have to act in this matter according to your own judgment, simply knowing my views.
>
> Is it possible that Banks will entrust such an expedition to the command of McClernand? I have so little confidence in his ability to command that I would not want the responsibility of entrusting men with him, without positive orders to do so. I send this by special messenger, who will await your return to Vicksburg, and who will bear any letters you may have for me.[7]

Henry Halleck believed the Red River was the best path for advancing into western Louisiana and Texas. In aggregate, Nathaniel Banks had around forty-two thousand to forty-five thousand men to conduct the campaign.[8]

Behind Confederate lines, Dick Taylor, Edmund Kirby-Smith, and District of Texas commander Maj. Gen. John Bankhead Magruder had expected Union thrusts at the coast of Texas and Louisiana and up the Red for the past year. They planned to make the going rough for any future Union expedition. The Confederates were determined to make the Yankees work for every inch of territory, no matter their direction.

Supported by Lincoln, Halleck green-lit a Union advance up the Red River. The campaign aimed to capture Shreveport and use that as a base to invade eastern Texas, destroy Richard Taylor's Confederate army, and overtly confiscate all the Confederate cotton they could lay their hands on. This decision set the stage for the upcoming campaign in northwestern Louisiana, the largest combined operation west of the Mississippi. Every decision hereafter can be tied to this decision by the general-in-chief. The choice to advance up the Red was also the opening act in one of the most spectacular Union failures of the Civil War.

Decision—The Command of the Union Operation

As the Union leadership began planning for a campaign up the Red River, conversations on the overall commander of such an operation started in earnest. The Red River Campaign was not the largest in terms of overall manpower that the Union conducted during the war, but it covered a vast geographic area. Given the size and scope of the operation, it made military sense to have a single individual in overall command.

Communication between the wildly dispersed Union departments in the Trans-Mississippi was unreliable on good days and almost impossible on bad ones. Messages often took days or weeks to reach New Orleans from the War Department in Washington, DC; maintaining contact between Steele's Arkansas and Banks's Louisiana forces was even more complicated. This proposed campaign required the coordination of Union forces from three separate departments and a schedule necessitating units' simultaneous arrival at designated locations. It included troops from the Gulf, Arkansas, and Mississippi Departments and the navy, which had its own internal communication challenges.[9]

The Union command was in a state of flux in early 1864. Grant's pending promotion to lieutenant general and likely supplanting of Halleck as general-in-chief put both men at a disadvantage. Grant did not yet have full authority to direct overall strategy, and Halleck was gradually becoming more hesitant to make changes that Grant might overturn. Believing Banks was the president's preferred choice, both men were disinclined to make a decision that might displace him in favor of a more qualified general.

In February, Henry Halleck wrote William T. Sherman and asserted that many of the decisions emanating from his office were not his own.

Communication from Halleck to Sherman, February 16, 1864

My Dear General: Yours of January 29, dated on board the Juliet, is received, and I thank you for the kind allusions to me in your Memphis speech. I saw some notice of it in the newspapers, but not so full as in your letter. You have probably seen the attempt in the newspapers to create difficulties and jealousies between me and General Grant. This is all for political effect. There is not the slightest ground for any such assertions. There cannot and will not be any differences between us. If he is made lieutenant-general, as I presume he will be, I shall most cordially welcome him to the command, glad to be relieved from so thankless and disagreeable a position. I took it against my will, and shall be most happy to leave it as soon as another is designated to fill it. The great difficulty in the office of General-in-Chief is, that it is not understood by the country. The responsibility and odium thrown upon it does not belong to it. I am simply a military adviser of the Secretary of War and the President, and must obey and carry out what they decide upon, whether I concur in their decisions or not. As a good soldier I obey the orders of my superiors. If I disagree with them in opinion, I say so, but when they decide it is my duty faithfully to carry out their decision. Moreover, I cannot say to the public I approve this and I disapprove that. I have no right to say this, as it might embarrass the execution of a measure fully decided on. My mouth is closed except when officially called on to give such opinion. It is my duty to strengthen the hands of the President as Commander-in-Chief, not to weaken them by factious opposition. I have, therefore, cordially co-operated with him in every plan decided upon, although I have never hesitated to differ in opinion. I must leave it to history to vindicate or condemn my own opinions and plans. They will be found at some future time on record. What we now have to do is to put down this rebellion. We have no time to quibble and contend for the pride of personal opinion. On this subject there seems to be a better feeling among the officers in the West than here. There is less jealousy and back-biting, and a greater disposition to assist each other. Here we have too much party politics and wire-pulling. Everybody wants you to turn a grindstone to grind his particular ax, and if you decline he regards you as an enemy and takes revenge by newspaper abuse.[10]

U. S. Grant, who was never supportive of the proposed Red River operation, was even less enthusiastic about Banks's military skills. On February 18, he also wrote Sherman, stating, "I have so little confidence in his [Banks's] ability to command that I would not want the responsibility of entrusting men with him, without positive orders to do so."[11]

Until the official word from the president and Congress on Grant's promotion came down, the command decision ultimately fell to Henry Halleck. Halleck, who was also not very encouraged about Nathaniel Banks's abilities, could put him in overall command, choose some other more competent general, or designate no overall commander and hope those involved would cooperate. Halleck expressed his concerns a month into the operation and the day the Battle of Mansfield took place.

Communication from Halleck to Sherman, April 8, 1864

We fully agree that the Departments of Arkansas and the Gulf should be under one commander as soon as the armies come within

> communicating distance, but the difficulty is to get a suitable commander. General Banks is not competent, and there are so many political objections to superseding him by Steele that it would be useless to ask the President to do it. Moreover, I fear the command would be too large for Steele. Nevertheless, if the proper man can be found for the place I shall not hesitate to advise a change now. No doubt the lines of departments of your command west of the Mississippi River might also be modified with advantage, but I would not advise making all three into one, for the reason it would make you a mere bureau general. You know there is an immense amount of official business, courts-martial, discharges of soldiers, furloughs, requisitions, &c., which the law and regulations require to be done by the commander of a department.[12]

Halleck decided to place no one individual in charge. Instead, he ordered each department commander to cooperate with the others. The most extensive campaign ever conducted west of the Mississippi would succeed or fail depending on the collaboration and communication of three independent commands. Incidentally, when Grant was promoted and made general-in-chief, he made no real effort to reverse Halleck's decision.

As the campaign moved forward, it became a series of uncoordinated moves by the Union units taking part. Each commander had to act on faith that his counterparts were all working from the same plan. The Rebel army took full advantage of this lack of coordination, which negated the benefit of overwhelming Union manpower. Without a cohesive and specific strategy, the Confederates could deal with one Federal threat and then the other. As a result, Kirby-Smith was able to bring a more significant force to bear on Banks's army at each critical battle of the campaign than he might have otherwise been able to.

Stop 2—Jackson Square, New Orleans, Louisiana
Corner of Decatur and Saint Peter Streets, New Orleans, LA 70116
(29.957263, -90.062627)

Decision—Banks Remains in New Orleans

From the US Custom House, go northwest 3 blocks and turn right on Chartres Street. Go 0.4 mile and turn right onto Wilkinson Street, then go about 420 feet and turn left onto Decatur Street. Jackson Square will be on your left. This area is also busy, so you may have to park a few blocks away and walk.

Detroit Publishing Co., Publisher. U.S. Custom House, New Orleans, La. United States New Orleans Louisiana, Unknown, circa, 1890 – 1899, Library of Congress Prints and Photographs Division Washington, DC 20540.

If you stand facing the statue of Andrew Jackson with Decatur Street at your back, you are facing northeast. The Mississippi River is behind you.

The equestrian statue of Jackson is a duplicate of the sculptor Clark Mills statue in Washington, DC, at Lafayette Square. In 1856, this version of Mills's famous figure was erected in New Orleans's historic Place d'Armes, which had been renamed Jackson Square in anticipation of the monument and recognition of Jackson's victory at the Battle of New Orleans in 1815. In 1864, this was the heart of a city nearly two years into Federal occupation. Still dealing with the mess his predecessor, Ben "the Beast" Butler, left for him, current Union commander Nathaniel Banks believed a more conciliatory stance with the locals would gain their favor. He and his wife held weekly receptions at the famous Saint Charles Hotel that stood just a mile southeast from where you are standing, inviting all the local socialites. Unfortunately, Southern animosity proved stronger than Union hospitality, and only Union loyalists dared attend.

Jackson Square has been the location of numerous celebrations over the years, including one by Banks.[13]

Decision—Banks Remains in New Orleans

As a skilled politician, Nathaniel P. Banks was happy to accommodate and further the administration's goals in the Trans-Mississippi. By the early spring of 1864, he was determined to shape the politics of Louisiana by the

Appendix I

Jackson Square - New Orleans, LA, Modern Image, Author.

force of his own will, even at the expense of military necessity. Banks did effectively implement President Lincoln's December 1863 Proclamation for Amnesty and Reconstruction. Lincoln's reconstruction plan for conquered Southern states was elementary. As each Confederate state capitulated, the Union would work to hold local elections. Federal officials always supported the pro-Union/pro-Lincoln candidates for key political positions. Additionally, if a particular state adopted a new constitution and 10 percent of its citizens took a loyalty oath, that state could be readmitted to the Union. Lincoln could count another state's electoral votes in his hand if this could be conducted in Louisiana before the 1864 election.[14]

By March 1864, and after much delay, the time had come to launch the campaign. It was agreed that Banks and his command would meet Smith's force and Porter's fleet at Alexandria, Louisiana, about 165 air miles northwest of New Orleans, on March 17. On March 10, Smith's command departed Vicksburg for Alexandria, meeting Porter's fleet at the mouth of the Red River. Smith and Porter entered the Red River two days later. The Red River Campaign had begun.[15]

Delayed by weather and poor communication, Banks's cavalry and the Union Thirteenth and Nineteenth Corps of the Department of the Gulf did not assemble at Brashear City (present-day Morgan City) near the mouth of the Atchafalaya River until March 7. These troops did not begin their advance until the following day. To reach Alexandria, their first objective, in nine days, these units had to march over 150 miles on narrow and rutted country roads through swampland and the unforgiving Cajun prairie.[16] Fort DeRussy fell to the Federals on March 14, and Richard Taylor subsequently abandoned Alexandria; Union forces occupied the city two days later with barely a shot fired.[17]

Meanwhile, in New Orleans, Nathaniel Banks, who had spent the better part of a year preparing for this day, was as busy as ever. His staff was firing off messages and working diligently to get all the logistical elements in place. Banks saw to other matters. George Michael Decker Hahn, enthusiastically supported by the general, won the governorship of Union-controlled Louisiana on February 22. Hahn's inauguration scheduled for March was to be a grand celebration.[18]

Banks decided to stay in New Orleans and revel in Hahn's victory; it was really Banks's victory. The celebration was all he had hoped for. On inauguration day, a banner behind the grandstand read, "Major General Banks, Hero of Port Hudson." A band of three hundred musicians played the "Anvil Chorus" while accompanied by fireworks, and a children's choir sang the officer's praises. Banks estimated that fifty thousand people attended the event.

In a letter to Halleck, Banks addressed some campaign details while seeming to confirm his political priorities.

Communication from Banks to Halleck, March 12, 1864

General: Major-General Sherman, of General Grant's department, arrived in this city on the evening of the 1st instant, having completed his expedition to Meridian to his entire satisfaction. He returned to Vicksburg on the evening of the 3rd, to arrange for his co-operation in the Red River movement. Unless delayed by want of steam transportation, of which we put everything we have at his command, he will be ready to join me on the Red River by the 17th, where I hope to be at that date. He expects to furnish 10,000 men for that purpose. . . . General Steele appears to have changed the plan entertained when he last communicated with me. Copies of his dispatch at that time have been forwarded to you. He then proposed to move by the way of Monroe for the Red River. He is now apprehensive, in consequence of the reduction of his forces, that he can only enter upon a movement for the diversion of the enemy in the direction of Arkadelphia, without any expectation of joining us at Shreveport or any other position on the river. General Sherman and myself have earnestly urged him to abandon this idea, which in any event could effect but little good, and to prepare for a movement direct upon the Red River in co-operation with us. I have hopes that he may accept this proposition, in which event the three forces in the course of thirty days would meet at Shreveport. General Steele represents that he will have about 6,000 men at his command. I respectfully request that orders may be given to him to co-operate with us upon the point named, in accordance with the plan originally proposed by you. I see nothing to defeat its success. Admiral Porter is ready to move up the river in co-operation with us as soon as his vessels can be admitted. . . .

The inauguration of Mr. Hahn, who was designated in the election of the 22nd February by the people as their candidate for Governor, in a poll numbering nearly 12,000 votes, occurred yesterday. Such a concourse of people has never, I think, been witnessed in this country. From 6,000 to 8,000 pupils of the public schools participated, and the number of people present is supposed not to have been less than 40,000 or 50,000. I have never witnessed such a spectacle elsewhere, and never conceived it possible that in this State a popular demonstration of such magnitude and friendly spirit to the Government could be attained. It is impossible to describe it with truth.

So far as the election of the 22nd is concerned, all has been accomplished that has been anticipated, and much more. The understanding is that, with the concurrence of the Government, Mr. Hahn will be invested with the authority heretofore exercised by the military governor. His position is subordinate to the military occupation of the State by the troops of the United States for the suppression of the rebellion and the full restoration of the authority of the United States. So far as we have gone, we have obtained the practical results of an election by the people, without the risk of losing the control of the State exercised by the officers of the Government. The other measures necessary for the complete restoration of the State are perfectly practicable. The only embarrassment that can occur will arise from the desperate efforts of interested men who profess unreserved loyalty to the Government for personal place and power. Should the officers of the Government be allowed to contest for the high offices of the State, and enter into factious combination for this purpose, some embarrassment may occur, but the object cannot be defeated.[19]

Banks, aboard his command vessel *Black Hawk*, did not arrive in Alexandria until March 25, two weeks after the campaign began. Tagging along with Banks was a cadre of reporters and cotton speculators. Almost instantly upon arrival, Banks was distracted again as his forces marched toward Shreveport days later. At the end of March, he called for elections in Alexandria and Grand Ecore.[20]

On March 24, Banks received a startling message from the new general-in-chief, U. S. Grant.

Communication from Grant to Banks, March 24, 1864

Inclosed herewith I send you copy of General Orders, Numbers 1, assuming command of the armies of the United States. You will see from the order it is my intention to establish headquarters for the present with the Army of the Potomac. I have not fully determined upon a plan of campaign for this spring, but will do so before the return of our veteran troops to the field. It will, however, be my desire to have all parts of the Army, or rather all the armies, act as much in concert as possible. For this reason I now write you.

I regard the success of your present move as of great importance in reducing the number of troops necessary for protecting the navigation of the Mississippi River. It is also important that Shreveport should be taken as soon as possible. This done, send Brigadier General A. J. Smith with his command back to Memphis as soon as possible. This force will be necessary for movements east of the Mississippi. Should you find that the taking of Shreveport will occupy ten to fifteen days more time than General Sherman gave his troops to be absent from their command, you will send them back at the time specified in his note of March, even if it leads to the abandonment of the main object of your expedition. Should your expedition prove successful, hold Shreveport and the Red River with such force as you may deem necessary, and return the balance of your troops to the neighborhood of New Orleans.

I would not at present advise the abandonment of any portion of territory now held west of the Mississippi, but commence no move for the further reacquisition of territory unless it be to make that now ours more easily held. This, of course, is not intended to restrain you from making any disposition of your troops or going anywhere to meet and fight the enemy wherever he may be in force. I look

Appendix I

upon the conquering of the organized armies of the enemy as being of vastly more importance than the mere acquisition of territory.

It may be a part of the plan for the spring campaign to move against Mobile. It certainly will be if troops enough can be obtained to make it without embarrassing other movements. In this case, New Orleans will be the point of departure for such an expedition. There is one thing, general, I would urge, and don't know but what you have already, and that is of supplying your army as far as possible from the country occupied. Mules, horses, forage, and provisions can be paid for, where taken from persons who have taken the amnesty oath prescribed by the President (if the oath be taken before the loss of property), with both economy and convenience. I have directed General Steele to make a real move as suggested by you instead of a demonstration, as he thought advisable.[21]

Jarvis, J. F., Publisher. Jackson Square, New Orleans, USA Jackson Square New Orleans Louisiana, circa 1891, Library of Congress Prints and Photographs Division Washington, DC 20540.

Banks's delays set the timeline for upcoming battles and provided Taylor and Kirby-Smith with additional time to gather the scattered forces they would not have had otherwise. Banks's decision meant the size of the enemy force his army would eventually face was significantly larger, contributing to the Confederate victory and the ultimate Union failure. This time frame set for the campaign and upcoming engagements all but ensured that Banks's army would be stopped short of its goal, and that events would happen on the date history now records.

Stop 3—Fort DeRussy State Historic Site
Fort DeRussy Road, Marksville, LA 71351
(31.176170217114883, -92.06127327193587)

Decision—The Availability of A. J. Smith's Command

From downtown Marksville, Louisiana, drive northeast on Main Street. Just outside of town, turn right onto LA 1192. After 2.0 miles, turn right on Fort DeRussy Road. After 0.5 mile, you will see a sign on your left marking the Fort DeRussy State Historic Site. This is a relatively quiet road, so you are usually good to pull off to the side; just be mindful of the traffic. If you desire a more extensive site tour, you must make arrangements with the administrators of the Forts Randolph & Buhlow State Historic Site in Pineville. You can reach them at 318-484-2390.

As you face the sign, you are looking north. The Red River, much closer in 1864, is just over 1.5 miles in that direction. Portions of the great bend in the river that DeRussy was built on can still be seen, just over 0.5 mile to your right. Alexandria is 25.0 miles to your left, with Grand Ecore 50.0 miles farther in the same direction.

Fort DeRussy was an earthen stronghold built to defend the Red River from naval intrusions during the Civil War. It was named for Col. Lewis G. DeRussy, the Confederate engineering officer and former West Pointer in charge of constructing the first fortifications in November 1862. The bastion was the site of three major Civil War engagements and numerous minor skirmishes. The Confederate army rebuilt Fort DeRussy and adjacent water batteries in March 1864, at the start of the Red River Campaign. It was the first of a series of fortifications and defensive points the Rebels constructed on the Red.

On March 13–14, DeRussy was attacked from the landside by Union general A. J. Smith's command. John Walker's Texans retreated before Smith's army, leaving a small force of three hundred men to defend the fort against Smith's ten thousand veterans. The stronghold was captured after a four-hour

Appendix I

Fort DeRussy State Historic Site, Modern Image, Author.

siege and assault. After the capture by Union forces, Fort DeRussy was used as a recruiting station for Black troops and as a "contraband camp" for escaped enslaved peoples for several weeks. The fort was never remanned after the Red River Campaign.[22]

Fort DeRussy is now a state historic site, and efforts are underway to develop and preserve the location. We will review the next decision here.

Decision—The Availability of A. J. Smith's Command

As plans for the Red River Campaign began to take shape, one of the earliest fundamentals decided was that William T. Sherman would make part of his Army of the Tennessee available to support the operation. On February 16, 1864, Henry Halleck and Grant exchanged several messages on the subject. Early in March, William T. Sherman traveled to New Orleans to confer with Nathaniel Banks on strategy and determine whether he was to command.[23]

U. S. Grant did not support the idea of a Red River operation. He had divergent thoughts on Union strategy in the West, and taking Mobile was more important to him than capturing Shreveport. While he did not think the Red River operation was an excellent idea, Grant did not yet have the authority to overrule Halleck. By February 1864, everyone at the highest levels of the Union army knew that the bill to promote Grant to the rank of lieutenant general had been making its way through Congress. When Lincoln signed this bill, Grant would become the highest-ranking officer in the Union army, and he likely would then displace Halleck as general-in-chief. Also, Federal leadership was planning multiple operations to commence once spring came. Having the manpower to cover all of these was a concern.[24]

In a message dated February 18, Grant ordered Sherman to supply men to support the Red River operation. However, Grant also told his lieutenant that he would likely lose these troops from his command if he (Sherman) did not lead the campaign. Nevertheless, Halleck was unlikely to assign leadership to Sherman, as Banks was the president's preferred choice. Determining that he was not interested in participating in the Red River Campaign if he had to answer to Banks, Sherman agreed to make forces available for the operation.[25]

Sherman supplied men Banks with the caveats that they do not go beyond Shreveport, that they operate with Admiral Porter's fleet exclusively, and that they are returned thirty days after entering the Red or by April 15.[26] This force consisted of the First and Third Divisions of the Sixteenth Corps and the Second Division of the Seventeenth Corps. These divisions under Brig. Gen. Andrew Jackson Smith's command totaled ten thousand men. Smith was considered one of the best division commanders in Sherman's army.[27]

Communication from Sherman to A. J. Smith, March 6, 1864

GENERAL: By an order this day issued you are to command a strong, well-appointed detachment of the Army of the Tennessee, sent to re-enforce a movement against the Red River line, but more especially the fortified positions at Shreveport. You will embark your command as soon as possible, but little encumbered with wagons or wheeled vehicles, but well supplied with fuel, provisions, and ammunition. Take with you the twelve mortars, with their ammunition, and all the 30-pounder Parrotts the ordnance officer will supply; proceed to the mouth of Red River and confer with Admiral Porter; confer with him and in all the expedition rely on him implicitly, as he is the approved friend of the Army of the Tennessee, and has been associated with us from the beginning.

I have undertaken with General Banks that you will be at Alexandria, La., on or before the 17th day of March, and you will, if time allows, co-operate with the navy in destroying Harrisonburg, up Black River on the Washita, but as I passed Red River yesterday I saw Admiral Porter, and he told me he had already sent an expedition to Harrisonburg, so that I suppose that part of the plan will be accomplished before you reach Red River; but in any event be

Appendix I

careful to reach Alexandria about the 17th of March. General Banks will start by land from Franklin, in the Teche country, either the 5th or 7th, and will march via Opelousas to Alexandria. You will meet him there, report to him, and act under his orders. My understanding with him is, his forces will still move by land via Natchitoches, &c., to Shreveport, whilst the gun-boat fleet is to ascend the river with your transports in company. Now, Red River is very low for the season, and I doubt if any of the boats can pass the falls or rapids at Alexandria. What General Banks proposes to do in that event I do not know, but my own judgment is that Shreveport ought not to be attacked until the gun-boats can reach it. Not that a force marching by land cannot do it alone, but it would be bad economy in war to invest the place with an army so far from heavy guns, mortars, ammunition, and provisions, which can alone reach Shreveport by water. Still, I do not know about General Banks' plans in that event, but whatever they may be, your duty will be to conform in the most hearty manner. My understanding with General Banks is that he will not need the co-operation of your force beyond thirty days from the date you reach Red River. As soon as he has taken Shreveport

The Capture of Fort De Russy, La. on the 15th of March, by the United States Forces under Gen. Andrew Jackson Smith. - From a sketch by our Special Artist, *Frank Leslie's Illustrated Newspaper*, April 9, 1864, p. 41.

> or as soon as he can spare you will return to Vicksburg with all dispatch, gather up your detachments, wagons, tents, transportation, and all property pertaining to so much of the command as belongs to the Sixteenth Army Corps, and conduct it to Memphis, where orders will await you.[28]

This self-imposed Union deadline was one of the most critical decisions made by either side. Banks made several subsequent choices based on this deadline that affected the course of the campaign. It drove Banks to change his line of march and determined the time and place for the future Battles of Mansfield and Pleasant Hill. Incidentally, the actions of Andrew Jackson Smith also played a crucial role in the campaign, including the Union tactical victory at Pleasant Hill.[29]

Stop 4—Forts Randolph & Buhlow State Historic Site
135 Riverfront Street, Pineville, LA 71360
(31.32433850935325, -92.44938131313081)

Decision—Banks Changes His Line of March

From I-49, take Exit 84A east to Bus 165 N toward Pineville. This turns into 10th Street. After 0.25 mile, turn right on Jackson Street. Drive across the river, and after 0.70 mile, make a U-turn at Main Street. Follow Main Street west for 450 feet, and turn right on Riverside Drive. Follow this road for 1.0 mile until you reach the entrance. About 750 feet north of the entrance is a parking spot on your left that overlooks the river.

Following the Red River Campaign, the Confederates constructed Forts Randolph and Buhlow across the Red River from Alexandria to defend against future Union advances via the Red River. Only completed in March 1865, two months before the war ended in Louisiana, the project was supervised by Capt. Christopher M. Randolph and Lieut. Alphonse Buhlow. Built with slave labor, the earthen forts were fortified with cannon and over eight hundred soldiers. The Confederate ironclad *Missouri* was anchored in the river opposite Fort Randolph, but the anticipated attack never came.

Forts Randolph & Buhlow State Historic Site also includes the remains of Bailey's Dam, remarkable for its design and the amount of time required to construct it. The dam allowed the Union fleet, under the command of Adm. David Porter, to escape below the rapids on the Red River at Alexandria during the Federal retreat after the Battles of Mansfield and Pleasant Hill.

The Red River at Forts Randolph & Buhlow State Historic Site, Modern Image, Author.

Located on the Red River in downtown Pineville, the site includes a visitor center with exhibits on the Civil War Red River Campaign, an elevated boardwalk around the fort area, and an overlook near the Bailey's Dam site. Open Wednesday through Sunday from 9:00 a.m. to 5:00 p.m. Forts Randolph and Buhlow are on the National Register of Historic Places. This is a fee site; you can pay at the visitor center. We will cover our next decision here.[30]

Decision—Banks Changes His Line of March

Nathaniel Banks envisioned his advance up the Red River with Adm. David Dixon Porter's heavily armed and armored fleet for support. Advancing at Shreveport via the Red River only made sense if the Federals could use the added firepower of Porter's fleet. Also, each of these elements, infantry and navy, depended on the other for support. The infantry guarded against enemy shore attacks and general harassment of the fleet. At the same time, the navy provided efficient transportation for troops and their supplies and carried large-caliber artillery that was difficult to transport overland.

This decision by Banks to detach his command from its naval support stands out as the one that significantly exposed his inability to grasp fundamental military acumen.

On April 3, after weeks of delay, Banks, Porter, and Smith had all their men and vessels concentrated at Grand Ecore, a few miles northeast of Natchitoches. Porter could only get thirteen gunboats and thirty transport vessels above Alexandria due to the shallowness of the river. The Union's combined force was now within striking distance of Shreveport, their objective. Banks's and Smith's commands could count approximately twenty thousand infantry and cavalry and seventy-six artillery pieces in and around Natchitoches. Richard Taylor assembled a Confederate force that would eventually number just under nine thousand men.[31]

The week before, in Alexandria, Banks received a startling communication from the new general-in-chief, Lieut. Gen. Ulysses S. Grant. Grant, who never considered the Red River expedition worthwhile, told Banks that he was to capture Shreveport as soon as possible. If Banks could not complete this objective by the end of April, he was to return Smith's force to Sherman regardless. Additionally, Grant ordered Banks to only garrison a captured Shreveport and return the bulk of his troops to New Orleans to support a move at Mobile. Last, Banks was told he was not to advance into Texas.[32]

Stunned by this communication, Banks found that his leisurely pace thus far was abruptly working against him. Combined with all the delays in the movement, the pressure on the already struggling Union commander increased. It was then that Banks procured the services of Wellington W. Withenbury. A self-described *"steamboat-man"*, Withenbury was considered an expert river pilot. It can be definitively stated that he was an influential figure concerning one critical decision and possibly more.[33] As an expert on the river and all things connected, Withenbury now counseled Banks and his staff on the road system adjacent to the river, including all possible avenues approaching Shreveport.

Banks could approach Shreveport in several ways. Two potential routes on the eastern and western sides of the Red veered away from the river at some point before connecting back to Shreveport. The "riverboat-man" informed Banks that the eastern approach had better roads, although it would likely add days to the march by forcing the Federals to maneuver around several lakes. In fact, two other roads ran right next to the river on either side, both beginning several miles above Grand Ecore. Evidence suggests that Withenbury omitted those details in his overview to Banks to protect his personal cotton supply or for some other unknown reason. Having few other reliable resources from which to derive a conclusion, Banks drew on the implied expertise of the riverboat pilot.[34]

David Dixon Porter provided the following perspective in a letter to William Sherman.

Communication from David Dixon Porter to Sherman, April 16, 1864

Dear General: I wrote you a hurried note the other day, by General Corse, and I imagine your disappointment at having your well-laid plans interfered with and having part of your command mixed up in an affair, the management of which would be discreditable to a boy 9 years of age. . . .

The rebels, frightened to death, went on before us, burning all the fine cotton (bales being hid in the woods), but destroying none of the corn or cattle. Of these we found an abundance, and though we only stopped at three or four places there was enough and more to satisfy the troops without touching the rations. It struck me very forcibly that this would have been the route for the army, where they could have traveled without all that immense train, the country supporting them as they proceeded along. The roads are good, wide fields on all sides, a river protecting the right flank of the army, and gunboats in company. An army would have no difficulty in marching to Shreveport in this way. There is Bayou Pierre to pass and some bridges to be built, but that is child's play to our Western men, and "not so bad as being beaten" in a pine barren with only one road through it, and that a narrow one, where troops can not pass carts. I send you correct map, which I think will give you a good idea of the views I have expressed, if you have not got it already, knowing this country as well as you do. Why General Banks went through a desert where he could not even find water (so he says) instead of a prolific country, I can not say. You know I have always said that Providence was fighting this great battle its own way and brings these reverses to teach us—a proud, stiff-necked, and unthankful people—how to be contented under a good government, if peaceful times come again. I hope it will teach us not to place the destinies of a great nation in the hands of political generals or volunteer admirals.[35]

Banks decided that the western road network made the most sense. As the clock was ticking, Banks still believed he would not face any significant Confederate resistance until he reached Shreveport. The general ordered his forces on a line of march that took them miles away from the river on a narrow, heavily wooded road directly at the towns of Pleasant Hill and Mans-

Porter's Fleet Passing Colonel Baily's Dam, *Frank Leslie's Illustrated History of the Civil War*, Mrs. Frank Leslie Pub., circa 1894, p.402.

field. As it happens, this was precisely what Richard Taylor was hoping for. He picked his spot and waited for Banks. This decision set up the next stage of the campaign, ensuring that the Battles of Mansfield and Pleasant Hill occurred at the time and place history now records.

Stop 5—Grand Encore Visitor Center
106 Tauzin Island Road, Natchitoches, LA 71457
(31.818263215688024, -93.08876850327073)

Decision—Banks's Order of March

From downtown Natchitoches, head north on Front Street toward Church Street. This turns into Washington Street and then into LA 6 E. After 4 miles, turn left onto Par / Tauzin Island Road.

The Grand Ecore Visitor Center is located on the banks of the Red River, just north of Natchitoches, Louisiana. It commands a panoramic view from a bluff 80 feet above the river. The US Army Corps of Engineers manages the site. Over the years, Grand Ecore has been occupied by Native peoples and settlers alike. In the spring of 1864, it was a Confederate outpost guarding the Red River and a staging area for Union troops during the Red River Campaign. Grand Ecore was also the Union fallback position after the retreat from Pleasant Hill.

The visitor center provides a splendid overview of the history of the river and its impact on the region. Open noon to 4:00 p.m. Wednesday through

Appendix I

The Red River at Grand Ecore, Louisiana, Author, Modern Image.

Saturday, the site is closed for all federal holidays.[36] An observation deck on the visitor center's north side offers a great river view and a suitable spot to review our next decision. As you face the river, Pleasant Hill Battlefield is roughly 20 miles northwest on your left. Mansfield is approximately 12 miles beyond that. New Orleans is 220 air miles to your right (southeast).

Decision—Banks's Order of March

On April 6, the Union army and naval forces were ready for the final dash to Shreveport. Adm. David Dixon Porter was preparing for action a smaller subset of his vessels still able to navigate the shallowing river. The Union infantry, cavalry, and artillery planned to march the one hundred miles northwest from Natchitoches on the Shreveport–Natchitoches Stage Line Road, passing through the villages of Pleasant Hill and Mansfield. Banks and Porter were to meet at Springfield Landing, just below Shreveport, on or about April 10. Porter was also to bring along the army transport/supply vessels for Banks's command.[37]

Thus far, Confederate forces had offered only token resistance to Banks's operation. The Union leadership was convinced this trend would continue.[38]

As they were severely outmanned in the campaign's early days, the Rebels were forced to skirmish with Banks's army and disappear into the landscape. Richard Taylor's men fell back almost two hundred miles, parrying with the

Union vanguard the whole way. Taylor was eager for a fight, but he had to be careful not to get drawn into a major battle before he was reinforced.[39]

After conferring with his staff, Banks now counted only 15,000 to 18,000 men of all arms available to continue his operation. The 1,000 men of the Mississippi Marine Brigade were summoned back to Vicksburg by Maj. Gen. John A. McClernand. General Banks was forced to leave the 3,600 men of Brig. Gen. Cuvier Grover's Second Division of the Nineteenth Corps at Alexandria as an occupation force. Brig. Gen. Andrew J. Smith's command was likewise reduced to roughly 7,500 men, as Brig. Gen. Thomas Kilby Smith's division of the Seventeenth Corps was assigned to accompany Porter's fleet. Banks still outnumbered his opponent by almost two to one, but he could only guess at the number of Confederates that might be waiting for him at Shreveport.[40]

Banks was concerned with how to supply his army. As his line of march took him away from the river, his naval support, and his supply base for an unknown period, having the soldiers haul a certain amount of provisions with them was essential. Considering all relevant factors, the question remained as to the best and most efficient way to do so. Banks could either have his men carry all their needed supplies or bring along his wagon trains to keep his army fed and supplied with ammunition.

The general decided to bring his supply trains with him on the march. And not just the bare minimum—one thousand wagons loaded with food, fodder, and ammunition accompanied the Federals. This was a staggering and unprecedented amount of supplies by any measure. Banks's decision altered the course of the campaign by setting the stage for the disaster at Mansfield and the subsequent retreat to Pleasant Hill.

When quizzed about the decision by the Joint Committee on the Conduct of the War, Banks replied in this way:

Testimony of Maj. Gen. Nathaniel P. Banks, USA, December 14, 1864

Question. Will you describe the order of march.

Answer. General Lee, with the cavalry, was in front on the 6th and 7th of April. General Lee had met the enemy in considerable force and had asked for assistance. It was a question whether he should have infantry assistance or not. I said to General Franklin, "Certainly; send forward a brigade of infantry to assist him in his march." I did it upon the idea that the advance guard should be composed of cavalry for celerity, artillery for force, and infantry for solidity; that General Lee could not safely march faster than the column, and therefore he might have this infantry to support him, but not for a general battle; only that they might not be stopped by a slight force of the enemy. If the enemy was in full strength they were to halt, if only in small force it would be otherwise. First, then, was General Lee with his cavalry, and General Ransom with two brigades of the 13th army corps, to support him. The infantry had just got up to him at this time. Then came the 13th corps, under General Cameron. General Ransom was commander of that corps in fact, but General Cameron was commander of the main body on the march. Then came General Emory and the 19th corps, a brigade of colored troops following the 19th corps.

Then came General Smith with the balance of his forces, amounting to about 5,000 men, 3,000 having gone back at the request of General McPherson, and 2,500 being on the river to protect the fleet. From Grand Ecore to Sabine Crossroads, where this encounter with the enemy took place, was fifty-six miles, but the troops were separated on the road by a distance of twenty or twenty-five miles from the front to the rear. General Smith's command reached Pleasant Hill on the evening of the 8th, at the same time, we beat back the enemy in the second encounter at the Sabine Crossroads.

Question. What made it necessary that they should advance in one column?

Answer. Because we were in a country occupied by the enemy. We were moving upon a single road through the woods; we were, therefore, likely to encounter the enemy at any step. Whenever we encountered the enemy, if our troops were in compact form, we could immediately engage him and take our chances for the battle; if, on the contrary, our advance guard was ten or fifteen miles in advance of the other troops, and should encounter the enemy and be compelled to fall back, whatever disaster we might incur in that encounter might be avoided by being in compact order.

Question. Why could you not have advanced on two or three different lines within supporting distance?

Answer. There was no other road except that upon which we were marching. There was no other route within ten or fifteen miles, probably no other parallel road.

Question. Who was responsible for that order of march?

Answer. General Franklin was in command of the troops on

War in Louisiana - View of Natchitoches, Louisiana, From a sketch by our special artist, C.E.H. Bonwill, *Frank Leslie's Illustrated Newspaper*, circa May 1864. Library of Congress Washington, DC 20540.

the march from Grand Ecore, as he had been from the beginning of the movement.

Question. Were there parallel roads there within convenient distance?

Answer. No, sir. We were upon one line with our trains and troops, and that was a narrow, crooked, circuitous road; merely a country road through a dense forest.[41]

Stop 6—Russell B. Long Lock and Dam and Picnic Ground

Porters Island Road, Martin, LA 71019-Red River Parish, Louisiana (31.9370083305882, -93.27238930640358)

Decision—Banks Withdraws to the Red River

From the Grand Ecore Visitor Center, head south and turn right onto LA 6 W. After 2.1 miles, turn right to stay on LA 6 W. Proceed 1.3 miles, and turn right onto LA 1 N. Follow this road for 16.7 miles, then turn right onto Porter's Island Road. After 2.8 miles, you will arrive at the parking lot. The Russell B. Long Lock and Dam and Picnic Ground gives a great view of the river while providing perspective on the US Army Corps of Engineers' twentieth-century efforts to control flooding and facilitate modern navigation.

If you face the river, you are looking northeast. Grand Ecore is about 14 miles to your right (southeast), and Alexandria is 50 miles beyond that. Pleasant Hill is behind you, roughly 15 miles to the southwest. The Mansfield Battlefield is 26 miles to the northwest, on your left.

About halfway between LA 1 N and the parking lot, on the northwest side of the road, is a marker for Confederate brigadier general Tom Green, who was killed at the Battle of Blair's Landing. On April 12, 1864, Green, 2,500 Texas Confederate cavalry, and a four-gun battery attempted to trap Porter's fleet here at Blair's Landing. The ships Green and his troopers found were the rear of Porter's flotilla, which had already begun retreating downriver. After a two-and-a-half-hour struggle, three Union vessels, *Osage*, *Lexington*, and *Black Hawk*, managed to drive off Green's men and escape. There were few casualties in this engagement, but among those killed was Thomas Green, decapitated by a Union canister round fired from the river monitor *Osage*.[42]

The inscription on the marker reads as follows:

> April 12, 1864, C.S.A. Brig. Gen. Tom Green was killed near here leading his Texas cavalry in a duel against the Union monitor Osage, gunboat Lexington, and the transport Black Hawk at the Battle of Blair's Landing. Of his passing Lt. Gen. Richard Taylor, said Green was "upright, modest, and with the simplicity of a child, danger seemed to be his element, and he rejoiced in combat. . . . His death was a public calamity and mourned as such by the people of Texas and Louisiana.[43]

Decision—Banks Withdraws to the Red River

The two armies disengaged on April 9, 1864, as the sun set in the western sky. Duplicating a scene that had played out on countless battlefields across the war-torn nation since the summer of 1861, the deafening clamor of combat was replaced by pitiful and agonizing cries from scores of grievously wounded men.

Richard Taylor's army had battled Banks's command for almost three straight days, beginning with Brig. Gen. Thomas Green's April 7 attack on Albert Lee's Union troopers at Wilson's Farm, the assault at Mansfield the next day, and the final assault at Pleasant Hill the day after that. While the

Russell B. Long Lock and Dam – Blair's Landing, Louisiana, Author, Modern Image.

Confederate army's more than 2,600 combined casualties were undoubtedly a grim reality facing its commanders, the damage to Taylor's officer corps was even more devastating. In Brig. Gen. Alfred Mouton's division alone, five brigade and regimental commanders were killed, including Mouton himself.[44]

Dick Taylor was determined to keep pressure on the enemy. Committed to driving Banks and his invading army out of Louisiana and into the Gulf of Mexico if necessary, Taylor would allow no amount of casualties or damage to his own command to get in the way of this objective. Convinced that the Union forces were beaten, Taylor wrote, "The enemy's campaign for conquest was defeated by an inferior force, and it was doubtful if his army and fleet could escape destruction." He continued, "Banks, with the remains of his beaten army, was before us and the fleet of Porter, with barely enough water to float upon. We had to strike vigorously to capture or destroy both."[45]

Despite his intent to strike Banks again, Taylor did recognize he and his men were close to exhaustion. The Confederate general finally gave in to his weariness, lying down for a well-earned rest.[46]

Union general Nathaniel Banks was busily consulting with his staff and senior commanders about his army's next move. Union forces not only stopped the main Confederate assault at Pleasant Hill, but they also, thanks to A. J. Smith, drove the Rebels back to where they started at the outset of the battle. Even though Banks could claim tactical victory, it is safe to say that

Richard Taylor's aggression had somewhat unnerved his Union counterpart. Banks likely anticipated further assaults on his position when dawn came.[47]

Since April 7, Banks's command had suffered just over 4,000 combined casualties, including 529 killed, 1,444 wounded, and approximately 2,051 men missing.[48] Each army had roughly ten thousand to twelve thousand men each to renew the fight the next day. The main difference was that Taylor's army was reaching the end of its endurance, while Banks's forces were not nearly so worn down.[49]

Despite the losses, the Union army still had a strong force at hand. Banks had a reserve available to him—the 3,600 men of Brig. Gen. Cuvier Grover's Second Division of the Nineteenth Corps were at Alexandria, and the 2,000 men of Brig. Gen. Thomas Kilby Smith's division of the Seventeenth Corps were with Porter's flotilla. The challenge here was that Banks was not precisely sure where Porter and Kilby Smith were, and Grover's command was almost seventy miles away.[50]

After conferring with his generals, Banks was eventually convinced to fall back to Grand Ecore. Sometime around midnight on April 10, he ordered a full retreat to the safety of the Red River. This decision determined that the remainder of the campaign would be a return trip down the river, signaling the beginning of the end of the operation.[51]

In his after-action report, Banks outlined his choice.

After-Action Report, Maj. Gen. Nathaniel P. Banks, USA

At the close of the engagement the victorious party found itself without rations and without water. To clear the field for the fight, the train had been sent to the rear upon the single line of communication through the woods, and could not be brought to the front during the night. There was neither water for man or beast, except such as the now exhausted wells had afforded during the day, for miles around. Previous to the movement of the army from Natchitoches orders had been given to the transport fleet, with a portion of the Sixteenth Corps, under the command of Brig. Gen. Kilby Smith, to move up the river, if it was found practicable, to some point near Springfield Landing with the view of effecting a junction with the army at that point on the river. The surplus ammunition and supplies were on board these transports. It was impossible to ascertain whether the fleet had been able to reach the point designated. The rapidly falling river and the increased difficulties of navigation made it appear almost certain that it would not be able to attain the point proposed. A squadron of cavalry sent down to the river, accompanied by Mr. Young, of the engineer corps, who was thoroughly acquainted with the country, reported on the day of the battle that no tidings of the fleet could be obtained on the river, and we were compelled to assume that the increasing difficulties of navigation had prevented it, even if disaster had not occurred from the obstructions which the enemy had placed in the river. These considerations, the absolute deprivation of water for man or beast, the exhaustion of rations, and the failure to effect a connection with the fleet on the river, made it necessary for the army, although victorious in the terrible struggle through which it had just passed, to retreat to a point where it would be certain in communicating with the fleet and where it would have an opportunity of reorganization. The shattered condition of the Thirteenth Army Corps and the cavalry made this indispensable. The wounded were gathered from the battlefield, placed in comfortable hospitals, and left under the care of competent surgeons and assistants. The dead remaining upon the field, as far as possible, were buried during the night. The next day medical supplies and provisions, with competent attendants, were sent in for the sustenance of the wounded, and at daybreak the army reluctantly fell back to its position at Grand Ecore.[52]

Neosho-class river monitor - USS *Osage*, U.S. Naval History and Heritage Command, Unknown, 1863–1865.

Stop 7—*Pleasant Hill Battlefield Park*
23271 LA-175, Pelican, LA 71063
(31.853476559302813, -93.51383074897632)

Decision—Churchill Fails to Find the Union Flank
Decision—A. J. Smith Counterattacks

From the Russell B. Long Lock and Dam and Picnic Ground, return to Porter's Island Road for 2.8 miles, and turn left onto LA 1 S.

After 0.3 mile, turn right onto LA 174 W. Proceed 10.7 miles on LA-174 W, then turn right onto Bob Wilson Road. After 1.4 miles, make a slight left onto LA 177 S. Drive 2.8 miles, then turn right onto LA 175 N. Drive for 800 feet, and the destination will be on your right. There are several places to park at the entrance.

In 1864, Pleasant Hill was a small village situated about 2 miles north of the current village of Pleasant Hill. The entire town moved to be closer to the railroad in 1881. Founded in 1844, the old village site is called Old Town or Old Pleasant Hill Battlefield today. The markers you see before you are all that is left to indicate where this engagement occurred; these include memorials and the old cemetery site, where several battle casualties are buried. A large monument near the cemetery was recently moved from the courthouse at Shreveport.[53]

You are at the Union end of the battlefield. If you stand with LA 175 at your back, you are facing north. The old Pleasant Hill was in front of you. Taylor's attack came from your left (about 1,000 yards away) on both sides of the road. Smith's Union lines were directly behind you, extending roughly 500 yards to the south. The Mansfield Battlefield is up that road 16 miles to the northeast. The Red River is not quite 14 miles to the northeast, on your right.

Decision—Churchill Fails to Find the Union Flank

When Kirby-Smith ordered Sterling Price to send reinforcements from his command to Shreveport, Brig. Gen. Thomas James Churchill was selected to lead a detachment of two small divisions of Arkansas and Missouri regiments, approximately 4,300 men of all arms. Leaving Arkansas on March 20, the men of Churchill's Command marched seventy miles to Shreveport, arriving on March 24.[54]

Remaining in Shreveport until April 3, Churchill's Division marched forty-five miles in thirty-six hours to reach the battlefield at Mansfield, reporting to Taylor sometime between 4:00 and 6:00 p.m. on April 8. Churchill was placed in reserve as the struggle at Mansfield was winding down. Taylor

Pleasant Hill Battlefield Park, Louisiana, Author, Modern Image.

ordered him to have his men prepare two days' worth of rations and get ready to advance. At 3:00 a.m. on April 9, Churchill's Command advanced toward Pleasant Hill.[55]

Richard Taylor had to act quickly if he intended to strike the Union army again. The Federals might just fall back to the Red River to link up with Porter's fleet via Grand Ecore. Or Banks might attempt to open communication with Porter via Blair's Landing on the Red, due east of Pleasant Hill. Taylor mistakenly believed that A. J. Smith's entire force was with Porter's fleet, when these troops were actually at Pleasant Hill. However, he soon discovered his mistake.

Determined to hold on to the initiative, Taylor ordered an advance. Following Green's cavalry, the head of Churchill's column reached a point west of Pleasant Hill sometime after 9:00 a.m. The rest of Taylor's Command followed them. Then the Confederates discovered the Union army in line of battle, waiting for them.[56] Dick Taylor spent the next several hours positioning his forces as they arrived while allowing his men time to rest. His lines on the west end of the clearing stretched north to south and were anchored in the wood line. Left to right were the commands of Green, Polignac, Walker, and Churchill. With the arrival of Churchill's Command, Taylor now had a force of about 12,500 men. Facing the Confederates was a Union force of just shy of 12,000 men.[57]

Banks and his generals positioned their troops in and around the village. The irregular Union line stretched for about a mile. On the right was the brigade of Brig. Gen. William Dwight of the Nineteenth Corps, with Col. William T. Shaw's brigade of the Sixteenth Corps just to his left. Brig. Gen. James W. McMillan's brigade from the Nineteenth was in reserve behind them. The men of Col. Lewis Benedict's brigade, also of the Nineteenth, positioned themselves on a line paralleling the Shreveport–Natchitoches Stage Line Road with the rest of Smith's command behind them. Just before noon, having arranged his men more or less where he wanted them, Banks returned to his headquarters for lunch, believing no battle would take place that day.[58]

The battle at Pleasant Hill began at 3:00 p.m. when Richard Taylor gave the order to advance. Churchill was to march south and east through the woods and get on the left flank of the Federals. Once this attack commenced, the rest of the Confederate force, starting with Walker, would advance en echelon, driving the Yankees from the field. A local man familiar with the roads was sent with Churchill as a guide. About ninety minutes later, Churchill's Command emerged from the woods. The Confederates from Arkansas and Missouri quickly discovered that they were not on the flank of A. J. Smith's veteran Union line, but facing its very center.[59] Realizing he was out of position, Churchill decided to advance and attempt to adjust his alignment simultaneously.

After-Action Report, Brig. Gen. Thomas James Churchill, CSA, Commanding Detachment, District of Arkansas

At the appointed hour the command, as directed, moved off upon the road leading to Pleasant Hill. On arriving within about two miles and a half of that town I was informed that the enemy was drawn up in line of battle three-fourths of a mile this side of Pleasant Hill. After halting and resting the troops for about an hour I was instructed by the major-general commanding to make a detour to the right and fall into the road leading to the town from the Sabine, which intersected the main Mansfield and Pleasant Hill road almost at a right angle. This movement was made for the purpose of turning the enemy's left flank. In about an hour and a half's march I gained the point indicated, and, as I thought, sufficiently far to the right, from the information given me by the guide. I here formed my line of battle—the Missouri division, under Brigadier-General Parsons, on the right, and the Arkansas division, under Brigadier-General Tappan, on the left, with the brigade under General Clark on the right of the road—and moved forward at 4.30. After advancing a few hundred yards in line of battle I discovered that I was not far enough to the right and ordered the command to move by the right flank until I had passed the whole of General Parsons' division to the right of the road. The line of battle was again advanced, and pressing forward we immediately and hotly engaged the enemy along the entire line. We drove him rapidly before us. The right by this time had reached an open field, where they found the enemy drawn up in several lines to receive them. They did not hesitate to charge and drove them across the open field of some 700 yards in width. It was as gallant a charge as ever made by any soldiers of the Confederacy. The left kept steadily advancing, but owing to a dense thicket and having to pass over trees blown down by a hurricane, which formed an almost impassable barrier, and behind which the enemy lay concealed in strong force, it was delayed some time in dislodging them and, in consequence, was unable to keep up with the right. The dead, which here lie piled before our lines, will amply testify to the courage of our gallant soldiers. In the charge on the right we captured several batteries and some 400 or 500 prisoners, 300 of whom were sent to the rear and secured, but as the artillery horses were killed it was impossible to bring off the captured guns. The impetuosity of the charge on the right carried them too far, and the enemy seeing this took advantage of it. Having heavy reserves he threw them around on our right and rear and opened a deadly enfilading fire upon them. Not having sufficient force to meet it, as a matter of necessity and protection they were compelled to fall back. I regret to state that this movement was accompanied with some little confusion, which was extended to the left, and the whole line had to be withdrawn to its original position.[60]

What seemed to be another Confederate victory suddenly turned into a defeat or, at the very least, a tie. Beaten and exhausted, Taylor's Command was forced to fall back, allowing Nathaniel Banks to reclaim the campaign's initiative. If Banks acted decisively, he could erase the stain of the previous day's debacle and continue with his advance. The only question remaining was whether he would have the strength and courage to do so.

Decision—A. J. Smith Counterattacks

By the first week of April 1864, Andrew Jackson Smith had been a part of the Red River Campaign since its opening days. Exposure to Banks's decision-making and command style for almost a month had begun to wear on the gruff, old-school army general. It is unknown how much of his negativity toward Banks was baked in and how much came from direct exposure during the campaign. But by the time the sun set on April 9, Smith had lost any respect for the political general from Massachusetts.

Until now, almost all Union successes in the campaign were credited to Smith's command. On March 14, Smith's men captured Fort DeRussy. They were among the first troops to advance on Alexandria, helping to drive Richard Taylor from the city. On March 21, a force under Brig. Gen. Joseph A. Mower surprised and captured nearly 250 Louisiana Confederates and a four-gun artillery battery at Henderson's Hill, almost without firing a shot.[61]

At the end of the Union column advancing to Shreveport, Smith and his 7,500 men left Grand Ecore on the morning of April 8, arriving near Pleasant Hill after a twenty-one-mile march. Hearing the sounds of battle emanating from Mansfield, Smith sent for instructions from Banks. Smith was told to wait at Pleasant Hill, and the rest of the army would fall back and join him. After allowing his men to rest, in the early morning hours of April 9, Smith moved into position south of the town, forming a line that crossed the road to Mansfield. Elements of the Thirteenth and Nineteenth Corps fell into line to his right. Banks's army now rested on their arms waiting for the Confederates.[62]

Richard Taylor's plan at Pleasant Hill was to have Churchill's Command attack the Union left flank. As Churchill was rolling up the Federal line, Taylor would throw the balance of his force at the Yankees. At 4:30 p.m., Taylor ordered his artillery to open fire. Shortly after hearing the sounds of Churchill's attack from his right, Taylor called for an en echelon attack.[63]

At the far left of the Union line was the brigade of Col. William F. Lynch of Smith's command. The brigade of Col. Lewis Benedict, First Division, Nineteenth Corps, was in front and slightly to his right. Lynch had also sent his Fifty-Eighth Illinois Regiment half a mile in front. The Illinois men took shelter behind a makeshift breastwork.

Churchill's attack drove the irregular Union line back on itself, while Green's Texas cavalry and the Frenchman Polignac leading a brigade of Texas infantry did the same on his right. But Churchill failed to position his command far enough to the right, exposing his own flank as he advanced. Lynch's brigade was now collapsing Brig. Gen. John Bullock Clark Jr.'s Confederate brigade at the far right of Churchill's line. Witnessing the desperate struggle unfolding was the old army brigadier Andrew Jackson Smith. [64]

Smith, sensing an opportunity, could either hold his ground or advance. In his after-action report, the veteran of more than a dozen battles described his critical decision:

After-Action Report, Brig. Gen. Andrew Jackson Smith, USA, Commanding Detachment, Army of the Tennessee

The enemy's skirmishers appeared on Colonel Shaw's front about noon, and there was desultory skirmishing at different parts of the line until about 4.30 p.m., when the enemy made his attack on the right center, driving in the outposts and the brigade of the Nineteenth Corps in my front through my line, they reforming in my rear. Advancing my line slightly to be able to close with and support Shaw's brigade, the battle immediately became general. The enemy had been re-enforced during the afternoon with two divisions of infantry from Price's command, and their troops, flushed with their success of the previous day, seemed determined to break through our line, charging it with desperate energy. Fearing that Shaw's brigade might be totally enveloped, I directed him to fall back and connect with my right. In the mean time the enemy's right had advanced beyond my extreme left and were taken in flank and rolled up by the First Brigade, Third Division, Col. William F. Lynch commanding. Seizing the opportunity I ordered a charge by the whole line, and we drove them back, desperately fighting, step by step across the field, through the wood, and into the open field beyond, fully a mile from the battlefield, when they took advantage of the darkness and fell back toward Mansfield thoroughly whipped and demoralized. In the charge we captured nearly 1,000 prisoners, five pieces of artillery, and six caissons. The artillery was brought off, but the caissons were left until morning. The casualties in my command were as follows: Killed, 98; wounded, 529; missing, 124; total, 751. A large proportion of the missing were of the Thirty-second Iowa, which was on the left of Shaw's brigade, and were nearly surrounded in the early part of the battle during the enemy's first charge. The loss of the enemy in killed was unusually severe. A brigade of cavalry which charged Shaw's brigade in the early part of the action were almost annihilated, he allowing them to approach within 50 yards before opening fire. The prisoners captured were many of them from Missouri regiments, belonging to the divisions that had re-enforced the enemy during the engagement. The darkness compelled us to cease pursuit. Anticipating the order to follow up our success by a vigorous pursuit, the next morning I sent the Third Brigade, Third Division, Col. R. M. Moore commanding, about 2 1/2 miles out on

Appendix I

> the road taken by the retreating enemy, with orders to watch their movements and gain all the information possible, and fell back with the remainder of my command and bivouacked in line on the field of battle. The opinion of Major-General Banks as to the action of the command and its results may be gathered from his own words to me on the field just after the final charge, when, riding up to me, he remarked, shaking me by the hand, "God bless you, general; you have saved the army."[65]

Even though many on both sides sensed another Confederate victory was in the offing, Smith's decision set off a general advance up and down the Union line. As the Federals pressed forward, the exhausted and fought-out Rebels were forced to fall back. The seemingly unstoppable momentum from two straight days of Confederate attacks was stopped, and Taylor's vision of a complete victory was likewise stymied. It was the next step in returning the campaign's momentum to the Federals. With this decision, Smith allowed the Union commanding general to return to the offensive and salvage the operation. In Smith's mind, that was the next logical move.[66]

The Battle of Pleasant Hill, PGA Bufford, Battle of Pleasant Hill, circa, Unknown, Library of Congress Washington, DC 20540.

Stop 8—Mansfield State Historic Site
15149 LA-175, Mansfield, LA 71052
(32.011164177328666, -93.66372564248209)

Decision—The Confederate Stand at Mansfield
Decision—Banks Retreats to Pleasant Hill

From the Pleasant Hill Battlefield site, turn right and drive 15.8 miles northwest on LA 175 N. The Mansfield State Historic Site will be on your right. Park at the visitor center, and walk to the cannon at the entrance. You can pay the entrance fee at the visitor center. Also, inside the visitor center is a movie on the campaign and a museum. A three-quarter-mile interpretive battlefield trail circles the site.

The visitor center sits in what was the middle of the Union lines on April 8, 1864. Facing southeast, you will be looking toward the Union lines. Pleasant Hill is 16 miles in that same direction. If you turn around and face northwest, the town of Mansfield is 3 miles in that direction. Taylor's attack came from that direction. Shreveport is approximately 35 miles due north. The Red River is roughly 15 miles east, on your right.

Preserving the Mansfield Battlefield began when the United Daughters of the Confederacy acquired four acres of land here in 1924. The first monument was placed that same year. Incremental improvements were made over time, and in 1954, custodianship of the site was transferred to the State of Louisiana. The initial construction of the visitor center and museum began that same year. By 2001, with the aid of groups like American Battlefield Trust, the Mansfield site has expanded to 177 acres of preserved land. The location is also listed on the National Register of Historic Places. The Louisiana Department of State Parks manages the Mansfield State Historic Site, and it is open daily from 9:00 a.m. to 5:00 p.m., excluding major holidays.[67]

Decision—The Confederate Stand at Mansfield

The decisions leading up to the clash at Mansfield were months in the making. The slow but steady concentration of thousands of armed men on both sides increased the likelihood of a significant battle. By the evening of April 7, 1864, all the previous decisions coalesced in a two-hundred-acre clearing southeast of this small Louisiana town.[68]

In February 1864, Taylor's and Kirby-Smith's suspicions that the Red River Valley was destined for a Union invasion were further reinforced when they learned that Nathaniel Banks had pulled troops from his foothold in Matagorda, Texas. In addition, the officers received reports from Confederate

Appendix I

Mansfield State Historic Site, Mansfield, Louisiana, Author, Modern Image.

spies in New Orleans that Union troops were massing. This could only mean Banks intended to use these forces to man a campaign up the Red River.[69]

Kirby-Smith began amassing an army from his widely scattered command to answer this new Federal threat. In March 1864, he ordered the various Trans-Mississippi subdepartments to send every available man either to Richard Taylor in northwestern Louisiana or directly to his garrison in Shreveport.

Maj. Gen. John B. Magruder was ordered to send Brig. Gen. Thomas J. Green's cavalry corps from Texas to Alexandria. The conspicuously named Brig. Gen. Camille Armand Jules Marie, Prince de Polignac, marched his brigade from Trinity, Texas. It was combined with the brigade of Col. Henry Gray under the command of Brig. Gen. Jean-Jacques-Alfred-Alexandre "Alfred" Mouton. Maj. Gen. John G. Walker's Texas Division (a.k.a. the Greyhounds), relieved from the backbreaking work of reinforcing Fort DeRussy, had been checking the Union advance since the fall of that position. These soldiers, too, were summoned to fall back and join the gathering

Confederate commands. Taylor also had an unknown number of "reserves"; these were likely unexchanged Confederate soldiers paroled at Vicksburg. Best estimates are that by the evening of April 7, Richard Taylor had assembled a force of between 8,800 and 9,000 men of all arms.[70]

Kirby-Smith also ordered Maj. Gen. Sterling Price in Arkansas and Brig. Gen Samuel B. Maxey in the Indian Territory to send all available reinforcements from their departments to Shreveport.[71]

Kirby-Smith had competing strategic priorities. Learning of Frederick Steele's departure from Little Rock on March 2, Kirby-Smith was concerned that Steele's column from the north might be a more imminent threat than Banks advancing from the south. Even though Banks's army was closer, Kirby-Smith began to hesitate, looking over both shoulders. The Confederate commander initially decided that his forces would concentrate on Banks's army moving up from New Orleans. Once that force was defeated, the Confederate troops would move north to take on Steele's command. However, Kirby-Smith suddenly changed his mind, believing Steele's command might be the most pressing threat.[72]

Kirby-Smith wanted to concentrate all available Trans-Mississippi forces at Shreveport and make a stand against the Federal troops near the town. Taylor had other ideas. He wanted all reinforcements in the theater sent to him so that he could strike Banks's army head-on as soon as it was practical and ideally below Mansfield. Once the enemy troops were eliminated, the unified Confederate commands could turn their attention to Steele. Convinced he was right, Taylor expressed his feelings to Kirby-Smith at every opportunity.[73]

The two generals exchanged numerous and often contentious communications. They clashed over everything, including reinforcements, defensive strategies, and the lack of cooperation from other Trans-Mississippi departments.[74]

Communication from Taylor to Kirby-Smith, April 4, 1864

Steele's advance has been long expected by me (refer to several dispatches on the subject), and his movements have been connected with those of the column in my front; hence my extreme anxiety to fight the latter before it gained too much territory. Like the man who has admitted the robber into his bed-chamber instead of resisting him at the door, our defense will be embarrassed by the cries of wives and children. Action, prompt, vigorous action, is required. While we are deliberating the enemy is marching. King James lost three kingdoms for a mass. We may lose three States without a battle. Banks is cold,

> timid, easily foiled. He depends principally on the river for transportation. The rapid fall in the river and the sinking of the Falls City may well be expected to delay him. Captain McCloskey has been ordered to sink the Falls City as low down as possible. Banks has a number of very light stern-wheel transports, plated to be musket-proof. These are evidently to bring up supplies after the advance by land has opened the river. Steele is bold, ardent, vigorous. Independent of rivers, his transportation has doubtless been made ample for his purposes. If he has anything like the force represented he will sweep Price from his path. He is the most dangerous and should be met and overthrown at once. Having but little knowledge of the roads and lines of supply above Shreveport, I am unable to express any definite opinion as to the point where Steele should be met.[75]

Having massed his forces southeast of Mansfield, Taylor was convinced the whole of Banks's army was within one day's march of his position. Taylor requested permission to attack Banks. Kirby-Smith, rather than simply ordering Taylor, merely suggested that all might be lost if Taylor's army was destroyed in a premature clash with Banks. Kirby-Smith returned to Shreveport on April 7, satisfied that the situation was understood.[76]

Richard Taylor could obey orders from Kirby-Smith and not bring on a significant engagement, or he could defiantly stand and fight at Mansfield.

Communication from Taylor to Kirby-Smith, April 7, 1864

> I have the honor to report that the enemy have driven in my pickets, and advanced some 7 miles, with considerable skirmishing, this side of Pleasant Hill. The force displayed thus far is about 4,000 men (cavalry and mounted infantry). This may be merely a reconnaissance in large force for the forerunner of a positive advance on the part of the enemy with his whole force. I respectfully ask to know if it accords with the views of the lieutenant-general commanding that I should hazard a general engagement at this point, and request an immediate answer, that I may receive it before daylight to-morrow morning.
>
> Very respectfully, your obedient servant,
> R. TAYLOR. Major- General.[77]

It is believed that Taylor sent this message at the last moment and by the slowest possible means, ensuring he would not receive a reply before the fighting erupted. Kirby-Smith replied, still urging his lieutenant not to bring on a general engagement.[78]

Richard Taylor spent almost the whole of April 8 waiting for Banks to foolishly and impulsively attack his army. Growing tired of the Union general's unwillingness to throw his army at the Rebel lines, Taylor ordered the Louisianians and Texans forward at 3:30 p.m. while riding among Mouton's Command. Turning to Brigadier General Polignac, Taylor shouted over the growing din of battle, "Little Frenchman, I am going to fight Banks here if he has a million men."[79]

Communication from Taylor to Kirby-Smith, April 8, 1864

I have the honor to report that the fighting continued until night. The fight then for water was very severe, the enemy being at that time re-enforced by the Nineteenth Corps. We fought the Thirteenth Army Corps all day, and late in the evening met the Nineteenth Army Corps; repulsed and drove them back. We have captured about 2,000 prisoners, 20 pieces of artillery, 200 wagons, and thousands of small-arms. Our loss in officers has been severe, and we have many wounded. Send all the medical assistance and medical stores you can, and if you have any re-enforcements hurry them down. Churchill's and Parsons' divisions, which did not take part in the fight to-day, have been ordered to the front before daylight to-morrow morning. I shall continue to push the enemy with the utmost vigor.

Very respectfully, your obedient servant,
R. TAYLOR, Major-General, Commanding.[80]

Seeing his opportunity slipping away, Dick Taylor decided to stand and fight. The Battle of Mansfield turned the campaign's momentum by halting the Union advance at Shreveport.

Decision—Banks Retreats to Pleasant Hill

In the saddle all afternoon and evening on April 8, Nathaniel Banks was moving from point to point shouting orders, rallying his men, and doing all he could to stem the deluge of retreating men, wagons, horses, and artillery. Despite his personal courage and appeals for them to stop, his men deserted the field. A soldier in the Thirty-Eighth Massachusetts described the chaos: "The teams were abandoned by the drivers; the traces cut and the animals ridden off by the frightened men. Bare-headed riders rode with agony in their faces, and for at least ten minutes it seemed as if all were going to destruction together."[81]

Banks's army suffered 240 men killed, 671 wounded, and 1,508 missing in the confrontation at Mansfield, a casualty rate of 20 percent of those engaged.[82] Nineteenth Corps commander William B. Franklin broke an arm, had a bullet glance off his leg, and had two horses shot from underneath him during the melee. The Thirteenth Corps Division of Brig. Gen. Robert A. Cameron endured nearly 50 percent casualties in the desperate attempt to stop Taylor's assaults. Brig. Gen. Thomas E. G. Ransom, commander of the Thirteenth Corps, was wounded and had to be carried from the field. In Col. William Landram's Fourth Division of the Thirteenth Corps, brigade commander Col. Frank Emerson was wounded and captured, and brigade commander Col. Joseph W. Vance was killed.[83]

As the sun was setting, three brigades of Brig. Gen. William H. Emory made a determined stand three miles south of the initial Federal position at Mansfield near a small creek called Chapman's Bayou. Thirteen miles southeast at Pleasant Hill, the uncommitted 7,500 men of Brig. Gen. A. J. Smith's command paused to rest, having marched the twenty-one miles that day from Grand Ecore.[84]

On the Confederate side, the battle's results were far better than Richard Taylor could have reasonably expected. Taylor reported that his army suffered one thousand men killed and wounded in the assault. Brig. Gen. Alexander Mouton's Second Division suffered grievously during the fight. Mouton was mortally wounded, reportedly shot several times in the back. All the field officers in Col. Henry Gray's First Brigade of Mouton's Command were either killed or wounded, save Gray himself. In the very eye of the storm, the Crescent Consolidated Louisiana Regiment saw nearly two hundred men, all of its field officers, and seven color-bearers killed. It has been estimated that Gray's Brigade of Mouton's Division sustained a casualty rate of 40 percent of those engaged.[85]

Taylor was pleased with the results. His men had stopped Banks's army dead in its tracks and pushed them back several miles south, capturing dozens of wagons full of supplies and hundreds of horses and mules in the process.[86]

Told by his commanding officer that the risk of a general engagement with Union forces outside of Shreveport was too high, Taylor must have felt vindicated by the day's outcome. He sent several messages to Kirby-Smith in Shreveport, extolling a largely one-sided victory while expressing his intention to press his advantage by pursuing Banks to finish him off.[87] Taylor repeated this self-satisfied tone in his memoir while disparaging his Union opponent: "With a much smaller force on the field, we invariably outnumbered the enemy at the fighting point; and foreseeing the possibility of this, I was justified in my confidence of success. The defeat of the federal army was largely due to the ignorance and arrogance of its commander, General Banks, who attributed my long retreat to his own wonderful strategy."[88]

At that moment, Nathaniel Banks worked feverishly to salvage his campaign, which was now at risk of coming entirely off the rails. Haunted by the prospect of additional combat come the morning and unsettled by an unusually aggressive opponent, Banks vacillated. The New Englander could stand and fight in his current position, fall back, or advance. Time, manpower, and logistics would influence his choice.

After conferring with his generals, Banks initially decided to continue the advance toward Shreveport. Still, after consulting with Franklin, Emory, and Dwight of the Nineteenth Corps, he was convinced to fall back to Grand

View of the Union position, Mansfield State Historic Site, Mansfield, Louisiana, Author, Modern Image.

Ecore. Sometime around midnight on April 10, Banks ordered a full retreat to the safety of the Red River.[89]

On April 13, in the aftermath of the Federal retreat, an article in the *St. Louis Republican* read in part, "He [Banks] has lost the confidence of the entire army. The privates are ridiculing him. Officers are not loudly but deeply cursing him and civilians are unanimous in the condemnation of the commanding general. . . . Personally, General Banks is a perfect gentleman. I have no prejudice against him, for he had invariably treated me with kindness and consideration. But the truth must be told. As a military man he is, as the vernacular has it, 'played out.'"[90]

Stop 9—Mansfield Cemetery, Mansfield, Louisiana
303-309 Van Buren Street, Mansfield, LA 71052
(32.039882770097456, -93.70585768729988)

Decision—Kirby-Smith Moves Forces to Arkansas

From the Mansfield State Historic Site visitor center, turn right on LA 175 N. After traveling 2.7 miles, turn left onto McArthur Drive, which turns into Polk Street. Drive for 0.2 mile, and turn right on Van Buren Street. After 850 feet, you will find yourself at the entrance to the cemetery.

Mansfield Cemetery, Mansfield, Louisiana, Author, Modern Image.

The city of Mansfield was first platted in 1843 and incorporated in 1847. The land for the Mansfield Cemetery was designated at the same time, and interments began shortly after that and continue to this day. As Mansfield is the seat of DeSoto Parish, the first parish courthouse was erected here in the early 1850s.

The Act to Establish and Protect National Cemeteries was passed in 1867. Part of its purpose was to ensure that every Union soldier who died during the war was placed in a national cemetery. Subsequently, Federal representatives visited DeSoto Parish to identify and rebury Union dead from the Battles of Mansfield and Pleasant Hill. When these agents identified a disinterred body as a Confederate, they turned it over to local communities like Mansfield. Eighty-seven unknown Confederate soldiers are buried in a mass grave in the cemetery's northwest corner.[91]

Facing the gate, you are looking due north. Shreveport is 34 miles in that same direction. The Red River is just over 18 miles to your right, and the border of Texas is just under 20 miles to your left. We will review our next decision here.

Decision—Kirby-Smith Moves Forces to Arkansas

Despite the Confederate setback at Pleasant Hill, by the evening of April 9, Richard Taylor was convinced he had stopped the Federal momentum north. Nathaniel Banks was withdrawing to Grand Ecore, giving Taylor the strategic victory.

The Rebel general was determined to operate from the same playbook as before. That book told him that continued pressure on Nathaniel Banks's infantry and David Dixon Porter's Union flotilla would shatter the Federals' resolve and push them back down the Red River.

Now that the fighting was over, most of Taylor's worn-out army fell back some six miles from the battlefield, except for two brigades of cavalry. Taylor had posted these horsemen on the Blair Landing Road earlier that day to block any Federal movement to the river and prevent a linkup with the Union navy.[92]

Dick Taylor had not stopped for nearly a week and had barely slept. Having made the needed arrangements for his army, he finally lay down to rest, overcome by exhaustion. Much to his disappointment, this respite was not to last. A renewed debate on Confederate strategy soon interrupted the general's much-needed sleep.

Having ridden all day to reach Taylor, a frustrated Kirby-Smith sought to rein in his irrepressible general. As was routine, Kirby-Smith and Taylor had very different thoughts on what the Confederates' subsequent actions should be. Taylor wanted to continue the attacks and crush the Union army and navy, leaving Sterling Price in Arkansas to check Steele's advance with whatever forces he had. Taylor argued that if Banks and Porter were forced to fall back downstream, Steele would have no choice but to retreat to Littlerock. He thought the best way to accomplish this was to direct all available Confederate strength at Banks and Porter. Taylor also pointed out that Union general Steele was still over one hundred miles from Shreveport and no immediate threat to the capital city.

Conversely, Kirby-Smith believed Taylor's army was worn down, paralyzed, and disorganized from continuous marching and fighting. Moreover, with his command moving south, Kirby-Smith was also concerned that Maj. Gen. Frederick Steele in Arkansas now posed a more significant danger to the Rebels. He wanted all the department's resources brought to bear against this threat from the north.[93] Indeed, Kirby-Smith could not help but continue to throw his gaze northward to Steele's Union force. Real or imagined, the Confederate commander saw only disaster in Arkansas.[94]

Meanwhile, Steele and his Federal command had reached Arkadelphia, Arkansas, on March 26. Here, the general paused for several days waiting for Brig. Gen. John Milton Thayer's 3,600 men from the Fort Smith garrison to join him. Thayer and Steele finally connected on April 7, five miles south of Elkins Ferry and about one hundred miles north of Shreveport. Steele now had over 10,000 to 11,000 men to continue his operation, while the Confederate brigadier general John S. Marmaduke had perhaps 3,600 mounted troops to oppose the Yankees. However, promised reinforcements were on the way.[95]

In Louisiana, the telltale sounds of an army on the move became evident to the Confederates. Stragglers soon confirmed to Edmund Kirby-Smith and Richard Taylor that Banks was in full retreat.[96]

On April 14, 1864, Kirby-Smith ordered the divisions of Walker, Churchill, and Parson to march north to reinforce Maj. Gen. Sterling Price's command in Arkansas. Hoping to keep some control over these units, Taylor offered to lead them. Kirby-Smith refused, taking command himself while keeping this quarrelsome general in Louisiana. Roughly speaking, about five thousand men were detached from Taylor's force for the campaign's duration.[97]

This decision impacted the campaign in several significant ways. First, it reduced the number of men available to Richard Taylor by roughly half. The determined general was now forced to try and destroy Banks's command with a fraction of the men he had before. For the next several weeks, Taylor tried unsuccessfully to land a decisive blow on Banks's army. While his men were undoubtedly willing, most of the Federals escaped across the Atchafalaya River.

Second, the choice drove a further wedge between Kirby-Smith and Taylor. Richard Taylor was promoted to lieutenant general as a reward for his recent performance, leaving him in charge at Shreveport while Kirby-Smith marched to Arkansas. Yet Taylor was anything but grateful. On April 19, he rejoined what remained of his army, facing Banks's command at Grand Ecore.[98] Increasingly incensed, Taylor then spent the last months of his tenure in the Trans-Mississippi battling his commander more than he did the enemy. On June 5, 1862, the officer demanded to be relieved of duty, no longer wanting to serve under Edmund Kirby-Smith.[99]

Frederick Steele had been getting intelligence regarding Banks's defeat and subsequent retreat, and by April 22 the rumors were confirmed. In an almost constant state of combat for a week, Steele's army was hemorrhaging men, supplies, arms, wagons, and mules. Learning of the approach of Kirby-Smith all but sealed his fate. The final battle at Jenkins Ferry was a strategic victory for Steele, as he could hold off Kirby-Smith and Sterling Price's combined forces. But in the end, the Federals were forced to fall back to Little Rock.[100]

Edmund Kirby-Smith convinced himself that his actions saved Shreveport and the Trans-Mississippi, later stating as much in his after-action report:

Confederate Grave, Mansfield Cemetery, Mansfield, Louisiana, Author, Modern Image.

Appendix I

> ### After-Action Report, Gen. Edmund Kirby-Smith, CSA, Commanding Department of the Trans-Mississippi
>
> I have written thus at length in advance of my report, delayed by being unable to get the reports of my subordinate commanders, because I learn that my policy and plans have been much discussed at Richmond, and that it has been charged that but for my errors much more important results would have been achieved. In this connection I have only to remark that I have honestly done what appeared to me to be right and proper. I claim that my combinations have resulted in great successes, and beg to doubt whether more could have been accomplished under a different system of operations.[101]

Stop 10—Stoner Avenue Park, Shreveport, Louisiana
857 E Stoner Avenue, Shreveport, LA 71101
(32.49958129228306, -93.71014550704226)

Decision—Edmund Kirby-Smith Takes Command
Decision—The Confederates Divert the Red River

Drive south on Van Buren Street from the Mansfield Cemetery, and turn right on Polk Drive. After 1,000 feet, turn left on Lake Drive. Drive for 0.45 mile, and exit onto LA 175 N toward Shreveport. After 13.0 miles, merge onto US 49 N. Drive for 20.0 miles, and take Exit 206 to merge onto I-20 E toward Monroe. After 1.1 miles, take Exit 19A to merge onto LA 1 S / Market Street. Drive 1.0 mile, and take a slight left onto N. Spring Street. Drive for 0.9 mile, and then turn left onto E. Stoner Avenue. Drive 1.25 miles, turn right, and follow the drive to the parking lot. Park near the river.

Founded in 1836 by the Shreve Town Company, Shreveport was established to develop a town at the juncture of the newly navigable Red River and the Texas Trail, an overland route into the newly independent Republic of Texas. In 1864, the town had become the home for the displaced Confederate state governments of Louisiana and Arkansas and the headquarters of the Confederate Department of the Trans-Mississippi. Receiving war materials from Texas, Shreveport was the most significant supply depot in the theater by the start of the Red River Campaign.

You are standing on what would have been the southernmost extension of the defensive works protecting the city in 1864. These were a series of trenches, breastworks, river batteries, and fortifications. As you face the river, you are

The Red River at Stoner Avenue Park, Shreveport, Louisiana, Author, Modern Image.

looking northeast. Little Rock is 163 miles in that direction. Grand Ecore and Natchitoches are about 60 miles southeast, on your right. Austin, the capital of Texas, is behind you, 280 miles southwest.[102]

Decision—Edmund Kirby-Smith Takes Command

Confederate forces under Robert E. Lee won a stunning victory over the Army of the Potomac at Fredericksburg in December 1862. However, Jefferson Davis and his Confederacy faced far more uncertain times in the West. By January 1863, Braxton Bragg and the Army of Tennessee had been forced to fall back to Tullahoma, Tennessee, after failing to win strategic victories at Perryville and Stones River. To add to Confederate misfortunes, Union forces under U. S. Grant had begun their dogged advance at the Rebel stronghold of Vicksburg.

Gen. Braxton Bragg presented one of Davis's primary dilemmas in the West. Dissatisfied with his handling of the Kentucky and Stones River Campaigns, several of Bragg's most senior lieutenants, including Edmund Kirby-Smith, demanded his removal. Determined to find a solution to the rapidly disintegrating situation, Davis sent Western Department commander Gen. Joe Johnston to investigate and report his findings.[103]

West of the Mississippi, affairs were not much better. Davis's overall commander of the Trans-Mississippi since October 1862 was the equally problematic Lieut. Gen. Theophilus H. Holmes. Holmes was banished to the theater, a victim of Robert E. Lee's purge of army commanders he had no further use for after the Seven Days Battles. From his headquarters in Little Rock, Holmes constantly complained about the inferior quality of his troops, the weapons he was provided, and the general lack of support he received from the Confederate War Department in Richmond. Holmes also refused to send troops to support Vicksburg, and he was primarily blamed for the Confederate losses at Prairie Grove and Dripping Springs in December 1862, resulting in the Union occupying most of northern Arkansas.[104]

With the situation on both banks of the Mississippi seeming to worsen by the moment, Jefferson Davis, who often functioned as his own secretary of war and general-in-chief, pondered a solution to his command woes west of the Mississippi. He could keep Holmes in place, move Bragg or Johnston to the Trans-Mississippi, divide command responsibilities, or give the job to Kirby-Smith.

Initially, it was decided to divide the responsibilities of the far-flung department.

> Special Orders, No. 11
> Adjt. and Insp. General's Office
> Richmond, January 14, 1863.
> Lieut. Gen. E. Kirby Smith is assigned to the command of the Southwestern Army, embracing the Department of West Louisiana and Texas. The geographical limits of this command will hereafter be separate and distinct from the command of the Trans-Mississippi Department, named in previous orders. Lieutenant-General Smith will proceed with his staff to Alexandria, La., and assume this command.
> By command of the Secretary of War:
> Jno. Withers,
> Assistant Adjutant-General.[105]

Before he could reach his new command, Kirby-Smith received countermanding orders.

> Richmond, February 9, 1863.
> Lieut. Gen. E. Kirby Smith,
> Care of General Pemberton, Jackson, Miss.:
> Your command of Southwestern Army has been enlarged so as to embrace the Trans-Mississippi Department. Lieutenant-General Holmes will still remain in that department, and it is suggested for

> your consideration to visit his headquarters before proceeding to West Louisiana.
>
> S. Cooper,
> Adjutant and Inspector General.[106]

Decision—The Confederates Divert the Red River

Brig. Gen. William Robertson Boggs followed Kirby-Smith to the Trans-Mississippi, becoming his chief of staff. Knowing the thirty-five-year-old officer's skill as an engineer, Kirby-Smith at once set Boggs to work improving the defensive fortifications and obstacles up and down the Red River.[107] Boggs subsequently became one of the most talented engineers the Confederacy ever produced. His fortifications along the Red and his understanding of the use of topography for defensive warfare provided a master class in military engineering.[108]

Boggs found himself amid the constant quarreling between his commander and Richard Taylor. Taylor and Kirby-Smith clearly had vastly different philosophies on warfare and how best to thwart any Union advance up the Red River Valley. Smith favored a solid defensive posture anchored by strong fixed fortifications. At the same time, Taylor's highly mobile fighting style, likely influenced by Stonewall Jackson, was at odds with any notion of static defense.[109]

The Red River was one of the main factors determining when Federal forces could launch their campaign at Louisiana's Confederate capital of Shreveport. The Red often ran shallow and was not navigable up to Shreveport during the winter. But it typically rose several feet in March and April with the ubiquitous spring rains. This seasonality was essential to Union plans, as Adm. David Dixon Porter's deep-draft vessels needed additional clearance to navigate up the river and accompany Federal land forces to Shreveport.[110]

Edmund Kirby-Smith recognized the challenges faced by Confederate forces and the need for proper defenses.

> ### "The Defense of the Red River," *Battles and Leaders*, Gen. E. Kirby-Smith, CSA
>
> Soon after my arrival in the Trans-Mississippi Department I became convinced that the valley of the Red River was the only practicable line of operations by which the enemy could penetrate the country. This fact was well understood and appreciated by their generals.

> I addressed myself to the task of defending this line with the slender means at my disposal. Fortifications were erected on the lower Red River; Shreveport and Camden were fortified, and works were ordered on the Sabine and the crossings of the upper Red River. Depots were established on the shortest lines of communication between the Red River valley and the troops serving in Arkansas and Texas. Those commands were directed to be held ready to move with little delay, and every preparation was made in advance for accelerating a concentration at all times difficult over long distances, and through a country destitute of supplies and with limited means of transportation.
>
> In February, 1864, the enemy were preparing in New Orleans, Vicksburg, and Little Rock for offensive operations. Though 25,000 of the enemy were reported on the Texas coast, my information convinced me that the valley of the Red River would be the principal theater of operations and Shreveport the objective point of the columns moving from Arkansas and Louisiana.[111]

Confederate efforts to frustrate an expected Union thrust up the Red River had been underway since 1862. However, preparations escalated dramatically once Kirby-Smith and his staff reached Louisiana. In just over twelve months, Boggs oversaw the installation of more than a dozen forts, artillery positions, strongpoints, and river obstructions from Fort DeRussy below Alexandria all the way northwest to the outskirts of Shreveport. The Confederate defenders even sunk a large side-wheeler, the 880-ton *New Falls City*, in the river about a dozen miles downstream of Shreveport.

Boggs had a truly inspired idea at a bend in the river just below Shreveport. In 1851 a somewhat disagreeable local planter named James Gilmer dug what came to be known as Tones Bayou. He planned to build a town below Shreveport and make it a competing shipping hub by diverting the flow of the Red into the bayou. Before the war, Louisiana state officials blocked this diversion, leaving the dam in place. Boggs, who knew the local history, realized that removing Tones Bayou would redirect as much as 75 percent of the Red River's flow—like a plug pulled on a bathtub's drain.[112]

Boggs and Kirby-Smith had contemplated eliminating the dam as early as 1863, understanding the challenges of supply it would create for Taylor's army downriver. Kirby-Smith could order Boggs to move forward with his plan or rely on the existing defensive works to do the job.

> **Communication from Boggs to Taylor, October 15, 1863**
> There are many points on the river above suitable for strong defense, with a small force, against gunboats. The position at Plaisance has the advantage of covering Cane River. I do not think it practicable to place permanent obstructions in the river. Lieutenant-General Smith has directed that the obstructions in the mouth of Tone's Bayou be removed, and steps be taken to stop the cut-off. This will take nearly all the water from Red River above Grand Ecore, and, owing to the scarcity of wagons, will make it difficult to supply your army from this region.
>
> I remain, very respectfully, your obedient servant,
> W. R. BOGGS,
> Brigadier-General, and Chief of Staff.[113]

Kirby-Smith and Boggs were convinced the scheme was worth the risk and removed the dam that blocked the Red from flowing into Tones Bayou. As the campaign began, the befuddled Union fleet waiting for the river to rise was astounded as the Red dropped to alarming levels day after day.

The dam's removal added to Union delays, as the US Navy sat idle and waited for the river to rise. While other factors were involved, the shallow-running river prevented Porter and his fleet from advancing farther than Loggy Bayou. Kirby-Smith and Boggs's decision determined that the Red River Campaign would be decided primarily by infantry actions and not by overwhelming Union naval strength. It took Porter several days to get his fleet turned around and safely back to Alexandria once Banks retreated, and the ships could go no farther, exposing them to additional attacks from Confederate forces.[114]

Stop 11—Jenkins Ferry Battleground State Park, Arkansas

Co Road 317 / Forest Road 9010, Leola, AR 72084
(34.21273892526126, -92.54814174105516)

Decision—Steele Advances at Shreveport

The Jenkins Ferry Battleground State Park is located on State Highway 46 in central Arkansas, just over 4 miles northeast of Leola. The Saline River runs adjacent to the park, and several interpretive makers describe the battle. You are looking northeast if you stand with Highway 46 at your back. Little Rock is roughly 38 miles to your right, or northeast. Shreveport is on your

Appendix I

McPherson & Oliver, photographer. Ironclad gunboat USS *Louisville* on the Red River, New Orleans. United States Red River Louisiana Texas, circa 1864, Library of Congress Washington, DC 20540.

left, about 136 miles to the southwest. Alexandria, Louisiana, is 184 miles due south from where you stand. The actual battlefield is about a mile to the southwest, on your left.

The land where this Civil War battle took place was settled by Thomas Jenkins, who started the ferry in 1815. His sons ran it until the beginning of the Civil War. The Battle of Jenkins Ferry on April 30, 1864, was the final significant engagement of the Camden Expedition, as it is called. With ten thousand men, Kirby-Smith and Sterling Price launched one unorganized attack after another, attempting to keep the pressure on Steele's army of twelve thousand and prevent it from crossing the Saline River. Despite a Union tactical victory, Steele was forced to fall back to Little Rock.[115]

Decision—Steele Advances at Shreveport

Part of the Red River Campaign plan was a coordinated Union advance with Steele's army moving south from Arkansas as Banks moved north. This strategy put Confederate forces at Shreveport at a significant disadvantage, forcing Kirby-Smith and Dick Taylor to defend against two separate Union armies attacking from two directions. An offensive drive by Steele from Little Rock might draw Rebels away from Banks and his army.

Frederick Steele was not enthusiastic about the campaign from the outset.

When told he was expected to support Banks's Red River operation in Louisiana, Steele began rationalizing why doing so was not feasible. He consistently dragged his feet, as he had no faith in Banks's ability as a commander. Steele resisted from February through March, until Grant summarily ordered him to provide support on March 15.[116]

Steele's lack of enthusiasm for the Red River expedition was likewise grounded in the difficulties he foresaw in supporting it. The road system in southwestern Arkansas was very problematic. Unmaintained dirt roads quickly turned to impassable bogs during the rainy season. Moreover, the local population was openly hostile to the Union army. Every citizen in this part of the state was a potential Southern sympathizer or an outright spy. Also, pockets of Confederate regular and partisan forces were very active throughout the southwestern part of Arkansas, and hostile Native American tribes just west beyond the frontier were an ongoing threat. These factions would no doubt take advantage of the Federals' diverted attention as they marched to Shreveport.[117]

The aggregate of all Union forces in Arkansas was about 20,000 men of all arms. Sixty percent of this command was garrisoned at Pine Bluff or far-off Fort Smith.[118] Despite all these challenges, Steele and his staff assembled about 10,000 to 11,000 men of all arms. In addition to Brig. Gen. Frederick Salomon's division with about 5,200 men from his own Little Rock command, Steele expected 3,200 men from Brig. Gen. John Milton Thayer's

Jenkins Ferry Battleground State Park, Arkansas, Curt Locklear, Modern Image.

Fort Smith garrison. Steele's force would also include a cavalry division commanded by Brig. Gen. Eugene Asa Carr with around 3,000 men. March 23 was set as the Federals' departure date from Little Rock.[119]

Steele's next step was to determine the best avenue of approach. The most apparent and shortest path would lead directly south toward Monroe, Louisiana, and then west. Steele decided to take a course southwest to link up with Thayer's command coming south from Fort Smith.[120]

The general had another critical factor to consider: his lines of communication and supply. Not knowing how long his forces would be in the field, Steele had to figure out how to keep his army adequately supplied with ammunition, food, and fodder. Shreveport was over 150 miles from Little Rock, and southern Arkansas was largely devoid of resources from which his army could forage.

Steele decided to load his wagons and men to the hilt and bring the needed supplies with him. On March 23, Steele's command left Little Rock, arriving in Arkadelphia on the twenty-ninth. Brig. Gen. John Thayer, the commander of the Fort Smith garrison, and his force of 3,600 men were to meet him.[121]

The results of Steele's decision were impactful, to say the least. Due to Thayer's delays, the Confederate counteroffensive, and mismanagement of his supply lines, he never got closer than Washington, Arkansas, or eighty miles from Shreveport. Steele would spend the better part of the next forty-three

Brigadier General Samuel Allen Rice, Department of Arkansas, mortally wounded at the Battle of Jenkins' Ferry, AK, circa 1862–1864, Library of Congress Washington, DC 20540.

days fighting off Confederate attacks while desperately working out how to feed and supply his army. With each subsequent engagement, his command fell back farther and farther from his objective, often losing men and valuable supplies in the process.

Five days before the Battle of Jenkins Ferry, Steele received the following communication from his quartermaster:

Communication from Capt. C. A. Henry to Frederick Steele, April 25, 1864

GENERAL: I have the honor to report that the wagon train of 211 wagons which left this post on the 23rd instant for Pine Bluff, for the purpose of loading with subsistence stores for the use of this command, was captured by the enemy, under command of General Fagan, to-day at a point some 30 miles north of this post. I am informed, general, by Mr. Coles, wagon-master in charge of the train, that a portion of the wagons were set on fire by shells from the enemy's artillery and entirely consumed, and that about 150 fell into the hands of the enemy. I most respectfully beg leave, general, again to call your attention to the impossibility of procuring forage for the public animals in this command. Our losses of animals by capture will amount to some 2,000. Since leaving Little Rock the wagoners have brought in from the two captured trains quite a number of mules, but we have still nearly 9,000 horses and mules to provide forage for, and in the present impoverished condition of this part of the State it is impassible to secure forage for even 1,000. Will you have the kindness, general, to give this question of supplying forage your immediate and earnest attention.[122]

APPENDIX II

UNION ORDER OF BATTLE

Abbreviations

k—killed, c—captured, mw—mortally wounded, w—wounded
Gen.—General
Lieut. Gen.—Lieutenant General
Maj. Gen.—Major General
Brig. Gen.—Brigadier General
Col.—Colonel
Lieut. Col.—Lieutenant Colonel
Maj.—Major
Capt.—Captain
Lieut.—Lieutenant
Sgt.—Sergeant
Surg.—Surgeon

Operations in Louisiana

Department of the Gulf

Maj. Gen. Nathaniel P. Banks, commanding

GENERAL STAFF
Chief of Staff
    Brig. Gen. Charles Pomeroy Stone

Aide-de-Camp
 Col. J. G. Wilson

GENERAL HEADQUARTERS
ESCORT
(Companies A and B)
 Capt. Richard W. Francis
(Company C)
 Capt. Frank Sayles

ENGINEER BRIGADE
 Col George D. Robinson

3rd Engineers, Corps d'Afrique (USCT)
 Lieut. Col. George A. Harmount
5th Engineers, Corps d'Afrique (USCT)
 Lieut. Col. Uri B. Pearsall

THIRTEENTH CORPS (Detachment)
 (1) Brig. Gen. Thomas E. G. Ransom (w 4/8)
 (2) Brig. Gen. Robert A. Cameron

THIRD DIVISION
 (1) Brig. Gen. Robert A. Cameron
 (2) Col. William H. Raynor

FIRST BRIGADE
 Lieut. Col. Aaron M. Flory

46th Indiana
 Capt. William M. DeHart
29th Wisconsin
 Maj. Bradford Hancock

SECOND BRIGADE
 Col. William H. Raynor

24th Iowa
 Maj. Edward Wright

28th Iowa
    (1) Col. John Connell (w and c 4/8)
    (2) Lieut. Col. Bartholomew W. Wilson
56th Ohio
    Capt. Maschil Manring

ARTILLERY
1st Missouri Light, Battery A
    Lieut. Elisha Cole
Ohio Light, 2nd Battery
    Lieut. William H. Harper

FOURTH DIVISION
    Col. William J. Landram

FIRST BRIGADE
    (1) Col. Frank Emerson (w and c 4/8)
    (2) Lieut. Col. Theodore E. Buehler

77th Illinois
    (1) Lieut. Col. Lysander R. Webb (k 4/8)
    (2) Maj. John A. Burdett
67th Indiana
    (1) Lieut. Col. Theodore E. Buehler
    (2) Maj. Francis A. Sears
19th Kentucky
    (1) Lieut. Col. John Cowan (c 4/8)
    (2) Capt. William T. Cummins
23rd Wisconsin
    Maj. Joseph E. Greene

SECOND BRIGADE
    (1) Col. Joseph W. Vance (k 4/8)
    (2) Lieut. Col. Albert H. Brown

130th Illinois
    (1) Maj. John B. Reid (w 4/8)
    (2) Capt. John H. Robinson

48th Ohio
    (1) Lieut. Col. Joseph W. Lindsey (c 4/8)
    (2) Capt. James R. Lynch
83rd Ohio
    Lieut. Col. William H. Baldwin
96th Ohio
    Lieut. Col. Albert H. Brown

ARTILLERY
    Indiana Light, 1st Battery
    Capt. Martin Klauss
    Chicago (Illinois) Mercantile Battery
    Lieut. Pinckney S. Cone

NINETEENTH CORPS
    Maj. Gen. William B. Franklin (w 4/8)

FIRST DIVISION
    Brig. Gen. William H. Emory

FIRST BRIGADE
    Brig. Gen. William Dwight

29th Maine
    Col. George L. Beal
114th New York
    (1) Lieut. Col. Henry B. Morse (w 4/8)
    (2) Maj. Oscar H. Curtis
116th New York
    Col. George M. Love
153rd New York
    Col. Edwin P. Davis
161st New York
    Lieut. Col. William B. Kinsey

SECOND BRIGADE
    Brig. Gen. James W. McMillan

13th Maine
    Col. Henry Rust Jr.

15th Maine
    Col. Isaac Dyer
160th New York
    Lieut. Col. John B. Van Petten
47th Pennsylvania
    Col. Tilghman H. Good

THIRD BRIGADE
    (1) Col. Lewis Benedict (k 4/9)
    (2) Col. Francis Fessenden

30th Maine
    (1) Col. Francis Fessenden
    (2) Lieut. Col. Thomas H. Hubbard
162nd New York
    Lieut. Col. Justus W. Blanchard
165th New York
    (1) Lieut. Col. Gouverneur Carr (w 4/8)
    (2) Capt. Henry C. Inwood
173rd New York
    Col. Lewis M. Peck

ARTILLERY
    Capt. George T. Hebard

New York Light, 25th Battery
    Lieut. Irving D. Southworth
1st United States, Battery L
    Lieut. Franck E. Taylor
Vermont Light, 1st Battery
    Capt. George T. Hebard

SECOND DIVISION (garrisoned at Alexandria, Louisiana, during the Battles of Mansfield and Pleasant Hill)
    Brig. Gen. Cuvier Grover

SECOND BRIGADE
    Col. Edward L. Molineux

13th Connecticut
    Col. Charles D. Blinn
1st Louisiana
    Col. William O. Fiske
90th New York (3 companies)
    Maj. John C. Smart
159th New York
    Lieut. Col. Edward L. Gaul

THIRD BRIGADE
    Col. Jacob Sharpe

38th Massachusetts
    Lieut. Col. James P. Richardson
128th New York
    Col. James Smith
156th New York
    Capt. James J. Hoyt
175th New York (3 companies)
    Capt. Charles McCarthey

ARTILLERY
    Capt. George W. Fox

Massachusetts Light, 7th Battery (G)
    Capt. Newman W. Storer
New York Light, 26th Battery
    Capt. George W. Fox
1st United States, Battery F
    Lieut. Hardman P. Norris
2nd United States, Battery C
    Lieut. John I. Rodgers

CAVALRY
3rd Maryland
    Col. Charles (Washington) Carroll Tevis

CORPS ARTILLERY RESERVE
    Capt. Henry W. Closson

Delaware Light, 1st Battery
    Capt. Benjamin Nields
1st Indiana Heavy (2 companies)
    Capt. William S. Hinkle

CORPS D'AFRIQUE (United States Colored Troops)

FIRST DIVISION

FIRST BRIGADE
    Col. William H. Dickey

1st Infantry (73rd USCT)
    Maj. Hiram E. Perkins
3rd Infantry (75th USCT)
    Col. Henry W. Fuller
12th Infantry (84th USCT)
    Capt. James H. Corrin
22nd Infantry (92nd USCT)
    Col. Henry N. Frisbie

ENGINEER BRIGADE
    Col. George D. Robinson

97th Regiment (USCT)
    Lieut. Col. George A. Harmount
99th Regiment (USCT)
    Lieut. Col. Uri B. Pearsall

CAVALRY DIVISION
    Brig. Gen. Albert L. Lee

FIRST BRIGADE
    Col. Thomas J. Lucas

16th Indiana Infantry (mounted)
    Lieut. Col. James H. Redfield
2nd Louisiana Infantry (mounted)
    Maj. Alfred Hodsdon

6th Missouri (howitzer battery under Capt. Herbert H. Rottaken, attached)
    Capt. Sidney A. Breese
14th New York
    Maj. Abraham Bassford

THIRD BRIGADE
    (1) Col. Harai Robinson (w 4/8)
    (2) Lieut. Col. John M. Crebs

87th Illinois Infantry (mounted)
    (1) Lieut. Col. John M. Crebs
    (2) Maj. George W. Land
1st Louisiana
    Maj. Algernon S. Badger

FOURTH BRIGADE
    Col. Nathan A. M. Duddley

2nd Illinois
    Maj. Benjamin F. Marsh Jr.
3rd Massachusetts
    Lieut. Col. Lorenzo D. Sargent
31st Massachusetts Infantry (mounted)
    Capt. Elbert H. Fordham
2nd New Hampshire
    Lieut. Col. George A. Flanders

FIFTH BRIGADE
    Col. Oliver P. Gooding

2nd New York Veteran
    Col. Morgan H. Chrysler
18th New York
    Col. James J. Byrne
3rd Rhode Island (detachment)
    Maj. George R. Davis

ARTILLERY BRIGADE
Massachusetts Light, 2nd Battery G
    Capt. Ormand F. Nims

Rawles's Battery—5th United States, Battery G
    Lieut. Jacob B. Rawles

ARMY OF THE TENNESSEE (detachment)
    Brig. Gen. Andrew J. Smith

SIXTEENTH CORPS

FIRST DIVISION

SECOND BRIGADE
    Col. Lucius F. Hubbard

47th Illinois
    Col. John D. McClure
5th Minnesota
    Maj. John C. Becht
8th Wisconsin
    Lieut. Col. John W. Jefferson

THIRD BRIGADE
    Col. Sylvester G. Hill

35th Iowa
    Lieut. Col. William B. Keeler
33rd Missouri
    Lieut. Col. William H. Heath (w 4/9)

THIRD DIVISION
    Brig. Gen. Joseph A. Mower

FIRST BRIGADE
    Col. William F. Lynch

58th Illinois
    Maj. Thomas Newlan
119th Illinois
    Col. Thomas J. Kinney
89th Indiana
    Col. Charles D. Murray

SECOND BRIGADE
    Col. William T. Shaw

14th Iowa
    (1) Lieut. Col. Joseph H. Newbold (k 4/9)
    (2) Capt. Warren C. Jones
27th Iowa
    Col. James I. Gilbert (w 4/9)
32nd Iowa
    Col. John Scott
24th Missouri
    Maj. Robert W. Fyan

THIRD BRIGADE
    Col. Risdon M. Moore

49th Illinois
    Maj. Thomas W. Morgan
117th Illinois
    Lieut. Col. Jonathan Merriam
178th New York
    Col. Edward Wehler

ARTILLERY
    Capt. James M. Cockefair

Indiana Light, 3rd Battery
    Capt. James M. Cockefair
Indiana Light, 9th Battery
    Capt. George R. Brown

SEVENTEENTH CORPS (assigned to Porter's fleet 4/6)

PROVISIONAL DIVISION
    Brig. Gen. Thomas Kilby Smith

FIRST BRIGADE
    Col. Jonathan B. Moore

41st Illinois
    Lieut. Col. John H. Nale

3rd Iowa
  Lieut. Col. James Tullis
33rd Wisconsin
  Maj. Horatio H. Virgin

SECOND BRIGADE
  Col. Lyman M. Ward

81st Illinois
  Lieut. Col. Andrew W. Rogers
95th Illinois
  Col. Thomas W. Humphrey
14th Wisconsin
  Capt. Carlos M. G. Mansfield

ARTILLERY
1st Missouri Light, Battery M
  Lieut. John H. Tiemeyer

MISSISSIPPI MARINE BRIGADE (returned to Vicksburg, Mississippi, 4/6)
  Brig. Gen. A. W. Ellet

Infantry Regiment
  Col. Charles R. Ellet
Cavalry Battalion
  Maj. James M. Hubbard

THIRTEENTH ARMY CORPS (Added as reinforcements after Mansfield and Pleasant Hill)
  Maj. Gen. John H. McClernand

FIRST DIVISION

SECOND BRIGADE
  Brig. Gen. Michael K. Lawler

49th Indiana
  Col. James Keigwin
69th Indiana
  Lieut. Col. Oran Perry

34th Iowa
    Col. George W. Clark
22nd Kentucky
    Col. George W. Monroe
16th Ohio
    Lieut. Col. Phillip Kreshner
114th Ohio
    Lieut. Col. John H. Kelley

Operations in Arkansas / Camden Expedition

SEVENTH CORPS (Department of Arkansas and Army of Arkansas)
    Maj. Gen. Frederick Steele

ESCORT
3rd Illinois Cavalry, Company D
    Lieut. Solomon M. Tabor
15th Illinois Cavalry, Company H
    Capt. Thomas J. Beebe

THIRD DIVISION
    Brig. Gen. Frederick Salomon

FIRST BRIGADE
    Brig. Gen. Samuel Allen Rice (mw 4/30)
    Col. Charles E. Salomon

50th Indiana
    Lieut. Col. Samuel T. Wells
29th Iowa
    Col. Thomas H. Benton Jr.
33rd Iowa
    Maj. Hiram D. Gibson
9th Wisconsin
    Col. Charles E. Salomon

SECOND BRIGADE
    Col. William E. McLean

43rd Indiana
    Maj. Wesley W. Norris

36th Iowa
    Col. Charles W. Kittredge
77th Ohio
    Col. William B. Mason

THIRD BRIGADE
    Col. Adolph Engelmann

43rd Illinois
    Lieut. Col. Adolph Dengler
40th Iowa
    Col. John A. Garrett
27th Wisconsin
    Col. Conrad Krez

ARTILLERY
Springfield Illinois Light Artillery (Vaughn's Independent Illinois Battery)
    Lieut. Charles W. Thomas
Battery E, 2nd Missouri Light Artillery
    Lieut. Charles Peetz
Voegele's Wisconsin Battery
    Capt. Martin Voegele

FRONTIER DIVISION
    Brig. Gen. John Milton Thayer

FIRST BRIGADE
    Col. John Edwards
1st Arkansas
    Lieut. Col. Elhanon J. Searle
2nd Arkansas (8 companies)
    Maj. Marshall L. Stephenson
18th Iowa
    Capt. William M. Duncan
2nd Indiana Battery
    Lieut. Hugh Espey

SECOND BRIGADE
    Col. Charles W. Adams

1st Kansas (USCT)
    Col. James M. Williams
2nd Kansas (USCT)
    Col. Samuel J. Crawford
12th Kansas
    Lieut. Col. Josiah E. Hayes
1st Battery, Arkansas Light Artillery
    Capt. Denton D. Stark

THIRD BRIGADE
    Col. Owen Bassett

2nd Kansas Cavalry
    Maj. Julius G. Fisk
6th Kansas Cavalry
    Lieut. Col. William T. Campbell
14th Kansas Cavalry
    Lieut. Col. John G. Brown

CAVALRY DIVISION
    Brig. Gen. Eugene Asa Carr

FIRST BRIGADE
    Col. John F. Ritter

3rd Arkansas Cavalry (4 companies)
    Maj. George F. Lovejoy
13th Illinois Cavalry (Company B)
    Capt. Adolph Bechand
3rd Iowa Cavalry (detachment)
    Lieut. Franz W. Arnim
1st Missouri Cavalry (8 companies)
    Capt. Miles Kehoe
2nd Missouri Cavalry
    Capt. William H. Higdon

THIRD BRIGADE
    Col. Daniel Anderson

10th Illinois Cavalry (detachment)
    Lieut. Col. James Stuart

1st Iowa Cavalry
   Lieut. Joseph W. Caldwell
3rd Missouri Cavalry
   Maj. John A. Lennon

INDEPENDENT CAVALRY BRIGADE
(post of Pine Bluff, Arkansas)
   Col. Powell Clayton

1st Indiana Cavalry (8 companies)
   Maj. Julian D. Owen
5th Kansas Cavalry (10 companies)
   Lieut. Col. Wilton A. Jenkins
7th Missouri Cavalry
   Maj. Henry P. Spellman
18th Illinois
   Lieut. Col. Samuel B. Marks
28th Wisconsin
   Lieut. Col. Edmund B. Gray

APPENDIX III

CONFEDERATE ORDER OF BATTLE

Abbreviations

k—killed, c—captured, mw—mortally wounded, w—wounded
Gen.—General
Lieut. Gen.—Lieutenant General
Maj. Gen.—Major General
Brig. Gen.—Brigadier General
Col.—Colonel
Lieut. Col.—Lieutenant Colonel
Maj.—Major
Capt.—Captain
Lieut.—Lieutenant
Sgt.—Sergeant
Surg.—Surgeon

DEPARTMENT OF THE TRANS-MISSISSIPPI
  Lieut. Gen. Edmund Kirby-Smith

GENERAL STAFF
  Chief of Staff
    Brig. Gen. William Robertson Boggs

Appendix III

Operations in Louisiana

Confederate District of West Louisiana

Maj. Gen. Richard S. Taylor

WALKER'S TEXAS DIVISION
Maj. Gen. John George Walker (w 4/9)

First Brigade
Brig. Gen. Thomas N. Waul (w 4/30)

12th Texas Infantry Regiment
    Col. Overton C. Young
18th Texas Infantry Regiment
    Col. William H. King
22nd Texas Infantry Regiment
    Col. Richard B. Hubbard
13th Texas Cavalry Regiment (dismounted)
    Col. Anderson F. Crawford
Haldeman's Texas Battery
    Capt. Horace Haldeman

Second Brigade
Brig. Gen. Horace Randal (mw 4/30)

11th Texas Infantry Regiment
    Col. Oran Milo Roberts
14th Texas Infantry Regiment
    Col. Edward Clark
28th Texas Cavalry Regiment (dismounted)
    Col. Eli H. Baxter
6th Texas Cavalry Battalion (dismounted)
    Lieut. Col. Robert S. Gould
Daniel's Texas Battery
    Capt. James M. Daniel

Third Brigade
Brig. Gen. William R. Scurry (k 4/30)

3rd Texas Infantry Regiment
   Col. Philip N. Luckett (stationed at Shreveport)
16th Texas Infantry Regiment
   Col. George Flournoy
17th Texas Infantry Regiment
   Col. George Washington Jones
19th Texas Infantry Regiment
   Col. Richard Waterhouse
16th Texas Cavalry Regiment (dismounted)
   Col. William Fitzhugh
1st Texas Field Battery
   Capt. William Edgar

MOUTON'S DIVISION
   (1) Brig. Gen. Alfred Mouton (k 4/8)
   (2) Brig. Gen. Camille de Polignac

POLIGNAC'S BRIGADE
   (1) Brig. Gen. Camille de Polignac
   (2) Col. James R. Taylor (k 4/8)
   (3) Lieut. Col. Robert D. Stone

17th Texas Cavalry Regiment (dismounted)
   Col. James R. Taylor (k 4/8)
22nd Texas Cavalry Regiment (dismounted)
   Lieut. Col. Robert D. Stone
31st Texas Cavalry Regiment (dismounted)
   Maj. Frederick Malone
34th Texas Cavalry Regiment (dismounted)
   Lieut. Col. John H. Caudle

GRAY'S BRIGADE
   Col. Henry Gray

18th Consolidated Louisiana Infantry Regiment
   Col. Leopold L. Armant (k 4/8)
Crescent Consolidated Louisiana Regiment
   Col. J. H. Beard (k 4/8)
28th Louisiana Infantry Regiment
   Lieut. Col. William Walker (k 4/8)

ARTILLERY
Maj. T. A. Faries

1st Louisiana Regular Battery
    Capt. James M. T. Barnes
Cornay's Battery
    (1) Capt. Florian O. Cornay (k 4/26)
    (2) Lieut. John B. Tarleton
Boone's Battery
    Lieut. Maunsel Bennett

GREEN'S CAVALRY CORPS
(1) Brig. Gen. Thomas Green (k 4/12)
(2) Brig. Gen. Hamilton P. Bee (w 4/9)
(3) Maj. Gen. John A. Warton

BEE'S CAVALRY DIVISION
Brig. Gen. Hamilton P. Bee (w 4/9)

DEBRAY'S BRIGADE
Brig. Gen. Xavier Debray (w 4/9)

23rd Texas Cavalry Regiment
    Col. Nicholas C. Gould
26th Texas Cavalry Regiment
    Lieut. Col. J. J. Meyers
36th Texas Cavalry Regiment
    Col. Peter C. Woods

BUCHEL'S BRIGADE
Col. Augustus Buchel (mw 4/9)
Col. Alexander Terrell

1st Texas Cavalry Regiment
    Lieut. Col. William O. Yager
35th Texas Cavalry Regiment
    Col. James B. Likens
37th Texas Cavalry Regiment
    Col. Alexander Terrell

MAJOR'S CAVALRY DIVISION
Brig. Gen. James Patrick Major (w 4/9)

Lane's Brigade
    (1) Col. Walter Lane (w 4/8)
    (2) Col. George W. Baylor

1st Texas Partisan Rangers Cavalry Regiment
    Lieut. Col. R. P. Crump
2nd Texas Partisan Rangers Cavalry Regiment
    Col. Isham Chisum
2nd Texas Cavalry Regiment (Arizona Brigade)
    Col. George Baylor
3rd Texas Cavalry Regiment (Arizona Brigade)
    Lieut. Col. George Madison

Bagby's Brigade
    Col. Arthur Bagby

4th Texas Cavalry Regiment
    Col. William Hardeman
5th Texas Cavalry Regiment
    Col. Henry C. McNeill
7th Texas Cavalry Regiment
    (1) Lieut. Col. Philemon Herbert (mw 4/8)
    (2) Lieut. Col. Gustave Hoffman
13th Texas Cavalry Battalion
    Lieut. Col. Edward Waller

Vincent's Brigade
    Col. William Vincent

2nd Louisiana Cavalry Regiment
    Maj. Winter Breazeale
4th Louisiana Cavalry Regiment
    Col. A. J. McNeill
4th Louisiana Cavalry Regiment (redesignated 7th Louisiana Cavalry Regiment 10/1864)
    Col. Louis Bush

STEELE'S CAVALRY DIVISION (arrived after Pleasant Hill)
Brig. Gen. William Steele

12th Texas Cavalry Regiment
  Col. William H. Parsons
19th Texas Cavalry Regiment
  Col. Nathaniel M. Burford
21st Texas Cavalry Regiment
  Col. George W. Carter
Morgan's Texas Cavalry Battalion
  Lieut. Col. Charles L. Morgan
10th Texas Field Battery
  Capt. J. H. Pratt

CORPS ARTILLERY (horse artillery)
Maj. Oliver J. Semmes

Moseley's Texas Battery
  Capt. William G. Moseley
Val Verde Texas Battery
  Capt. T. D. Nettles
McMahan's Texas Battery
  Capt. M. V. McMahan
West's Louisiana Battery (the Grosse Tete Flying Artillery)
  Capt. John A. A. West

LOUISIANA STATE GUARDS CAVALRY
Louisiana governor (CSA) Brig. Gen. Henry Allen

1st Louisiana State Guards Cavalry Battalion
  Lieut. Col. Benjamin Clark
2nd Louisiana State Guards Cavalry Battalion
  Lieut. Col. Henry Favrot

UNATTACHED CAVALRY
2nd Louisiana Cavalry Regiment (Rendered combat ineffective at the Battle of Henderson's Hill [3/21]. What soldiers remained acted as scouts for the remainder of the campaign.)
  Col. William G. Vincent

DETACHMENT FROM STERLING PRICE'S ARMY
(joined Taylor's army on the evening of 4/8)
    Brig. Gen. Thomas James Churchill

FIRST DIVISION / ARKANSAS DIVISION
    Brig. Gen. James Camp Tappan

Tappan's Brigade
    Col. H. L. Grinsted (k 4/29)

19th and 24th Arkansas Infantry Regiments
    Col. Robert G. Shaver
24th and 33rd Arkansas Infantry Regiments
    Lieut. Col. Thomas D. Thomson

Chruchill's Brigade
    Col. Lucien C. Gause

26th Arkansas Infantry Regiment
    Lieut. Col. Iverson L. Brooks
32nd Arkansas Infantry Regiment
    Lieut. Col. William Hicks
36th Arkansas Infantry Regiment
    Col. James M. Davie

Artillery
    6th Arkansas Field Battery
    Capt. Chambers B. Etter

SECOND DIVISION / MISSOURI INFANTRY DIVISION
    Brig. Gen. Mosby Monroe Parsons

First Brigade
    Brig. Gen. John Bullock Clark Jr.

8th Missouri Infantry Regiment
    Col. Charles S. Mitchell
9th Missouri Infantry Regiment
    Col. Richard H. Musser

SECOND BRIGADE
    Col. Simon P. Burns

10th Missouri Infantry Regiment
    Col. William M. Moore
11th Missouri Infantry Regiment
    Lieut. Col. Thomas H. Murray
12th Missouri Infantry Regiment
    Col. Willis M. Ponder
16th Missouri Infantry Regiment
    Lieut. Col. P. W. H. Cumming
9th Missouri Sharpshooter Battalion
    Maj. L. A. Pindall

ARTILLERY
Etter's Arkansas Artillery Battery
    Capt. Chambers Brady Etter

Subdistrict of North Louisiana (operated east of the Red River during the campaign)

(1) Brig. Gen. St. John R. Liddell (relieved 4/10)
(2) Col. Isaac F. Harrison

HARRISON'S BRIGADE
    Col. Isaac F. Harrison

3rd Louisiana Cavalry
    Lieut. Col. Francis W. Moore
4th Louisiana Cavalry
    Col. A. J. McNeill
5th Louisiana Cavalry
    Col. Richard L. Capers
8th Missouri Cavalry (detachment)
    Lieut. Col. Samuel J. Ward
35th Texas Cavalry (Likens's)
    (1) Col. James B. Likens
    (2) Lieut. Col. James R. Burns

Operations in Arkansas / Camden Expedition

District of Arkansas

Maj. Gen. Sterling Price

ESCORT
14th Missouri Battalion
    Maj. Robert C. Wood

FAGAN'S CAVALRY DIVISION
    Brig. Gen. James Fleming Fagan

Cabell's Brigade
    Brig. Gen. William Lewis Cabell

1st Arkansas Cavalry
    Col. James C. Monroe
2nd Arkansas Cavalry
    Col. T. J. Morgan
4th Arkansas Cavalry
    Col. A. Gordon
7th Arkansas Cavalry
    Col. John F. Hill
Gunter's Arkansas Cavalry Battalion
    Lieut. Col. Thomas M. Gunter
Blocher's Arkansas Battery
    Capt. William D. Blocher

Dockery's Brigade
    Brig. Gen. Thomas Pleasant Dockery

18th Arkansas Infantry Regiment (Carroll's)
    Col. Robert Hamilton Crockett
19th and 15th Consolidated Infantry
    Lieut. Col. H. G. P. Williams
20th Arkansas Infantry Regiment
    Col. Daniel W. Jones
12th Arkansas Infantry Battalion (sharpshooters)
    Maj. William F. Rapley

CRAWFORD'S BRIGADE
    Col. William A. Crawford

2nd Arkansas Cavalry Regiment (Slemons's)
    Capt. O. B. Tebbs
Crawford's Arkansas Cavalry
    Col. William A. Crawford
Wright's Arkansas Cavalry
    Col. John Crowell Wright
Poe's Arkansas Cavalry Battalion
    Maj. James T. Poe
McMurtrey's Arkansas Cavalry Battalion
    Maj. Elisha L. McMurtrey
Hughey's Arkansas Battery
    Capt. William M. Hughey

MARMADUKE'S CAVALRY DIVISION
    Brig. Gen. John S. Marmaduke

GREENE'S BRIGADE
    Col. Colton Greene

3rd Missouri Cavalry
    Lieut. Col. Leonidas A. Campbell
4th Missouri Cavalry
    Lieut. Col. William J. Preston
7th Missouri Cavalry
    Col. Solomon G. Kitchen
8th Missouri Cavalry
    Col. William L. Jeffers
10th Missouri Cavalry
    Col. Robert R. Lawther
Harris's Missouri Battery
    Capt. S. S. Harris

SHELBY'S BRIGADE
    Brig. Gen. Joseph O. Shelby

1st Missouri Battalion
    Maj. Benjamin Elliott

5th Missouri Cavalry
    Col. B. Frank Gordon
11th Missouri Cavalry
    Col. M. W. Smith
12th Missouri Cavalry
    Col. David Shanks
Hunter's Regiment
    Col. DeWitt C. Hunter
Collins's Missouri Battery
    Capt. Richard A. Collins

MAXEY'S CAVALRY DIVISION
    Brig. Gen. Samuel B. Maxey

GANO'S BRIGADE
    Col. Charles DeMorse

29th Texas Cavalry
    Maj. J. A. Carroll
30th Texas Cavalry
    Lieut. Col. N. W. Battle
31st Texas Cavalry
    Maj. Michael Looscan
Welch's Company
    Lieut. Frank M. Gano
Krumbhaar's Texas Battery
    Capt. W. Butler Krumbhaar

CHOCTAW BRIGADE
    Col. Tandy Walker

1st Regiment: Lieut. Col. James Riley
2nd Regiment: Col. Simpson W. Folsom

WALKER'S TEXAS DIVISION (arrived 4/20; attached to Price's Command 4/26)
    Maj. Gen. John George Walker (w 4/9)

FIRST BRIGADE
    Brig. Gen. Thomas N. Waul (w 4/30)

12th Texas Infantry Regiment
    Col. Overton C. Young
18th Texas Infantry Regiment
    Col. William H. King
22nd Texas Infantry Regiment
    Col. Richard B. Hubbard
13th Texas Cavalry Regiment (dismounted)
    Col. Anderson F. Crawford
Haldeman's Texas Battery
    Capt. Horace Haldeman

SECOND BRIGADE
    Brig. Gen. Horace Randal (mw 4/30)

11th Texas Infantry Regiment
    Col. Oran Milo Roberts
14th Texas Infantry Regiment
    Col. Edward Clark
28th Texas Cavalry Regiment (dismounted)
    Col. Eli H. Baxter
6th Texas Cavalry Battalion (dismounted)
    Lieut. Col. Robert S. Gould
Daniel's Texas Battery
    Capt. James M. Daniel

THIRD BRIGADE
    Brig. Gen. William R. Scurry (k 4/30)

3rd Texas Infantry Regiment
    Col. Philip N. Luckett (stationed at Shreveport)
16th Texas Infantry Regiment
    Col. George Flournoy
17th Texas Infantry Regiment
    Col. George Washington Jones
19th Texas Infantry Regiment
    Col. Richard Waterhouse
16th Texas Cavalry Regiment (dismounted)
    Col. William Fitzhugh
1st Texas Field Battery
    Capt. William Edgar

FIRST DIVISION / ARKANSAS DIVISION (arrived 4/20; attached to Price's Command 4/26)
    Brig. Gen. Thomas J. Churchill

TAPPAN'S BRIGADE
    Brig. Gen. James C. Tappan

19th and 4th Consolidated Arkansas Infantry
    Lieut. Col. William R. Hardy
27th and 38th Consolidated Arkansas Infantry
    Col. Robert G. Shaver
33rd Arkansas Infantry Regiment
    (1) Col. Hiram L. Grinsted (k 4/30)
    (2) Lieut. Col. Thomas D. Thomson

GAUSE'S BRIGADE
    Col. Lucien C. Gause

26th Arkansas Infantry
    Lieut. Col. Iverson L. Brooks
32nd Arkansas Infantry
    Lieut. Col. William Hicks
36th Arkansas Infantry
    Col. James M. Davie
39th Arkansas Infantry
    Col. James W. Rogan
Marshall's Arkansas Battery
    Capt. John G. Marshall

HAWTHORN'S BRIGADE
    Brig. Gen. Alexander T. Hawthorn

34th Arkansas Infantry
    Col. William H. Brooks
35th Arkansas Infantry
    Col. Henry J. McCord
37th Arkansas Infantry
    Col. Samuel S. Bell
Cocke's Arkansas Infantry
    Col John B. Cocke (k 4/30)

SECOND DIVISION / MISSOURI DIVISION (arrived 4/20; attached to Price's Command 4/26)
    Brig. Gen. Mosby M. Parsons

FIRST BRIGADE
    Brig. Gen. John Bullock Clark Jr.

8th Missouri Infantry
    Col. Charles S. Mitchell
9th Missouri Infantry
    Col. R. H. Musser
Ruffner's Missouri Battery
    Capt. Samuel T. Ruffner

SECOND BRIGADE
    Col. Simon P. Burns

10th Missouri Infantry
    Col. William M. Moore
11th Missouri Infantry
    Lieut. Col. Thomas H. Murray
12th Missouri Infantry
    Col. Willis M. Ponder
16th Missouri Infantry
    Col. P. W. H. Cumming
9th Missouri Battalion Sharpshooters
    Maj. L. A. Pindall
Lesueur's Missouri Battery
    Capt. A. A. Lesueur

APPENDIX IV

RED RIVER CAMPAIGN

UNIT STRENGTH AND NAVAL VESSELS

The figures contained in the following tables are compiled from these sources:

"Confederate Ships" Naval History and Heritage Command Website, Last accessed: 12-25-2023, https://www.history.navy.mil/research/histories/ship-histories/confederate_ships.html.

Gary D, Joiner, Through the Howling Wilderness: The 1864 Red River Campaign and Failure in the West, (Knoxville: The University of Tennessee Press, 2006), 187-190.

Gary D. Joiner, The Red River Campaign: The Union's Final Attempt to Invade Texas, (Buffalo, Gap TX: State House Press, 2013), 169-171.

James M. Merrill, *"Confederate Shipbuilding at New Orleans."* The Journal of Southern History 28, no. 1 (1962): 87–93; Gary McQuarrie & Neil P. Chatelain, *"Confederate Shipyards"* in Civil War Navy Magazine Website, Last accessed: 12-25-2023, https://civilwarnavy.com/confederate-shipyards/.

Richard B. Irwin, *"The Red River Campaign,"* in Battles and Leaders of the Civil War, ed. Robert Underwood Johnson and Clarence Clough Buel (New York: Century, 1887), 4: 350-351.

Appendix IV

United States Government Printing Office, *Report of the Joint Committee on the Conduct of the War: Vol. 2, Red River Expedition*, (Washington D.C., United States Government, 1865), pp. 192-193, 322.

United States War Department, *The War of the Rebellion: Official Records of the Union and Confederate Armies,* (Washington, DC: United States Government Printing Office, 1874–1880), vol. 34, pt. 1, pp. 167—76, 203, 657, vol. 34, pt. 2, pp. 814, 1051, Series III, Vol. 3, p. 59.

United States War Department, The War of the Rebellion: Official Records of the Union and Confederate Navies, (Washington, DC: United States Government Printing Office, 1874–1880), vol. 26, pp. 24-25.

Total Strength of Union Forces, March 31, 1864

Department of the Gulf		Present for Duty				
General HQ	Maj. Gen. Nathaniel P. Banks	Officers	Men	Aggregate Present	Aggregate Present & Absent	Pieces of Artillery
Staff and Escorts	NA	20	47	106	160	0
Eng. Troops	Col. George D. Robinson	40	681	872	807	0
Total		60	728	978	967	0
Thirteenth Army Corps	Brig. Gen. Thomas E. G. Ransom					
Third Division	Brig. Gen. Robert A Cameron	94	2,020	2,275	4,413	8
Fourth Division	Col. William J. Landram	132	2,527	2,990	5,971	10
*First Division, Second Brigade	Maj. Gen. John H. McClernand	112	2,069	2,383	4,903	0
Total		226	4,547	7,648	10,384	18
Nineteenth Army Corps	Maj. Gen. William B. Franklin					
HQ		2	0	10	12	0
First Division	Brig. Gen. William H. Emory	294	6,193	7,134	9,733	14
Second Division	Brig. Gen. Cuvier Grover	146	3,700	4,477	5,950	18
Artillery Reserve	Capt. George W. Fox	6	270	280	373	14
Total		448	10,163	11,901	16,068	46
Corps d' Afrique	Col. William H. Dickey	88	1,447	1,745	2,034	0
Cavalry Division	Brig. Gen. Albert L. Lee	205	4,448	5,333	8,996	12
Total DotG		1,027	21,333	27,605	38,449	76

* Did not join the campaign until 04/18/1864

Red River Campaign Unit Strength and Naval Vessels

Army of the Tennessee (Detachment)

Sixteenth Army Corps, First Division	Brig. Gen. Andrew J. Smith	Present for Duty Officers	Present for Duty Men	Aggregate Present	Aggregate Present & Absent	Pieces of Artillery
HQ		3	0	4	4	0
First Division, Second Brigade	Col. Lucius F. Hubbard					
First Division, Third Brigade	Col. Sylvester G. Hill					
Total First Division		103	1,899	2,431	4,351	0
Total		106	1,899	2,435	4,355	0
Third Division	Brig. Gen. Joseph A. Mower					
Third Division, First Brigade	Col. William F. Lynch					
Third Division, Second Brigade	Col. William T. Shaw					
Third Division, Third Brigade	Col. Risdon M. Moore					
Artillery						
Total Third Division		237	4,791	6,151	7,732	10
Seventeenth Corps, Second (Provisional) Division	Brig. Gen. Thomas Kilby Smith					
Second Division, First Brigade	Col. Jonathan B. Moore					
Second Division, Second Brigade	Col. Lyman M. Ward					
Artillery						
Total		73	1,648	2,039	3,838	4
Total AotT		416	8,338	10,625	15,925	14
Brig. Gen. A.W. Ellet	*Mississippi Marine Brigade				1,034	0

* The actual number of men in the Mississippi Marine Brigade that participated in the Campaign is an estimate. The number varies from 1,000 to 3,000, depending on the source

Department of Arkansas

General HQ	Maj. Gen. Frederick Steele	Present for Duty Officers	Present for Duty Men	Aggregate Present	Aggregate Present & Absent	Pieces of Artillery
Staff and Escorts	NA	19	88	117	187	0
3rd Division	Brig. Gen. Fredrick Salmon	193	4,657	5,127	8,411	16
Total		212	4,745	5,244	8,598	16
Cavalry Div.	Brig. Gen. Eugene Asa Carr					
Cavalry	Brig. Gen. Eugene Asa Carr	77	2,611	3,248	4,421	0
Frontier Div.	Brig. Gen. John M. Thayer					
Infantry	1st Brig. - Edwards/2nd Big. - Adams	115	2,893	3,864	4,979	10
Cavalry	Bassett	40	913	1,218	2,934	4
Total		155	3,806	5,082	7,913	14
Pine Bluff Garrison						
Infantry	Col. Powell Clayton	21	688	1,113	1,705	0
Cavalry	Col. Powell Clayton	42	885	1,322	1,900	11
Total		63	1,573	2,435	3,605	11
Total DoA		367	8,551	16,009	20,116	30

Appendix IV

Total Strength of Confederate Forces, January 1, 1864

Department of The Trans-Mississippi	Lt. Gen. Edmund Kirby-Smith						
		Present for Duty			Effective Total Present	Aggregate Present	Aggregate Present & Absent
District	Commander	Officers	Men	Aggregate			
Arkansas	Maj. Gen. Sterling Price	1,032	10,354	11,386	11,520	13,905	25,623
Indian Territory	Maj. Gen. Samuel B Maxey	161	1,665	1,826	1,895	2,241	8,885
Texas	Maj. Gen. John B. Magruder	719	9,103	9,822	9,815	11,400	16,952
Western Louisiana	Maj. Gen. Richard Taylor	890	10,657	11,547	11,615	13,441	21,829
Total		2,802	31,779	34,581	34,845	40,987	73,289

Union Vesseles and Types Participating in the Red River Campaign

Rear Admiral David Dixon Porter's - Mississippi Squadron	
Converted Ironclads	Ironclads
USS Benton	USS Carondelet
USS Choctaw	USS Louisville
USS Eastport*	USS Mound City
USS Essex	USS Pittsburg
USS Lafayette	USS Chillicothe
River Monitors	Large Tinclads
USS Neosho	USS Black Hawk
USS Osage	USS Ouachita
USS Ozark	
Tinclads/Side-Wheeler	Tinclads/Stern-Wheelers Cont.
USS Avenger	USS Argosy
USS Covington*	USS Cricket
USS Fort Hindman	USS Forest Rose
USS Gazelle	USS Juliet
Tinclads/Stern-Wheelers	USS General Bragg
USS Signal*	USS Naiad
USS Saint Clair	USS Nymph
USS General Sterling Price	
Timberclads	Ram Armed Supply Vessels
USS Lexington	USS General Sterling Price
Mail/Supply/Receiving Vessels	Ordnance/Stores, Dispatch Vessels
USS New National	USS General Lyon
River Service Vessels/Side-Wheeler	Tug-Pump Boats/Side-Wheeler
USS Benefit	USS Champion No. 3*
USS Willam H. Brown	USS Champion No. 5*
Tugs	Ordnance Boats
USS Dahlia	USS Judge Torrance
USS Fern	
USS Thistle	
Floating Machine Shop Vessels	Mississippi Marine Brigade Transports
USS Sampson	USS Autocrat
Mississippi Marine Brigade Gunboats	USS Baltic
USS Little Rebel	USS Diana
Mississippi Marine Brigade Tugs	USS John Rain
USS Alf Cutting	USS T.D. Horner
USS Cleveland	Mississippi Marine Brigade Hospital Ship
USS Bell Darlington	USS Woodford*
	Mississippi Marine Brigade Ram
* Lost during the Campaign	USS Lioness

Red River Campaign Unit Strength and Naval Vessels

United States Army Quartermaster Corps	
Transport Vessels	Transport Vessels
USS Adriatic	USS Laurel Hill
USS Alice Vivian	USS Liberty
USS Any One	USS Little Rebel
USS Arizona	USS Louisiana Belle
USS Bella Donna	USS Luminary
USS Belle Creole	USS Madison
USS Black Hawk	USS Mars
USS City Belle*	USS Meteor
USS Clarabelle	USS Mittie Stephens
USS Colonel Cowles	USS Ohio Belle
USS Des Moines	USS Pauline
USS Diadem	USS Polar Star
USS Emarald	USS Red Chief No. 2
USS Emma*	USS Rob Roy
USS Gillum	USS Satie Robinson
USS Hamilton	USS Shenango
USS Hastings*	USS Shreveport
USS Henry Chouteau	USS Silver Lake No. 2
USS Ike Davis	USS Silver Wave
USS Illinois	USS Sioux City
USS J.C. Lacy	USS South Wester
USS James Battle	USS Starlight
USS Jennie Rogers	USS Superior
USS John H. Groesbeck	USS Texas
USS John Warner*	USS Thomas E. Tutt
USS Kate Dale	USS Universe
USS La Crosse*	USS W.L. Ewing
* Lost during the Campaign	

Confederate Vessels and Types Participating in the Red River Campaign

Confederate Vessels	
Name	Type
CSS Anna Perrette	Side Wheeler/Transport
CSS Beauregard	Steamer/Gunboat
CSS Colonel Terry	Transport
CSS Countess	Side Wheeler/Transport
CSS Dixie	Unknown
CSS Frolic	Side Wheeler
CSS Gen. Quitman	Side Wheeler/Transport
CSS Indian No. 2	Transport
CSS Lafourche	Unknown
CSS Louis D'Or	Side Wheeler/Cargo
CSS Mary T - Cotton II	Side Wheeler/Gun Boat
CSS Missouri	Casemate Ironclad/Ram
CSS New Falls City	Side Wheeler/Transport
CSS Osceola	Side Wheeler
CSS Paulene	Transport
CSS T. D. Hine	Side Wheeler/Transport
CSS Web	Side Wheeler/Ram
Four Unnamed Hunley Class	Submersible

NOTES

Preface

1. James M. McPherson, *The Illustrated Battle Cry of Freedom: The Civil War Era* (New York: Oxford University Press, 2003), 271–72; Earl J. Hess, *The Civil War in the West: Victory and Defeat from the Appalachians to the Mississippi* (Chapel Hill: University of North Carolina Press, 2012), xi–xii.
2. Paul Schneider, *Old Man River: The Mississippi River in North American History* (New York: Picador, 2014), 1–2; "Mississippi River Facts," National Park Service, updated April 14, 2021, https://www.nps.gov/miss/riverfacts.htm; Ralph Grizzle, "Paddle-Wheelers on the Mississippi, Steamboats on the Rhine & the Rise of KD River Line," River Cruise Advisor, updated February 18, 2021, https://www.rivercruiseadvisor.com/2021/02/kd-cruises/.
3. McPherson, *Battle Cry of Freedom*, 271–72.
4. Carl Newton Tyson, *The Red River in Southwestern History* (Norman: University of Oklahoma Press, 1981), 1–9, 177–83.
5. Gary D. Joiner, One Damn Blunder from Beginning to End: The Red River Campaign of 1864 (Wilmington, DE: Scholarly Resources, 2003), xix.
6. Gary D. Joiner, *The Red River Campaign: The Union's Final Attempt to Invade Texas* (Buffalo, Gap TX: State House Press, 2013), xi.

Introduction

1. James. D. Hollandsworth, *Pretense of Glory: The Life of General Nathaniel P. Banks*, (Baton Rouge, LA: Louisiana State University Press, 1998), 199-200; Gary D. Joiner, *The Red River Campaign: The Union's Final Attempt to Invade Texas*, (Buffalo, Gap TX: State House Press, 2013), 131, 144, 172-176.

2. McPherson, *Battle Cry of Freedom*, 549, 593–99, 625–28.

3. Ron Chernow, *Grant* (New York: Penguin, 2017), 356–57.

4. Hollandsworth, *Pretense of Glory*, 3, 5, 13, 28, 35, 83–84.

5. Some sources distinguish between a major general of volunteers and a major general of the regular army. They point out that because Banks was the former, he did not outrank regular army major generals. However, in a letter home in March 1864, William T. Sherman suggested that Banks outranked him and Grant. John H. Eicher and David J. Eicher, *Civil War High Commands* (Stanford, CA: Stanford University Press, 2001), 773; William T. Sherman, letter dated March 10, 1864, in *Home Letters of General Sherman*, ed. M. A. DeWolf Howe, (New York: Scribner and Sons, 1909), 284–86.

6. United States War Department, *The War of the Confederatelion: Official Records of the Union and Confederate Armies* (Washington, DC: United States Government Printing Office, 1874–180), vol. 15, pp. 590–91. Hereafter, this source will be cited in the following format: *OR*, vol. 15, pp. 590–91; Hollandsworth, *Pretense of Glory*, 44, 45; Ezra J. Warner, *Generals in Blue: Lives of the Union Commanders* (Baton Rouge: Louisiana State University, 1964), 17–18.

7. Joiner, *One Damn Blunder*, 8–10; Gary D. Joiner, *Through the Howling Wilderness: The 1864 Red River Campaign and Failure in the West* (Knoxville: University of Tennessee Press, 2006), 13–14.

8. Hollandsworth, *Pretense of Glory*, 132; Lawrence Lee Hewitt, *Port Hudson: Confederate Bastion on the Mississippi* (Baton Rouge: Louisiana State University Press, 1987), 123.

9. According to the returns of January 1, 1864, Smith had 73,289 men in his department. He listed only 34,845 as present for duty. He probably had something like 34,000 to 40,000 effectives. *OR*, vol. 34, pt. 2, p. 814.

10. Charles L. Dufour, *Nine Men in Grey* (Garden City, NY: Doubleday, 1963), 3.

11. Samuel W. Mitcham Jr., *Richard Taylor and the Red River Campaign of 1864*, (Gretna, LA: Pelican, 2012), 47–55; Ludwell H. Johnson, *Red

River Campaign: Politics & Cotton in the Civil War (Kent, OH: Kent State University Press, 1993), 88–89.

12. Mitcham, *Richard Taylor*, 47–55; Ezra J. Warner, *Generals in Gray: Lives of the Confederate Commanders* (Baton Rouge: Louisiana State University, 1959), 299–300; John D. Winters, *The Civil War in Louisiana* (Baton Rouge: Louisiana State University Press, 1963), 152.

13. United States Government Printing Office, *Report of the Joint Committee on the Conduct of the War: Vol. 2, Red River Expedition* (Washington, DC: United States Government, 1865), iv. Hereafter, this source will be cited in the following format: *RJCCW, Vol. 2, RRE*, iv.

14. Mitcham, *Richard Taylor*, 61.

Chapter 1

1. *OR*, vol. 34, pt. 2, pp. 895–96.

2. Joseph Howard Parks, *General Kirby-Smith, CSA* (Baton Rouge: Louisiana State University Press, 1954), 1–19; Bvt. Maj. Gen. George W. Cullum, *Biographical Register of the Officers and Graduates of the U.S. Military Academy at West Point, N.Y.* (Boston: Houghton, Mifflin, 1891), 2:208–49.

3. Parks, *General Kirby-Smith, CSA*, 110, 116–17.

4. Warner, *Generals in Gray*, 279–80.

5. Earl J. Hess, *Braxton Bragg: The Most Hated Man of the Confederacy* (Chapel Hill: University of North Carolina Press, 2016), 113, 120–21.

6. Joseph G. Dawson III, "Theophilus H. Holmes and Confederate Generalship," in *Confederate Generals of the Trans-Mississippi*, ed. Lawrence L. Hewitt, Arthur W. Bergeron Jr., and Thomas E. Schott (Knoxville: University of Tennessee Press, 2013), 1:30–38.

7. Dawson, "Theophilus H. Holmes," 27–29, 32–34.

8. Warner, *Generals in Gray*, 161–62.

9. Craig L. Symonds, *Joseph E. Johnston: A Civil War Biography* (New York: W. W. Norton, 1992), 126–28, 138.

10. Hess, *Braxton Bragg*, xii–xiii, 2–4, 113–17; Warner, *Generals in Gray*, 30–31.

11. Parks, *General Kirby-Smith, CSA*, 247–50; Larry Peterson, *Decisions of the 1862 Kentucky Campaign: The Twenty-Seven Critical Decisions That Defined the Operation* (Knoxville: University of Tennessee Press, 2019), 95–97.

12. *OR*, vol. 15, p. 948; *OR*, vol. 22, pt. 2, pp. 786–87; Dawson, "Theophilus H. Holmes," 39–40.
13. *OR*, vol. 24, pt. 3, p. 948.
14. Jeffery S. Prushankin, "To Carry Off the Glory: Edmund Kirby-Smith in 1864," in *Confederate Generals of the Trans-Mississippi*, ed. Lawrence L. Hewitt, Arthur W. Bergeron Jr., and Thomas E. Schott (Knoxville: University of Tennessee Press, 2013), 1:57, 60, 83.
15. Mitcham, *Richard Taylor*, 117–18, 291–93; *OR*, vol. 34, pt. 1, pp. 541–42; Gen. D. H. Maury, *Sketch of General Richard Taylor*, in *Southern Historical Society Papers*, ed. Rev. J. William Jones (Richmond, VA: 1879), 7:343-345; Johnson, *Red River Campaign*, 89.
16. William. R. Boggs, *Military Reminiscences of Gen. Wm. R. Boggs, C.S.A.*, introduction and notes by William K. Boyd (Durham, NC: Seeman Printery, 1913), 54–57.
17. Pinning down the exact number of Confederates engaged in the Red River Campaign is challenging. Several battles were fought, and not all Confederate forces fought at the same place at the same time. In his after-action report, Smith pointed to several conflicting sets of numbers. *OR*, vol. 34, pt. 1, pp. 476–88; *OR*, vol. 34, pt. 2, p. 814; see also Appendix IV of this book.
18. Little Rock fell to Union forces in September 1863. Dawson, "Theophilus H. Holmes," 47.
19. Warner, *Generals in Blue*, 195–97; Stephen W. Sears, *Lincoln's Lieutenants: The High Command of the Army of the Potomac* (Boston: Houghton Mifflin Harcourt, 2017), 285–86; Curt Anders, *Henry Halleck's War: A Fresh Look at Lincoln's Controversial General-in-Chief* (Carmel: Guild Press of Indiana, 1999), 3–8; Stephen E. Ambrose, *Halleck: Lincoln's Chief of Staff* (Baton Rouge: Louisiana State University Press, 1962), 3–8; Cullum, *Biographical Register*, 1:729-48, 2:1–24.
20. Donald S. Frazier, *Tempest over Texas: The Fall and Winter Campaigns of 1863–1864* (Kerrville, TX; State House Press at Schreiner University, 2020), 24–31, 199–200.
21. Chernow, *Grant*, 212–319.
22. *OR*, vol. 34, pt. 1, pp. 266–67; *RJCCW, Vol. 2, RRE*, xvii.
23. *OR*, vol. 34, pt. 1, pp. 167–76; see also Appendix IV of this book.
24. McPherson, *Battle Cry of Freedom*, 628; Johnson, *Red River Campaign*, 42.
25. Joiner, *Through the Howling Wilderness*, 12, 48.

26. Ralph A. Wooster and Robert Wooster, "People at War: East Texans during the Civil War," *East Texas Historical Journal* 28, no. 1 (1990): 3–16.
27. *OR*, vol. 34, pt. 1, pp. 266–67.
28. Joiner, *One Damn Blunder*, 3–4; Henry O. Robertson, *The Red River Campaign and Its Toll: 69 Bloody Days in Louisiana, March–May 1864* (Jefferson, NC: McFarland, 2016), 68–71.
29. *OR*, vol. 34, pt. 2, pp. 45–46.
30. *OR*, vol. 34, pt. 1, pp. 211–12.
31. In May 1863, Shreveport became Louisiana's Confederate capital. The state's exiled government fled from Baton Rouge and then Opelousas as Union forces made their way deeper into Louisiana. Shreveport remained the capital until the end of the war. Eric Brock, *Eric Brock's Shreveport* (Gretna, LA: Pelican, 2001), 33; Johnson, *Red River Campaign*, 5, 47; *OR*, vol. 34, pt. 2, pp. 15–16, 295–96.
32. William A. Dobak, *Freedom by the Sword: The U.S. Colored Troops, 1862–1867* (2011; repr., Alexandria, VA: St. John's Press, 2016), 103–9.
33. According to returns on March 31, 1864, Banks, Steele, and Smith's combined forces had 51,677 men present for duty. Subtracting 15 percent of that number to account for noncombatants, you get a total of 42,891. Joiner estimates the number at 42,900 in his book. Also, the Mississippi Marine Brigade exited the campaign before the battle at Mansfield. This number does not include sailors. Joiner, *Through the Howling Wilderness*, 55; "The Mississippi Flotilla in the Red River Expedition," in *Battles and Leaders of the Civil War*, ed. Robert Underwood Johnson and Clarence Clough Buel (New York: Century, 1887), 4:366; *OR*, vol. 34, pt. 1, pp. 167–76; see also Appendix IV of this book.
34. Mitcham, *Richard Taylor*, 61.
35. Winters, *Civil War in Louisiana*, 176.
36. Cullum, *Biographical Register*, 1:592–619.
37. William T. Sherman to John Sherman, January 4, 1862, January 8, 1862, in *Sherman's Civil War: Selected Correspondence of William T. Sherman, 1860–1865*, ed. Brooks D. Simpson, Jean V. Berlin (Chapel Hill: University of North Carolina Press, 1999), 174, 176.
38. Warner, *Generals in Blue*, 441–44.
39. *OR*, vol. 32, pt. 2, pp. 401–2; Joiner, *Through the Howling Wilderness*, 50.
40. Chernow, *Grant*, 518.
41. *OR*, vol. 34, pt. 1, pp. 424–25; William T. Sherman, letter dated March

10, 1864, in *Home Letters of General Sherman*, ed. M. A. DeWolf Howe (New York: Scribner and Sons, 1909), 284–86.

42. *OR*, vol. 34, pt. 2, pp. 494, 496–97.
43. *OR*, vol. 32, pt. 2, p. 402.
44. *OR*, vol. 32, pt. 2, p. 496.
45. Joiner, *Through the Howling Wilderness*, 40–41. See Appendix II for the Union Order of Battle.
46. *OR*, vol. 32, pt. 2, pp. 424–25; *OR*, vol. 34, pt. 2, pp. 340–41, 494, 481, 496–97; Joiner, *Through the Howling Wilderness*, 50.
47. *OR*, vol. 34, pt. 1, pp. 303–12; *OR*, vol. 34, pt. 2, pp. 610–11, 714; *OR*, vol. 34, pt. 3, pp. 26; Joiner, *One Damn Blunder*, 76–78.
48. Warner, *Generals in Blue*, 454–55.
49. Cullum, *Biographical Register*, 2:515–71; Warner, *Generals in Gray*, 28; Boggs, *Military Reminiscences*, vii–xxi.
50. Boggs, *Military Reminiscences*, xxii.
51. Joiner, *Through the Howling Wilderness*, 18.
52. *OR*, vol. 34, pt. 2, pp. 221, 223, 424.
53. Clifton D. Cardin, *Bossier Parish History: The First 150 Years. 1843–1993* (Shreveport: Image Press, 1993), 62; Joiner, *One Damn Blunder*, 16–17, 23–24, 26–27; *OR*, vol. 34, pt. 2, p. 1056.
54. The aggregate of all railroad mileage in the Confederacy at the beginning of the war was between seven thousand and nine thousand miles. I have yet to find a reference that indicates precisely what percentage of that mileage was in the Trans-Mississippi. However, maps showed it was likely less than 5 percent of the total. Robert C. Black, *The Railroads of the Confederacy* (1952; repr., Chapel Hill: University of North Carolina Press, 1998), 1–5; William G. Thomas, *The Iron Way: Railroads, the Civil War, and the Making of Modern America* (New Haven, CT: Yale University Press, 2011), 215.
55. Chester G. Hern, *Admiral David Dixon Porter: The Civil War Years* (Annapolis, MD: Naval Institute Press, 1996), 249–51.
56. Joiner, *Through the Howling Wilderness*, 49.
57. *OR*, vol. 32, pt. 2, p. 408.
58. *OR*, vol. 32, pt. 2, pp. 410–13.
59. *OR*, vol. 32, pt. 2, pp. 424–25.
60. *OR*, vol. 32, pt. 2, pp. 424–25; *OR*, vol. 32, pt. 3, p. 289.

61. William T. Sherman, *The Personal Memoirs of William T. Sherman* (1885; repr., New York: Da Capo, 1984), 144.
62. Richard M. McMurry, *Two Great Confederate Armies: An Essay in Confederate Military History* (Chapel Hill: University of North Carolina Press, 1989) 128.
63. Hollandsworth, *Pretense of Glory*, 169–70; *OR*, vol. 32, pt. 2, pp. 424–25.
64. *OR*, vol 34, pt. 2, p. 423.
65. Joiner, *Through the Howling Wilderness*, 66, 71
66. *OR*, vol. 34, pt. 1, pp. 661–62.
67. *RJCCW, Vol. 2, RRE*, 19.
68. Johnson, *Red River Campaign*, 27–28, 89–91; Hollandsworth, *Pretense of Glory*, 83–84, 88–98, 158–60, 162–63; Carl Sandburg, *Abraham Lincoln: The Prairie Years and the War Years*, one volume edition (New York: Harcourt, Brace, 1954), 657; Abraham Lincoln, "The Proclamation of Amnesty and Reconstruction by the President of the United States of America," in *U.S. Statutes at Large, Treaties, and Proclamations of the United States of America*, ed. George P. Sanger (Boston: Little, Brown & Co.,1866), 13:737–39.
69. *OR*, vol. 34, pt. 2, pp. 514–16.
70. William Franklin testified he was not informed of the March 17 assembly date until March 10. *RJCCW, Vol. 2, RRE*, xxv.
71. Joiner, *Through the Howling Wilderness*, 60–61; Richard Taylor, *Destruction and Reconstruction: Personal Experiences of the Late War* (New York: D. Appleton, 1883), 155–56.
72. Hollandsworth, *Pretense of Glory*, 167–68.
73. *OR*, vol. 34, pt. 1, pp. 179–80.
74. Joiner, *Red River Campaign*, 54; *OR*, vol. 34, pt. 2, pp. 512–13.
75. Hollandsworth, *Pretense of Glory*, 170–71; *OR*, vol. 34, pt. 2, p. 512; *RJCCW, Vol. 2, RRE*, 280–81.
76. In aggregate, Green's cavalry corps numbered twenty-two regiments of cavalry, three cavalry battalions, and two horse artillery batteries, or three thousand men of all arms. Sources indicate Green had at Mansfield sixteen cavalry regiments, two state guards cavalry battalions, and two horse artillery batteries (three thousand men). Three Texas cavalry regiments—the Twenty-Third, Thirty-Fifth, and Thirty-Sixth—did not come into the area of operations until April 10. Also not present was Parson's Texas cavalry brigade (three cavalry regiments and one

cavalry battalion), which arrived after the Battle of Pleasant Hill. Taylor indicated that only two regiments of Green's Command (five hundred to six hundred troopers) arrived on March 30, 1864. Taylor also wrote that half of the forces that arrived on that date were unarmed. Joiner, *Through the Howling Wilderness*, 218–19; Taylor, *Destruction and Reconstruction*, 157–58; *OR*, vol. 34, pt. 1, p. 514.

77. Some sources indicate that Taylor had many Vicksburg parolees in his army that had not been exchanged. These men could have been shot if captured again. *RJCCW, Vol. 2, RRE*, 194; *OR*, vol. 34, pt. 1, p. 198; Taylor, *Destruction and Reconstruction*, 162; Joiner, *Red River Campaign*, 68–69; United States War Department, *The War of the Confederatelion: Official Records of the Union and Confederate Navies* (Washington, DC: United States Government Printing Office, 1874–80), 26:50–51. Hereafter, this source will be cited in the following format: *ORN*, 26:50–51.

78. *OR*, vol. 34, pt. 2, pp. 494, 610–11; *OR*, vol. 34, pt. 1, pp. 203–4.

79. Joiner, *Through the Howling Wilderness*, 68.

80. *RJCCW, Vol. 2, RRE*, 281, 285; Gary D. Joiner, *Mr. Lincoln's Brown Water Navy: The Mississippi Squadron* (Lanham, MD: Rowman and Littlefield, 2007), 151.

81. *RJCCW, Vol. 2, RRE*, 286–87; Johnson, *Red River Campaign*, 113–15; William Riley Brooksher, *War along the Bayous: The 1864 Red River Campaign in Louisiana* (Lincoln, NE: Potomac Books / University of Nebraska Press, 1998), 75.

82. Joiner, *Mr. Lincoln's Brown Water Navy*, 148–54; *RJCCW, Vol. 2, RRE*, 274–78.

83. Joiner, *Through the Howling Wilderness*, 73–74.

84. Johnson, *Red River Campaign*, 115; Hern, *Admiral David Dixon Porter*, 249.

85. John G. Nicolay and John Hay, *Abraham Lincoln: A History* (New York: Century, 1890), 8:291.

86. Cullum, *Biographical Register*, 2:152–91; Warner, *Generals in Blue*, 474–75.

87. *OR*, vol. 34, pt. 2, pp. 149–50, 246–47, 546–47, 576, 616.

88. Daniel E. Sutherland, "1864: A Strange and Wild Time," in *Rugged and Sublime: The Civil War in Arkansas*, ed. Mark K. Christ (Fayetteville: University of Arkansas Press, 1994), 105–8.

89. *OR*, vol. 34, pt. 1, p. 657.

90. *OR*, vol. 34, pt. 2, pp. 175, 403.

91. *OR*, vol. 34, pt. 1, pp. 657, 692; *OR*, vol. 34, pt. 2, pp. 638, 707; Johnson, *Red River Campaign*, 170–71.
92. Johnson, *Red River Campaign*, 170–71.
93. *OR*, vol. 34, pt. 1, pp. 661, 667–71.
94. *OR*, vol. 34, pt. 1, pp. 693; *OR*, vol. 34, pt. 3, pp. 77–79.
95. Johnson, *Red River Campaign*, 171–72; Joiner, *One Damn Blunder*, 124; *OR*, vol. 34, pt. 1, p. 693.
96. *OR*, vol. 34, pt. 1, pp. 10, 684, 770–71, 779–80; Johnson, *Red River Campaign*, 203–4; Joiner, *Through the Howling Wilderness*, 129.

Chapter 2

1. The number of Confederate casualties for both days is based on several sources. There is room for speculation, as many of these are contradictory as to the number of Confederates captured at Pleasant Hill. In his memoir, Richard Taylor stated that his combined losses for both battles were 2,626, with 1,000 killed, wounded, and missing at Mansfield and 1,626 at Pleasant Hill, including 426 men captured in the latter action. In his book, Ludwell H. Johnson also puts the total number of Confederate losses at 2,626. Several conflicting Union reports indicated between 400 and 1,000 Confederates were captured at Pleasant Hill. Nathaniel Banks reported 500 captured, while Charles Stone, his chief of staff, placed the number at 400 to 500. A. J. Smith had the most significant number, reporting "nearly 1,000" Confederates captured at Pleasant Hill. In his manuscript, Blessington put the number of Confederates captured at "about 250." Zac Cowsert, "The Civil War's Bloodiest Battles West of the Mississippi River," *Civil Discourse: A Civil War Era Blog*, May 20, 2019, http://civildiscourse-historyblog.com/blog/2018/10/13/battle-in-the-trans-mississippi-a-cursory-quantative-analysis#:~:text=The%20ten%20bloodiest%20battles%20of,%20Ferry%2C%20Arkansas%20(1%2C700)%3B; Taylor, *Destruction and Reconstruction*, 171; Johnson, *Red River Campaign*, 169; *OR*, vol. 34, pt. 1, pp. 184, 260, 309, 313, 553; *OR*, vol. 34, pt. 3, p. 100; Joseph Palmer Blessington, *The Campaigns of Walker's Texas Division: By a Private Soldier, Containing a Complete Record of the Campaigns in Texas, Louisiana, and Arkansas* [. . .], (New York: Lange, Little, 1875), 199; Joiner, *One Damn Blunder*, 99, 103, 116; Joiner, *Red River Campaign*, 79, 89–90.
2. James Kendall Ewer, *The Third Massachusetts Cavalry in the War for the*

Union: Company C, Third Mass. Cav. (Maplewood, MA: Historical Committee of the Regimental Association, 1903), 142, 439.

3. John Scott, *Story of the Thirty-Second Iowa Infantry Volunteers* (Nevada, IA: self-published, 1896), 136; *An Historical Sketch of the 162d Regiment N.Y. Vol. Infantry: (3d Metropolitan Guard), 19th Army Corps, 1862–1865* (Albany, NY: Weed, Parsons, 1867), 25; Johnson, *Red River Campaign*, 118; *RJCCW, Vol. 2, RRE*, 323; William H. Stewart Diary, entry for April 2, 1864, Southern Historical Collection, Wilson Library, University of North Carolina at Chapel Hill; Frank M. Flinn, *Campaigning with Banks in Louisiana, '63 and '64, and with Sheridan in the Shenandoah Valley in '64 and '65* (Boston: W. B. Clark, 1889), 97.

4. Taylor, *Destruction and Reconstruction*, 162.

5. *RJCCW, Vol. 2, RRE*, 275–76, 323; Richard B. Irwin, "The Red River Campaign," in *Battles and Leaders of the Civil War*, ed. Robert Underwood Johnson and Clarence Clough Buel (New York: Century, 1887), 4:363.

6. Hollandsworth, *Pretense of Glory*, 182.

7. Hollandsworth, *Pretense of Glory*, 182–83; Taylor, *Destruction and Reconstruction*, 155–59.

8. Johnson, *Red River Campaign*, 110; Joiner, *One Damn Blunder*, 79–81; *RJCCW, Vol. 2, RRE*, 192–93; *OR*, vol. 34, pt. 1, p. 308.

9. This math assumes two thousand pounds of materiel per wagon. *RJCCW, Vol. 2, RRE*, 32, 58; Earl J. Hess, *Civil War Logistics: A Study of Military Transportation* (Baton Rouge, Louisiana State University Press, 2017), 136, 142.

10. *RJCCW, Vol. 2, RRE*, 32.

11. *RJCCW, Vol. 2, RRE*, 32, 323; Johnson, *Red River Campaign*, 117.

12. *RJCCW, Vol. 2, RRE*, 192–95; *OR*, vol. 34, pt. 1, p. 449–52; Theo [Theophilus] A. Noel, *A Campaign from Santa Fe to the Mississippi: Being a History of the Old Sibley Brigade from Its First Organization to the Present Time; Its Campaigns in New Mexico, Arizona, Texas, Louisiana, and Arkansas, in the Years of 1861–2–3–4* (Shreveport, LA: Shreveport News Printing Establishment, 1865), 77.

13. *RJCCW, Vol. 2, RRE*, 192–95; *OR*, vol. 34, pt. 1, pp. 264–68, 389–92, 447–52; Hollandsworth, *Pretense of Glory*, 185–89; Taylor, *Destruction and Reconstruction*, 162–64; Wickham Hoffman, *Camp, Court and Siege: A Narrative of Personal Adventure and Observation during Two Wars, 1861–1865; 1870–1871* (New York: Harper and Brothers, 1877), 87–89.

14. Richard Bache Irwin, *History of the Nineteenth Army Corps* (New York:

G.P. Putnam and Sons, 1892), 306; Richard Brady Williams, *Chicago's Battery Boys: The Chicago Mercantile Battery in the Civil War's Western Theater*, (New York: Savis Beatie LLC, 2005), 240.

15. *RJCCW, Vol. 2, RRE*, 79.
16. Hoffman, *Camp, Court and Siege*, 93; Scott, *Thirty-Second Iowa*, 136.
17. Blessington, *Campaigns of Walker's Texas Division*, 182–83; "Joseph Palmer Blessington—the Sixteenth Texas Infantry, Company H," Military History Online, added August 20, 2015, https://www.military historyonline.com/Genealogy/Regiment/Texas/4/2595/40347.
18. *OR*, vol. 26, pt. 1, p. 526–27.
19. Taylor, *Destruction and Reconstruction*, 160–61; Kerby, *Kirby Smith's Confederacy*, 284–85.
20. *OR*, vol. 26, pt. 2, pp. 41–42, 117.
21. *OR*, vol. 26, pt. 2, p. 294; *OR*, vol. 34, pt. 2, p. 1035; Johnson, *Red River Campaign*, 86–87.
22. Taylor, *Destruction and Reconstruction*, 153–54.
23. *OR*, vol. 34, pt. 1, pp. 478–80, 494, 496, 500, 578; *OR*, vol. 34, pt. 2, pp. 1027, 1029; Joiner, *Red River Campaign*, 69; Taylor, *Destruction and Reconstruction*, 153, 156, 162.
24. *OR*, vol. 34, pt. 1, p. 479; *OR*, vol. 34, pt. 2, pp. 1056, 1062–63; *OR*, vol. 34, pt. 3, pp. 745, 760–61.
25. Taylor, *Destruction and Reconstruction*, 157; *OR*, vol. 34, pt. 2, pp. 1074, 1079.
26. *OR*, vol. 34, pt. 1, p. 480; Boggs, *Military Reminiscences*, 75.
27. Taylor, *Destruction and Reconstruction*, 154, 158–59; Joiner, *One Damn Blunder*, 33, 84–85.
28. Both men's after-action reports provide a good overview of these communications. *OR*, vol. 34, pt. 1, pp. 476–528, 560–95.
29. *OR*, vol. 34, pt. 1, p. 522.
30. Taylor, *Destruction and Reconstruction*, 158–59, 160; Kerby, *Kirby Smith's Confederacy*, 303; *OR*, vol. 34, pt. 1, pp. 522, 525–26.
31. Robertson, *Red River Campaign and Its Toll*, 20.
32. Taylor, *Destruction and Reconstruction*, 159; *OR*, vol. 34, pt. 1, p. 522.
33. *OR*, vol. 34, pt. 1, p. 526.
34. Joiner, *One Damn Blunder*, 94; Mitcham, *Richard Taylor*, 141–42; *OR*, vol. 34, pt. 1, p. 528.

35. *OR*, vol. 34, pt. 1, p. 527.
36. Jeff Kinard, *Lafayette of the South: Prince Camille de Polignac and the American Civil War* (College Station: Texas A&M University Press, 2001), 119.
37. Sarah A. Dorsey, *Recollections of Henry Watkins Allen: Brigadier General Confederate States Army and Governor of Louisiana* (New York: M. Doolady, 1866), 263.
38. Irwin's middle name is listed as Bache in some sources and Biddle in others. "LTC Richard Biddle Irwin," Find a Grave, updated October 9, 2005, https://www.findagrave.com/memorial/11918187/richard-biddle-irwin.
39. Irwin, *History of the Nineteenth Army Corps*, 310–12.
40. Flinn, *Campaigning with Banks in Louisiana*, 109.
41. Joiner, by investigating regimental records, gives a higher casualty rate than the official Union estimate of 2,235. Joiner, *Red River Campaign*, 79.
42. *OR*, vol. 34, pt. 1, p. 267; Joiner, *Red River Campaign*, 77; Williams, *Chicago's Battery Boys*, 240; Mark A. Snell, *From First to Last: The Life of Major General William B. Franklin* (New York: Fordham University Press, 2002), 308–9.
43. *OR*, vol. 34, pt. 1, pp. 307, 389–92.
44. Johnson, *Red River Campaign*, 139; Hollandsworth, *Pretense of Glory*, 67–68.
45. Taylor, *Destruction and Reconstruction*, 163; *OR*, vol. 34, pt. 1, p. 553, 564; Arthur W. Bergeron Jr., *Guide to Louisiana Confederate Military Units, 1861–1865* (Baton Rouge: Louisiana State University Press, 1989), pp. 119, 138–39, 146–47; Arthur W. Bergeron Jr., "A Colonel Gains His Wreath: Henry Gray and His Louisiana Brigade at the Battle of Mansfield, April 8, 1864," in *The Red River Campaign: Union and Confederate Leadership and the War in Louisiana*, ed. Theodore P. Savas, David A. Woodbury, and Gary D. Joiner (Shreveport, LA: Parabellum, 2003), 21–23.
46. Taylor, *Destruction and Reconstruction*, 165.
47. *OR*, vol. 34, pt. 1, pp. 526–28.
48. Taylor, *Destruction and Reconstruction*, 164.
49. *RJCCW, Vol. 2, RRE*, 77, 179; *OR*, vol. 34, pt. 1, pp. 392, 422; Joiner, *One Damn Blunder*, 104.
50. Irwin, *History of the Nineteenth Army Corps*, 311–12.
51. Don Montgomery, "Thomas James Churchill (1824–1905)," *Encyclopedia Of Arkansas*, updated November 19, 2020, https://encyclopediaofarkansas.net/entries/thomas-james-churchill-92/; David Sesser,

"Sterling Price (1809–1867)," *Encyclopedia Of Arkansas*, updated April 9, 2022, https://encyclopediaofarkansas.net/entries/sterling-price-2815/#:~:text=Sterling%20Price%20was%20a%20farmer,and%20during%20the%20Camden%20Expedition; Warner, *Generals in Gray*, 49–50, 246–47; Mark K. Christ, "Not Fortunate in War: Major General Thomas James Churchill," in *Confederate Generals of the Trans-Mississippi*, ed. Lawrence L. Hewitt, Arthur W. Bergeron Jr., and Thomas E. Schott, (Knoxville: The University of Tennessee Press, 2013), 1:167–85.

52. In his after-action report, Parsons indicated his division had 2,200 men in seven regiments and one artillery battery. Tappan did not indicate a number, but he had five regiments and one artillery battery. Churchill indicated he had 4,300 muskets in his entire command on April 8. If both figures are correct, Tappan should have had 2,100 men in his five regiments. *OR*, vol. 34, pt. 1, pp. 601–6; *OR*, vol. 53, p. 477; Ethan Allen Pinnell, entries for March 20, 1864, and March 24, 1864, in *Serving with Honor: The Diary of Captain Ethan Allen Pinnell of the Eighth Missouri Infantry (Confederate)*, ed. Michael E. Banasik (Iowa City, IA: Press of the Camp Pope Bookshop, 1999), 146–47.

53. *OR*, vol. 34, pt. 1, p. 523; *OR*, vol. 34, pt. 2, p. 1056; *OR*, vol. 53, p. 477; Taylor, *Destruction and Reconstruction*, 164–65; Pinnell, entries for April 3, 1864, through April 9, 1864, in *Serving with Honor*, 150–52.

54. *OR*, vol. 34, pt. 1, pp. 565–66, 607–8.

55. Elias Porter Pellet, *History of the 114th Regiment, New York State Volunteers: Containing a Perfect Record of Its Services, Embracing All Its Marches, Campaigns, Battles, Sieges and Sea-Voyages, with a Biographical Sketch of Each Officer, and a Complete Register of the Regiment [. . .]* (Norwich, NY: Telegraph and Chronicle Power Press Print, 1866), 193–94; Dr. Harris H. Beecher, *Record of the 114th Regiment, N.Y.S.V.: Where It Went, What It Saw, and What It Did* (Norwich, NY: J. F. Hubbard, 1896), 308; Taylor, *Destruction and Reconstruction*, 165–68; Johnson, *Red River Campaign*, 150, 168.

56. *OR*, vol. 34, pt. 1, p. 183; *RJCCW, Vol. 2, RRE*, 176; Hollandsworth, *Pretense of Glory*, 191.

57. Brooksher, *War along the Bayous*, 125–35.

58. *OR*, vol. 53, p. 477.

59. *OR*, vol. 53, p. 477.

60. *OR*, vol. 53, p. 477.

61. Taylor, *Destruction and Reconstruction*, 170.

62. Joiner, *Red River Campaign*, 87–88.
63. Edwin C. Bearss, *Protecting Sherman's Lifeline: The Battles of Brice's Cross Roads and Tupelo*, (Washington, DC: Office of Publications, National Park Service, US Department of the Interior, 1971); Eicher and Eicher, *Civil War High Commands*, 492.
64. Warner, *Generals in Blue*, 454–55; Cullum, *Biographical Register*, 1:697–729; Edwin C. Bearss and Edwin S. Bearss, "The Battle of the Post of Arkansas," *Arkansas Historical Quarterly* 18, no. 3 (1959): 237–79; *OR*, vol. 53, pp. 477–78.
65. Bearss, *Protecting Sherman's Lifeline*; Hollandsworth, *Pretense of Glory*, 175; Steven Woodworth, "General A. J. Smith's Guerrillas and the Battle of Nashville," talk presented at 1864: The Western Theater symposium, Civil War Center, Kennesaw State University, Kennesaw, GA, March 22, 2014, C-SPAN—the Civil War Series, American History TV, https://www.c-span.org/video/?318492-2/general-aj-smiths-guerrillas-battle-nashville.
66. *OR*, vol. 34, vol. 1, pp. 303, 305, 307; *ORN*, 26:26–27; Brooksher, *War along the Bayous*, 55–56; Johnson, *Red River Campaign*, 97.
67. *OR*, vol. 34, vol. 1, pp. 307–8.
68. Taylor, *Destruction and Reconstruction*, 167–68.
69. *OR*, vol. 34, vol. 1, pp. 308–9, 563–68.
70. James Lee McDonough, *William Tecumseh Sherman: In the Service of my Country; A Life* (New York: W. W. Norton, 2016), 362–65; Edwin C. Bearss, *The Campaign for Vicksburg*, vol. 1, *Vicksburg Is the Key* (Dayton, OH: Morningside House, 1985), 205–10.
71. *OR*, vol. 34, vol. 1, pp. 309.
72. Taylor, *Destruction and Reconstruction*, 170; Joiner, *One Damn Blunder*, 114–15.
73. *OR*, vol. 34, vol. 1, pp. 309
74. *RJCCW, Vol. 2, RRE*, 35.
75. Johnson, *Red River Campaign*, 166.

Chapter 3

1. Thomas W. Cutrer, "Medford, Harvey C. (1831–1902)," *Handbook of Texas*, updated April 1, 1995, https://www.tshaonline.org/handbook/entries/medford-harvey-c; United States Census Bureau, 1860 Census:

Population of the United States, State of Texas, updated December 16, 2021, https://www2.census.gov/library/publications/decennial/1860/population/1860a-34.pdf.

2. Harvey C. Medford, entry for April 9, 1864, in "The Diary of H. C. Medford, Confederate Soldier, 1864," ed. Rebecca W. Smith and Marion Mullins, *Southwestern Historical Quarterly* 34, no. 3 (January 1931): 222.

3. *RJCCW, Vol. 2, RRE*, 199, 208.

4. The number of Confederate casualties for both days is based on several sources. There is room for speculation as many of these are contradictory as to the number of Confederates captured at Pleasant Hill. In his memoir, Richard Taylor stated his combined losses for both battles were 2,626, with 1,000 killed, wounded, and missing at Mansfield and 1,626 at Pleasant Hill, including 426 men captured in the latter action. In his book, Ludwell H. Johnson, also puts the total number of Confederate losses at 2,626. Several conflicting Union reports indicated between 400 and 1,000 Confederates were captured at Pleasant Hill. Nathaniel Banks reported 500 Confederates captured, while Charles Stone, his chief of staff, placed the number at 400 to 500. A. J. Smith had the most significant number, reporting "nearly 1,000" Confederates captured at Pleasant Hill. In his manuscript, Blessington put the number of Confederates captured at "about 250." Taylor, *Destruction and Reconstruction*, 171; Johnson, *Red River Campaign*, 169; *OR*, vol. 34, pt. 1, pp. 184, 260, 309, 313, 553; *OR*, vol. 34, pt. 3, p. 100; Blessington, *Campaigns of Walker's Texas Division*, 199; Joiner, *One Damn Blunder*, 99, 103, 116.

5. Taylor, *Destruction and Reconstruction*, 171, 178.

6. Taylor, *Destruction and Reconstruction*, 178; Blessington, *Campaigns of Walker's Texas Division*, 200; Gen. E. Kirby-Smith, "The Defense of the Red River," in *Battles and Leaders of the Civil War*, ed. Robert Underwood Johnson and Clarence Clough Buel (New York: Century, 1887), 4:366.

7. *RJCCW, Vol. 2, RRE*, 12–13.

8. By investigating regimental records, Joiner gives a higher casualty rate than the official Union estimate of 2,235. Joiner, *Red River Campaign*, 79, 89–90.

9. Johnson, *Red River Campaign*, 168–69; *RJCCW, Vol. 2, RRE*, 13; *OR*, vol. 34, pt. 1, pp. 553, 568.

10. Johnson, *Red River Campaign*, 110; Joiner, *One Damn Blunder*, 79–81; *RJCCW, Vol. 2, RRE*, 192–93; *OR*, vol. 34, pt. 1, p. 308.
11. *RJCCW, Vol. 2, RRE*, 35; Snell, *From First to Last*, 312–13.
12. *OR*, vol. 34, pt. 1, p. 309.
13. Brig. Gen. William H. Emory commanded the First Division, Nineteenth Corps, and Brig. Gen. William Dwight commanded his First Brigade. *RJCCW, Vol. 2, RRE*, 13.
14. *RJCCW, Vol. 2, RRE*, 35.
15. Scott, *Thirty-Second Iowa*, 233–36.
16. *OR*, vol. 41, pt. 1, p. 123.
17. *OR*, vol. 41, pt. 1, pp. 566, 568, 596; Taylor, *Destruction and Reconstruction*, 171.
18. Taylor, *Destruction and Reconstruction*, 177.
19. Taylor, *Destruction and Reconstruction*, 170, 179; Kerby, *Kirby Smith's Confederacy*, 311.
20. Parks, *General Kirby-Smith, CSA*, 394–96.
21. *OR*, vol. 34, pt. 3, pp. 77–79; Johnson, *Red River Campaign*, 204.
22. Kirby-Smith, "Defense of the Red River," 4:372.
23. While Kirby-Smith never overtly expressed concern for Price's leadership ability, the fact that he personally assumed command of Confederate forces in Arkansas seems to point to his doubts. Kerby, *Kirby Smith's Confederacy*, 299, 311; Boggs, *Military Reminiscences*, 77–78.
24. Joiner, *Red River Campaign*, 174–75.
25. Kirby-Smith, "Defense of the Red River," 4:372.
26. The exact number of Confederates sent to Arkansas to support Sterling Price after the Battle of Pleasant Hill is up for debate—the records are imperfect. I estimate the number to be roughly 5,000. Joseph Parks puts the number as approximately 4,000 to 5,000 men in his book on Kirby-Smith, citing Sterling Price's after-action report on the Camden Expedition as the source. In his memoir, Richard Taylor indicated he had 13,000 men when the campaign started and had 5,200 men left under his command after Walker and Churchill were sent north. The 5,200 included the command of Brig. Gen. St. John R. Liddell (600 men) operating east of the Red River. That is a difference of 7,800. Subtracting for casualties at Mansfield and Pleasant Hill (2,626—see note 4 of this chapter) leaves 5,174 men sent north. Additional losses and straggling would probably place the number just below 5,000.

Parks, *General Kirby-Smith, CSA*, 380; *OR*, vol. 34, pt. 3, pp. 633, 779; Taylor, *Destruction and Reconstruction*, 191–92.

27. Taylor, *Destruction and Reconstruction*, 180; T. Michael Parrish, *Richard Taylor: Soldier Prince of Dixie* (Chapel Hill: University of North Carolina Press, 1992), 375.

28. *OR*, vol. 34, pt. 1, p. 476; Taylor, *Destruction and Reconstruction*, 180, 196.

29. *OR*, vol. 34, pt. 1, pp. 662–63.

30. *OR*, vol. 34, pt. 1, p. 487.

31. Johnson, *Red River Campaign*, 275–76.

Conclusions and Consequences

1. Blessington, *Campaigns of Walker's Texas Division*, 196.

2. Richard Lowe, *Walker's Texas Division C.S.A.: Greyhounds of the Trans-Mississippi* (Baton Rouge: Louisiana State University Press, 2004), 79–95, 135–43, 175–77, 188–99.

3. Scott, *Story of the Thirty-Second Iowa Infantry Volunteers*, (Nevada, IA: Self Published, 1896), 140.

4. Lowe, *Walker's Texas Division*, 204–10.

5. Lowe, *Walker's Texas Division*, 20, 23; Thomas W. Cutrer, "Allen, Robert Thomas Pritchard (1813–1888)," *Handbook of Texas*, updated November 1, 1994, https://www.tshaonline.org/handbook/entries/allen-robert-thomas-pritchard.

6. Elijah P. Petty, *Journey to Pleasant Hill: The Civil War Letters of Captain Elijah P. Petty, Walker's Texas Division, CSA*, ed. Norman D. Brown (San Antonio: University of Texas, Institute of Texan Cultures, 1982), x–xi, xii.

7. Petty was likely struck by a canister round. Grape was used very little in field artillery. Men in the war often used the words *canister* and *grape* interchangeably, as both were antipersonnel rounds. Petty, *Journey to Pleasant Hill*, 412–14.

8. In the twenty-seven years before the Civil War, the Texas population exploded from 39,000 in 1836 to 604,000 in 1860. The Americans who immigrated to Texas primarily came from southern states. While many Anglos brought slaves with them to Texas, many more did not, and just over 5 percent of Texans owned slaves in 1860. The 1860 population number includes 182,000 enslaved people. T. R. Fehrenbach, *Lone Star: A History of Texas and the Texans* (New York: American Legacy,

1983), 287; *Texas in the Civil War* (Austin: Texas Historical Commission, 2013), 2; Jenny Bourne, "Slavery in the United States," EH.Net Encyclopedia of Economic and Business History, ed. Robert Whaples, updated March 26, 2008, http://eh.net/encyclopedia/slavery-in-the-united-states/.

9. Petty, *Journey to Pleasant Hill*, 414–15.
10. Petty, *Journey to Pleasant Hill*, xii–xvi, 420.
11. *ORN*, 26:44–54.
12. Gary Joiner, "To Defend the Sacred Soil of Texas: Tom Green and the Texas Cavalry in the Red River Campaign," *East Texas Historical Journal* 46, no. 1 (2008): 15–16; Johnson, *Red River Campaign*, 211–13; *ORN*, vol. 26, p. 49.
13. Hollandsworth, *Pretense of Glory*, 204.
14. *OR*, vol. 34, pt. 1, pp. 190–92; *ORN*, vol. 26, pp. 60–63; Joiner, *Red River Campaign*, 125; David Dixon Porter, *Incidents and Anecdotes of the Civil War* (New York: D. Appleton, 1886), 235–36; Hollandsworth, *Pretense of Glory*, 204; Homer B. Sprague, *History of the 13th Infantry Regiment of Connecticut Volunteers during the Great Confederatelion* (Hartford, CT: Case, Lockwood, 1867), 192–20.
15. Blaine Lamb, *The Extraordinary Life of Charles Pomeroy Stone: Soldier, Surveyor, Pasha, Engineer*, (Yardly, PA: Westholme, 2015), 177; *OR*, vol. 34, pt. 1, pp. 187–88; *OR*, vol. 34, pt. 3, p. 211; Joiner, *Red River Campaign*, 146; Hoffman, *Camp, Court and Siege*, 97; J. Cutler Andrews, *The North Reports the Civil War* (1955; repr., Pittsburgh, PA: University of Pittsburgh Press, 1985), 510.
16. *ORN*, vol. 26, pp. 62, 68–69; *OR*, vol. 34, pt. 1, p. 190; Johnson, *Red River Campaign*, 254; Michael J. Goc, *The Hero of the Red River: The Life and Times of Joseph Bailey* (Friendship, WI: B. E. Gussel and New Past, 2007), 214–15, 218–29, 234–35.
17. Taylor, *Destruction and Reconstruction*, 190–91; Johnson, *Red River Campaign*, 274–76; Joiner, *Through the Howling Wilderness*, 161.
18. Hollandsworth, *Pretense of Glory*, 206–7.
19. The actual miles marched by individual commands are unknown, but Walker's Texans were reported to have marched over 620 miles during the campaign. Johnson, *Red River Campaign*, 278, *ORN*, vol. 26, p. 172, vol. 34, pp. 162–63, 653–54; Lowe, *Walker's Texas Division*, 228.
20. *RJCCW, Vol. 2, RRE*, iii–xv; Hollandsworth, *Pretense of Glory*, 216–17; Warner, *Generals in Blue*, 18; Fred Harvey Harrington, *Fighting Poli-*

tician: Major General N. P. Banks (London: Oxford University Press, 1948), 164–68; Mitcham, *Richard Taylor*, 298–300.

21. *OR*, vol. 34, pt. 1, pp. 546–48.
22. *OR*, vol. 34, pt. 1, pp. 540–41; Warner, *Generals in Gray*, 300; Mitcham, *Richard Taylor*, 300–302; Taylor, *Destruction and Reconstruction*, 196.
23. L. F. Andrews, "The Word 'Iowa'—What It Means," *Annals of Iowa*, 3rd series. 2, no. 6 (1896): 465–69.
24. Leland L. Sage, *A History of Iowa* (Ames: Iowa State University Press, 1974), 35, 90–91, 153–54; J. L. Anderson, "The Vacant Chair on the Farm: Soldier Husbands, Farm Wives, and the Iowa Home Front, 1861–1865," *Annals of Iowa* 66 (Summer–Fall 2007): 245–46.
25. Scott, *Story of the Thirty-Second Iowa*, 1–23, 141, 153–57, 170–72.
26. Scott, *Story of the Thirty-Second Iowa*, 281–82.

Appendix I

1. "U.S. Custom House, New Orleans, LA," United States General Services Administration, updated August 13, 2017, https://www.gsa.gov/historic-buildings/us-custom-house-new-orleans-la#overview.
2. Porter, *Incidents and Anecdotes*, 95–96.
3. *United States Department of the Interior*, "History & Culture—Vicksburg Military Park," National Park Service, updated July 26, 2019, https://www.nps.gov/vick/learn/historyculture/index.htm.
4. Abraham Lincoln to James Conkling, August 26, 1863, in *The Collected Works of Abraham Lincoln, in Eight Volumes*, ed. Roy Basler (New Brunswick, NJ: Rutgers University Press, 1953), 6:409.
5. *OR*, vol. 32, pt. 2, p. 41.
6. *OR*, vol. 34, pt. 1, pp. 266–67; *RJCCW, Vol. 2, RRE*, xvii.
7. *OR*, vol. 32, pt. 2, pp. 424–25.
8. *OR*, vol. 34, pt. 1, pp. 167–76.
9. Joiner, *Through the Howling Wilderness*, 49.
10. *OR*, vol. 32, pt. 2, pp. 407–8.
11. *OR*, vol. 32, pt. 2, pp. 424–25.
12. *OR*, vol. 32, pt. 3, p. 289.
13. "Jackson Square in the French Quarter," Experience New Orleans, accessed July 9, 2023, https://www.experienceneworleans.com/jackson-square.html; Winters, *Civil War in Louisiana*, 206.

14. Johnson, *Red River Campaign*, 27–28, 89–91; Hollandsworth, *Pretense of Glory*, 83–84, 88–98, 158–60, 162–63; Sandburg, *Abraham Lincoln*, 657; Lincoln, "Proclamation of Amnesty and Reconstruction," 13:737–39.
15. *OR*, vol. 34, pt. 2, pp. 514–16.
16. William Franklin testified he was not informed of the March 17 assembly date until March 10. *RJCCW, Vol. 2, RRE*, xxv.
17. Joiner, *Through the Howling Wilderness*, 60–61; Taylor, *Destruction and Reconstruction*, 155–56.
18. Hollandsworth, *Pretense of Glory*, 167–68.
19. Joiner, *Red River Campaign*, 54; *OR*, vol. 34, pt. 2, pp. 512–13.
20. Hollandsworth, *Pretense of Glory*, 170–71; *OR*, vol. 34, pt. 2, p. 512, *RJCCW, Vol. 2, RRE*, 280–81.
21. *OR*, vol. 34, pt. 2, pp. 610–11.
22. "A Brief History of Fort DeRussy," Friends of Fort DeRussy, Inc., accessed April 10, 2014, http://www.fortderussy.org/index.html.
23. *OR*, vol. 32, pt. 2, pp. 401–2; Joiner, *Through the Howling Wilderness*, 50.
24. Chernow, *Grant*, 518.
25. *OR*, vol. 34, pt. 1, pp. 424–25; William T. Sherman, letter home dated March 10, 1864, in *Home Letters of General Sherman*, ed., M. A. DeWolf Howe (New York: Scribner and Sons, 1909), pp. 284–86.
26. *OR*, vol. 32, pt. 2, p. 496.
27. Joiner, *Through the Howling Wilderness*, 40–41. See appendix II for Union order of battle.
28. *OR*, vol. 34, pt. 2, pp. 514–16.
29. *OR*, vol. 34, pt. 1, pp. 303–12; *OR*, vol. 34, pt. 2, pp. 610–11, 714; *OR*, vol. 34, pt. 3, pp. 26; Joiner, *One Damn Blunder*, 76–78.
30. "Forts Randolph & Buhlow State Historic Site," Louisiana State Parks, accessed July 9, 2023, https://www.lastateparks.com/historic-sites/forts-randolph-buhlow-state-historic-site.
31. Some sources indicate that Taylor had many Vicksburg parolees in his army that had not been exchanged. These men could have been shot if captured again. *RJCCW, Vol. 2, RRE*, 194; *OR*, vol. 34, pt. 1, p. 198; Taylor, *Destruction and Reconstruction*, 162; Joiner, *Red River Campaign*, 68–69; *ORN*, 26:50–51.
32. *OR*, vol. 34, pt. 2, pp. 494, 610–11; *OR*, vol. 34, pt. 1, pp. 203–4.
33. *RJCCW, Vol. 2, RRE*, 281, 285; Joiner, *Mr. Lincoln's Brown Water Navy*, 151.

34. *RJCCW, Vol. 2, RRE*, 286–87; Johnson, *Red River Campaign*, 113–15; Brooksher, *War along the Bayous*, 75.

35. *ORN*, vol. 26, p. 60.

36. "Welcome to the Grand Ecore Visitor Center," US Army Corps of Engineers, Vicksburg District website, accessed July 9, 2023, https://www.mvk.usace.army.mil/Missions/Recreation/Grand-Ecore-Visitor-Center/.

37. *RJCCW, Vol. 2, RRE*, 275–76, 323; Irwin, "Red River Campaign," 4:363.

38. Hollandsworth, *Pretense of Glory*, 182.

39. Hollandsworth, *Pretense of Glory*, 182–83; Taylor, *Destruction and Reconstruction*, 155–59.

40. Johnson, *Red River Campaign*, 110; Joiner, *One Damn Blunder*, 79–81; *RJCCW, Vol. 2, RRE*, 192–93; *OR*, vol. 34, pt. 1, p. 308.

41. *RJCCW, Vol. 2, RRE*, 11–12.

42. Joiner, "To Defend the Sacred Soil of Texas," 15–16; Johnson, *Red River Campaign*, 211–13; *ORN*, vol. 26, p. 49.

43. Craig Swain, "C.S.A. Brigadier General Tom Green," Historical Marker Database, updated April 24, 2022, https://www.hmdb.org/m.asp?m=7575.

44. The number of Confederate casualties for both days is based on several sources. There is room for speculation, as many of these are contradictory as to the number of Confederates captured at Pleasant Hill. In his memoir, Richard Taylor stated his combined losses for both battles were 2,626, with 1,000 killed, wounded, and missing at Mansfield and 1,626 at Pleasant Hill, including 426 men captured in the latter action. In his book, Ludwell Johnson also puts the total number of Confederate losses at 2,626. Several conflicting Union reports indicated between 400 and 1,000 Rebels were captured at Pleasant Hill. Nathaniel Banks reported 500 Confederates captured, while Charles Stone, his chief of staff, placed the number at 400 to 500. A. J. Smith had the most significant number, reporting "nearly 1,000" Confederates taken at Pleasant Hill. Blessington put the number of Confederates captured in his manuscript at "about 250." Taylor, *Destruction and Reconstruction*, 171; Johnson, *Red River Campaign*, 169; *OR*, vol. 34, pt. 1, pp. 184, 260, 309, 313, 553; *OR*, vol. 34, pt. 3, p. 100; Blessington, *Campaigns of Walker's Texas Division*, 199; Joiner, *One Damn Blunder*, 99, 103, 116.

45. Taylor, *Destruction and Reconstruction*, 171, 178.

46. Taylor, *Destruction and Reconstruction*, 178; Blessington, *Campaigns of Walker's Texas Division*, 200; Kirby-Smith, "Defense of the Red River," 4:366.
47. *RJCCW, Vol. 2, RRE*, 12–13.
48. By investigating regimental records, Joiner gives a higher casualty rate than the official Union estimate of 2,235. Joiner, *Red River Campaign*, 79, 89–90.
49. Johnson, *Red River Campaign*, 168–69, *RJCCW, Vol. 2, RRE*, 13; *OR*, vol. 34, pt. 1, pp. 553, 568.
50. Johnson, *Red River Campaign*, 110; Joiner, *One Damn Blunder*, 79–81; *RJCCW, Vol. 2, RRE*, 192–93; *OR*, vol. 34, pt. 1, p. 308.
51. Brig. Gen. William H. Emory commanded the First Division, Nineteenth Corps, and Brig. Gen. William Dwight commanded his First Brigade. *RJCCW, Vol. 2, RRE*, 13.
52. *OR*, vol. 34, pt. 1, pp. 184–85.
53. "History of the Battle of Pleasant Hill," BattleofPleasantHill.com, accessed July 9, 2023, https://battleofpleasanthill.com/history/.
54. In his after-action report, Parsons indicated his division had 2,200 men in seven regiments and one artillery battery. Tappan did not indicate a number, but he had five regiments and one artillery battery. Churchill indicated he had 4,300 muskets in his entire command on April 8. If both figures are correct, Tappan should have had 2,100 men in his five regiments. *OR*, vol. 34, pt. 1, pp. 601–6; *OR*, vol. 53, p. 477; Pinnell, entries for March 20, 1864, and March 24, 1864, in *Serving with Honor*, 146–47.
55. *OR*, vol. 34, pt. 1, p. 523; *OR*, vol. 34, pt. 2, p. 1056; *OR*, vol. 53, p. 477; Taylor, *Destruction and Reconstruction*, 164–65; Pinnell, entries for April 3, 1864, through April 9, 1864, in *Serving with Honor*, 150–52.
56. *OR*, vol. 34, pt. 1, pp. 565–66, 607–8.
57. Pellet, *History of the 114th Regiment*, 193–94; Beecher, *Record of the 114th Regiment*, 308; Taylor, *Destruction and Reconstruction*, 165–68; Johnson, *Red River Campaign*, 150, 168.
58. *OR*, vol. 34, pt. 1, p. 183; *RJCCW, Vol. 2, RRE*, 176; Hollandsworth, *Pretense of Glory*, 191.
59. Brooksher, *War along the Bayous*, 125–35.
60. *OR*, vol. 53, p. 477–78.
61. *OR*, vol. 34, vol. 1, pp. 303, 305, 307; Brooksher, *War along the Bayous*, 55–56; Johnson, *Red River Campaign*, 97.

62. *OR*, vol. 34, vol. 1, pp. 307–8.
63. Taylor, *Destruction and Reconstruction*, pp. 167-68
64. *OR*, vol. 34, vol. 1, pp. 308–9, 563–68.
65. *OR*, vol. 34, vol. 1, pp. 308–9.
66. Taylor, *Destruction and Reconstruction*, p. 170; Joiner, *One Damn Blunder*, 114–15.
67. Ethel G. Hellerman, "Dixie's Daughters to Deed Mansfield Battle Park to State," *Alexandria (LA) Daily–Town Talk*, August 9, 1954; "Mansfield Battle Park Survey Is Underway," *Shreveport (LA) Journal*, July 8, 1955; "Mansfield State Historic Site," Louisiana State Parks, accessed July 2, 2023, https://www.lastateparks.com/historic-sites/mansfield-state-historic-site.
68. Taylor, *Destruction and Reconstruction*, 160–61; Kerby, *Kirby Smith's Confederacy*, 284–85.
69. *OR*, vol. 26, pt. 2, p. 294; *OR*, vol. 34, pt. 2, p. 1035; Johnson, *Red River Campaign*, 86–87.
70. *OR*, vol. 34, pt. 1, pp. 478–80, 494, 496, 500, 578; *OR*, vol. 34, pt. 2, pp. 1027, 1029; Joiner, *Red River Campaign*, 69; Taylor, *Destruction and Reconstruction*, 153, 156, 162.
71. *OR*, vol. 34, pt. 1, p. 479; *OR*, vol. 34, pt. 2, pp. 1056, 1062–63; *OR*, vol. 34, pt. 3, pp. 745, 760–61.
72. *OR*, vol. 34, pt. 1, p. 480; Boggs, *Military Reminiscences*, 75.
73. Taylor, *Destruction and Reconstruction*, 154, 158–59; Joiner, *One Damn Blunder*, 33, 84–85.
74. A good overview of these communications is contained in both men's after-action reports. *OR*, vol. 34, pt. 1, pp. 476–528, 560–95.
75. *OR*, vol. 34, pt. 1, p. 522.
76. Taylor, *Destruction and Reconstruction*, 158–59, 160; Kerby, *Kirby Smith's Confederacy*, 303; *OR*, vol. 34, pt. 1, pp. 522, 525–26.
77. *OR*, vol. 34, pt. 1, p. 526.
78. Joiner, *One Damn Blunder*, 94; Mitcham, *Richard Taylor*, 141–42; *OR*, vol. 34, pt. 1, p. 528.
79. Kinard, *Lafayette of the South*, 119.
80. *OR*, vol. 34, pt. 1, p. 527.
81. Flinn, *Campaigning with Banks in Louisiana*, 109.
82. By investigating regimental records, Joiner gives a higher casualty rate

than the official Union estimate of 2,235. Joiner, *Red River Campaign*, 79.

83. *OR*, vol. 34, pt. 1, p. 267; Joiner, *Red River Campaign*, 77; Snell, *From First to Last*, 308–9.
84. *OR*, vol. 34, pt. 1, pp. 307, 389–92.
85. Taylor, *Destruction and Reconstruction*, 163; *OR*, vol. 34, pt. 1, p. 553, 564; Bergeron, *Guide to Louisiana Confederate Military Units*, 119, 138–39, 146–47; Bergeron, "Colonel Gains His Wreath," 21–23.
86. Taylor, *Destruction and Reconstruction*, 165.
87. *OR*, vol. 34, pt. 1, pp. 526–28.
88. Taylor, *Destruction and Reconstruction*, 164.
89. Brig. Gen. William H. Emory commanded the First Division, Nineteenth Corps, and Brig. Gen. William Dwight commanded his First Brigade. *RJCCW, Vol. 2, RRE*, 13.
90. Andrews, *North Reports the Civil War*, 516.
91. "Civil War and National Cemeteries (1867)," US Department of Veterans Affairs, National Cemetery Administration, updated August 18, 2021, https://www.cem.va.gov/cem/history/timeline/timeline-1867.asp; Telephone interview with Judson Rives (member of the Mansfield Cemetery Association), October 9, 2023.
92. *OR*, vol. 41, pt. 1, pp. 566, 568, 596; Taylor, *Destruction and Reconstruction*, 171.
93. Taylor, *Destruction and Reconstruction*, 170, 179; Kerby, *Kirby Smith's Confederacy*, 311.
94. Parks, *General Kirby-Smith, CSA*, 394–96.
95. *OR*, vol. 34, pt. 3, pp. 77–79; Johnson, *Red River Campaign*, 204.
96. Kirby-Smith, "Defense of the Red River," 4:372.
97. The exact number of Confederates sent to Arkansas to support Sterling Price after the Battle of Pleasant Hill is up for debate—the records are imperfect. I estimate the number to be roughly 5,000. In his book on Kirby-Smith, Joseph Parks puts the number as approximately 4,000 to 5.000 men. He cites Sterling Price's after-action report on the Camden Expedition as the source. In his memoir, Richard Taylor indicated he had 13,000 men when the campaign started and 5,200 men under his command after Walker and Churchill were sent north. The 5,200 included the command of Brig. Gen. St. John R. Liddell (600 men) operating east of the Red River. That is a difference of 7,800. Subtracting

for casualties at Mansfield and Pleasant Hill (2,626—see note 4 for chapter 2) leaves 5,174 men sent north. Additional losses and straggling would probably place the number just below 5,000. Parks, *General Kirby-Smith, CSA*, 380; *OR*, vol. 34, pt. 3, pp. 633, 779; Taylor, *Destruction and Reconstruction*, 191–92.

98. Taylor, *Destruction and Reconstruction*, 180; Parrish, *Richard Taylor*, 375.

99. *OR*, vol. 34, pt. 1, p. 476; Taylor, *Destruction and Reconstruction*, 180, 196.

100. *OR*, vol. 34, pt. 1, pp. 662–63.

101. *OR*, vol. 34, pt. 1, p. 487.

102. Brock, *Eric Brock's Shreveport*, 17–22, 33–37; Alma Burba, "Ft. Humbug Was a Monumental Joke of War between the States," *Shreveport (LA) Times*, June 28, 1935.

103. Hess, *Braxton Bragg*, 113, 120–21.

104. Dawson, "Theophilus H. Holmes and Confederate Generalship," 30–38.

105. *OR*, vol. 15, p. 948.

106. *OR*, vol. 22, pt. 2, pp. 786–87.

107. Cullum, *Biographical Register*, 2:515–71; Warner, *Generals in Gray*, 28; Boggs, *Military Reminiscences*, vii–xxi.

108. Boggs, *Military Reminiscences*, xxii.

109. Joiner, *Through the Howling Wilderness*, 18.

110. *OR*, vol. 34, pt. 2, pp. 221, 223, 424.

111. Kirby-Smith, "Defense of the Red River," 4:369.

112. Joiner, *One Damn Blunder*, 16–17, 23–24, 26–27; *OR*, vol. 34, pt. 2, p. 1056.

113. *OR*, vol. 26, pt. 2, p. 322.

114. Chester G. Hern, *Admiral David Dixon Porter: The Civil War Years* (Annapolis, MD: Naval Institute Press, 1996), 249–51.

115. "Jenkins Ferry Battleground State Park," Arkansas State Parks, accessed July 9, 2023, https://www.arkansasstateparks.com/parks/jenkins-ferry-battleground-state-park#.UqYAHpCJD4w .

116. *OR*, vol. 34, pt. 2, pp. 149–50, 246–47, 546–47, 576, 616.

117. Sutherland, "1864: A Strange and Wild Time," 105–8.

118. *OR*, vol. 34, pt. 1, p. 657.

119. *OR*, vol. 34, pt. 1, pp. 657, 692; *OR*, vol. 34, pt. 2, pp. 638, 707; Johnson, *Red River Campaign*, 170–71.
120. Johnson, *Red River Campaign*, 170–71.
121. *OR*, vol. 34, pt. 1, pp. 661, 667–71.
122. *OR*, vol. 34, pt. 1, p. 683.

BIBLIOGRAPHY

Ambrose, Stephen E. *Halleck: Lincoln's Chief of Staff.* Baton Rouge: Louisiana State University Press, 1962.

Anders, Curt. *Henry Halleck's War: A Fresh Look at Lincoln's Controversial General-in-Chief.* Carmel: Guild Press of Indiana, 1999.

Anderson, J. L. "The Vacant Chair on the Farm: Soldier Husbands, Farm Wives, and the Iowa Home Front, 1861–1865." *Annals of Iowa* 66 (Summer–Fall 2007): 241–65.

Andrews, J. Cutler. *The North Reports the Civil War.* 1955. Reprint. Pittsburgh, PA: University of Pittsburgh Press, 1985.

Andrews, L. F. "The Word 'Iowa'—What It Means." *Annals of Iowa*, 3rd series, 2, no. 6 (1896): 465-69.

Bearss, Edwin C. *The Campaign for Vicksburg.* Vol. 1, *Vicksburg Is the Key.* Dayton, OH: Morningside House, 1985.

———. *Protecting Sherman's Lifeline: The Battles of Brice's Cross Roads and Tupelo.* Washington, DC: Office of Publications, National Park Service, US Department of the Interior, 1971.

Bearss, Edwin C., and Edwin S. Bearss. "The Battle of the Post of Arkansas." *Arkansas Historical Quarterly* 18, no. 3 (1959): 237-79.

Beecher, Dr. Harris H. *Record of the 114th Regiment, N.Y.S.V.: Where It Went, What It Saw, and What It Did.* Norwich, NY: J. F. Hubbard, 1896.

Bergeron, Arthur W., Jr. "A Colonel Gains His Wreath: Henry Gray and His Louisiana Brigade at the Battle of Mansfield, April 8, 1864." In *The Red River Campaign: Union and Confederate Leadership and the War in Louisiana*, edited by Theodore P. Savas, David A. Woodbury, and Gary D. Joiner. Shreveport, LA: Parabellum, 2003: 1-25.

———. *Guide to Louisiana Confederate Military Units, 1861–1865*. Baton Rouge: Louisiana State University Press, 1989.

Black, Robert C. *The Railroads of the Confederacy*. 1952. Reprint. Chapel Hill: University of North Carolina Press, 1998.

Blessington, Joseph Palmer. *The Campaigns of Walker's Texas Division: By a Private Soldier, Containing a Complete Record of the Campaigns in Texas, Louisiana, and Arkansas* [. . .]. New York: Lange, Little, 1875.

Boggs, William R. *Military Reminiscences of Gen. Wm. R. Boggs, C.S.A.* Introduction and notes by William K. Boyd. Durham, NC: Seeman Printery, 1913.

Bourne, Jenny. "Slavery in the United States." EH.Net Encyclopedia of Economic and Business History. Edited by Robert Whaples. Updated March 26, 2008. http://eh.net/encyclopedia/slavery-in-the-united-states/.

"A Brief History of Fort DeRussy." Friends of Fort DeRussy, Inc. Updated April 10, 2014. http://www.fortderussy.org/briefhistory.html.

Brock, Eric. *Eric Brock's Shreveport*. Gretna, LA: Pelican, 2001.

Brooksher, William Riley. *War along the Bayous: The 1864 Red River Campaign in Louisiana*. Lincoln: Potomac Books / University of Nebraska Press, 1998.

Burba, Alma. "Ft. Humbug Was a Monumental Joke of War between the States." *Shreveport (LA) Times*, June 28, 1935.

Cardin, Clifton D. *Bossier Parish History: The First 150 Years. 1843-1993* (Shreveport: Image Press, 1993)

Chernow, Ron. *Grant*. New York: Penguin, 2017.

Christ, Mark K. "Not Fortunate in War: Major General Thomas James Churchill." In *Confederate Generals of the Trans-Mississippi*, edited by Lawrence L. Hewitt, Arthur W. Bergeron Jr., and Thomas E. Schott, 1:167-194. Knoxville: University of Tennessee Press, 2013.

"Civil War and National Cemeteries (1867)." US Department of Veterans Affairs, National Cemetery Administration. Updated August 18, 2021. https://www.cem.va.gov/cem/history/timeline/timeline-1867.asp.

Cowsert, Zac. "The Civil War's Bloodiest Battles West of the Mississippi River." *Civil Discourse: A Civil War Era Blog*, May 20, 2019. http://civil discourse-historyblog.com/blog/2018/10/13/battle-in-the-trans-mississippi -a-cursory-quantative-analysis#:~:text=The%20ten%20bloodiest%20battles %20of,' %20Ferry%2C%20Arkansas%20(1%2C700)%3B.

Cullum, Bvt. Maj. Gen. George W. *Biographical Register of the Officers and Graduates of the U.S. Military Academy at West Point*, 2 vols. N.Y. Boston: Houghton, Mifflin, 1891.

Cutrer, Thomas W. "Allen, Robert Thomas Pritchard (1813–1888)." *Handbook of Texas*. Updated November 1, 1994. https://www.tshaonline.org /handbook/entries/allen-robert-thomas-pritchard.

———. "Medford, Harvey C. (1831–1902)." *Handbook of Texas*. Updated April 1, 1995. https://www.tshaonline.org/handbook/entries/medford -harvey-c.

Dawson, Joseph G., III. "Theophilus H. Holmes and Confederate Generalship." In *Confederate Generals of the Trans-Mississippi*, edited by Lawrence L. Hewitt, Arthur W. Bergeron Jr., and Thomas E. Schott, 1:25-55. Knoxville: University of Tennessee Press, 2013.

Dobak, William A. *Freedom by the Sword: The U.S. Colored Troops, 1862–1867*. 2011. Reprint. Alexandria, VA: St. John's Press, 2016.

Dorsey, Sarah, A. *Recollections of Henry Watkins Allen: Brigadier General Confederate States Army and Governor of Louisiana*. New York: M. Doolady, 1866.

Dufour, Charles L. *Nine Men in Gray*. Garden City, NY: Doubleday, 1963.

Eicher, John H., and David J. Eicher. *Civil War High Commands*. Stanford, CA: Stanford University Press, 2001.

Ewer, James Kendall. *The Third Massachusetts Cavalry in the War for the Union: Company C, Third Mass. Cav.* Maplewood, MA: Historical Committee of the Regimental Association, 1903.

Fehrenbach, T. R. *Lone Star: A History of Texas and the Texans*. New York: American Legacy, 1983.

Flinn, Frank M. *Campaigning with Banks in Louisiana, '63 and '64, and with Sheridan in the Shenandoah Valley in '64 and '65.* Boston: W. B. Clark, 1889.

"Forts Randolph & Buhlow State Historic Site." Louisiana State Parks. Accessed July 9, 2023. https://www.lastateparks.com/historic-sites/forts -randolph-buhlow-state-historic-site.

Frazier, Donald S. *Tempest Over Texas: The Fall and Winter Campaigns of 1863–1864*. Kerrville, TX: State House Press at Schreiner University, 2020.

Goc, Michael J. *The Hero of the Red River: The Life and Times of Joseph Bailey*. Friendship, WI: B. E. Gussel and New Past, 2007.

Grizzle, Ralph. "Paddle-Wheelers on the Mississippi, Steamboats on the Rhine & the Rise of KD River Line." River Cruise Advisor. Updated February 18, 2021. https://www.rivercruiseadvisor.com/2021/02/kd-cruises/.

Harrington, Fred Harvey. *Fighting Politician: Major General N. P. Banks*. London: Oxford University Press, 1948.

Hellerman, Ethel G. "Dixie's Daughters to Deed Mansfield Battle Park to State." *Alexandria (LA) Daily-Town Talk*, August 9, 1954.

Hern, Chester G. *Admiral David Dixon Porter: The Civil War Years*. Annapolis, MD: Naval Institute Press, 1996.

Hess, Earl J. *Braxton Bragg: The Most Hated Man of the Confederacy*. Chapel Hill: University of North Carolina Press, 2016.

———. *The Civil War in the West: Victory and Defeat from the Appalachians to the Mississippi*. Chapel Hill: University of North Carolina Press, 2012.

———. *Civil War Logistics: A Study of Military Transportation*. Baton Rouge: Louisiana State University Press, 2017.

Hewitt, Lawrence Lee. *Port Hudson: Confederate Bastion on the Mississippi*. Baton Rouge: Louisiana State University Press, 1987.

An Historical Sketch of the 162nd Regiment N.Y. Vol. Infantry: (3d Metropolitan Guard), 19th Army Corps, 1862–1865. Albany, NY: Weed, Parsons, 1867.

"History of the Battle of Pleasant Hill." BattleofPleasantHill.com. Accessed July 9, 2023. https://battleofpleasanthill.com/history/.

Hoffman, Wickham. *Camp, Court and Siege: A Narrative of Personal Adventure and Observation during Two Wars, 1861–1865; 1870–1871*. New York: Harper and Brothers, 1877.

Hollandsworth, James. D. *Pretense of Glory: The Life of General Nathaniel P. Banks*. Baton Rouge: Louisiana State University Press, 1998.

Irwin, Richard B. *History of the Nineteenth Army Corps*. New York: G. P. Putnam and Sons, 1892.

———. "The Red River Campaign." In *Battles and Leaders of the Civil War*, edited by Robert Underwood Johnson and Clarence Clough Buel, 4: 345-361. New York: Century, 1887.

"Jackson Square in the French Quarter." Experience New Orleans. Accessed July 9, 2023. https://www.experienceneworleans.com/jackson-square.html.

"Jenkins Ferry Battleground State Park." Arkansas State Parks. Accessed July 9, 2023. https://www.arkansasstateparks.com/parks/jenkins-ferry-battleground-state-park#.UqYAHpCJD4w.

Johnson, Ludwell H. *Red River Campaign: Politics & Cotton in the Civil War.* Kent, OH: Kent State University Press, 1993.

Joiner, Gary D. *Mr. Lincoln's Brown Water Navy: The Mississippi Squadron.* Lanham, MD: Rowman and Littlefield, 2007.

———. *One Damn Blunder from Beginning to End: The Red River Campaign of 1864.* Wilmington, DE: Scholarly Resources, 2003.

———. *The Red River Campaign: The Union's Final Attempt to Invade Texas.* Buffalo Gap, TX: State House Press, 2013.

———. *Through the Howling Wilderness: The 1864 Red River Campaign and Failure in the West.* Knoxville: University of Tennessee Press, 2006.

———. "To Defend the Sacred Soil of Texas: Tom Green and the Texas Cavalry in the Red River Campaign." *East Texas Historical Journal* 46, no. 1 (March 2008): 11-17.

Kerby, Robert L. *Kirby Smith's Confederacy: The Trans-Mississippi South, 1863–1865.* New York: Columbia University Press, 1972.

Kinard, Jeff. *Lafayette of the South: Prince Camille de Polignac and the American Civil War.* College Station: Texas A&M University Press, 2001.

Kirby-Smith, Gen. E. "The Defense of the Red River." In *Battles and Leaders of the Civil War,* edited by Robert Underwood Johnson and Clarence Clough Buel. New York: Century, 1887: 4:369-378.

Lamb, Blaine. *The Extraordinary Life of Charles Pomeroy Stone: Soldier, Surveyor, Pasha, Engineer.* Yardley, PA: Westholme, 2015.

Lincoln, Abraham. *The Collected Works of Abraham Lincoln, in Eight Volumes.* 8 vols. Edited by Roy Basler. New Brunswick, NJ: Rutgers University Press, 1953.

———. "The Proclamation of Amnesty and Reconstruction by the President of the United States of America." In *U.S. Statutes at Large, Treaties, and Proclamations of the United States of America,* vol. 13:737–39. Boston: Little, Brown, 1866.

Lowe, Richard. *Walker's Texas Division C.S.A.: Greyhounds of the Trans-Mississippi.* Baton Rouge: Louisiana State University Press, 2004.

"LTC Richard Biddle Irwin." Find a Grave. Updated October 9, 2005. https://www.findagrave.com/memorial/11918187/richard-biddle-irwin.

"Mansfield Battle Park Survey Is Underway." *Shreveport (LA) Journal*, July 8, 1955.

"Mansfield State Historic Site." Louisiana State Parks. Accessed July 02, 2023. https://www.lastateparks.com/historic-sites/mansfield-state-historic-site.

Maury, Gen. D. H. "Sketch of General Richard Taylor." In *Southern Historical Society Papers*, edited by Rev. J. William Jones, 7: 343-345. 1879.

McDonough, James Lee. *William Tecumseh Sherman: In the Service of My Country; A Life*. New York: W. W. Norton, 2016.

McMurry, Richard M. *Two Great Rebel Armies: An Essay in Confederate Military History*. Chapel Hill: University of North Carolina Press, 1989.

McPherson, James M. *The Illustrated Battle Cry of Freedom: The Civil War Era*. New York: Oxford University Press, 2003.

Medford, Harvey C. "The Diary of H. C. Medford, Confederate Soldier, 1864." Edited by Rebecca W. Smith, Marion Mullins. *Southwestern Historical Quarterly* 34, no. 3: 106-230 (January 1931).

"The Mississippi Flotilla in the Red River Expedition." In *Battles and Leaders of the Civil War*, edited by Robert Underwood Johnson and Clarence Clough Buel. New York: Century, 1887: 4:366.

"Mississippi River Facts." National Park Service. Updated April 14, 2021. https://www.nps.gov/miss/riverfacts.htm.

Mitcham, Samuel W., Jr. *Richard Taylor and the Red River Campaign of 1864*. Gretna, LA: Pelican, 2012.

Montgomery, Don. "Thomas James Churchill (1824–1905)." *Encyclopedia of Arkansas*. Updated November 19, 2020. https://encyclopediaofarkansas.net/entries/thomas-james-churchill-92/.

Nicolay, John G., and John Hay. *Abraham Lincoln: A History*. 10 vols. New York: Century, 1890.

Noel, Theo [Theophilus] A. *A Campaign from Santa Fe to the Mississippi: Being a History of the Old Sibley Brigade from Its First Organization to the Present Time; Its Campaigns in New Mexico, Arizona, Texas, Louisiana, and Arkansas, in the Years of 1861–2–3–4*. Shreveport, LA: Shreveport News Printing Establishment, 1865.

Parks, Joseph Howard. *General Kirby-Smith, CSA*. Baton Rouge: Louisiana State University Press, 1954.

Parrish, T. Michael. *Richard Taylor: Soldier Prince of Dixie*. Chapel Hill: University of North Carolina Press, 1992.

Pellet, Elias Porter. *History of the 114th Regiment, New York State Volunteers: Containing a Perfect Record of Its Services, Embracing All Its Marches, Campaigns, Battles, Sieges and Sea-Voyages, with a Biographical Sketch of Each Officer, and a Complete Register of the Regiment* [. . .]. Norwich, NY: Telegraph and Chronicle Power Press Print, 1866.

Peterson, Larry. *Decisions of the 1862 Kentucky Campaign: The Twenty-Seven Critical Decisions That Defined the Operation*. Knoxville: University of Tennessee Press, 2019.

Petty, Elijah P. *Journey to Pleasant Hill: The Civil War Letters of Captain Elijah P. Petty, Walker's Texas Division, CSA*. Edited by Norman D. Brown. San Antonio: University of Texas, Institute of Texan Cultures, 1982.

Pinnell, Ethan Allen. *Serving with Honor: The Diary of Captain Ethan Allen Pinnell of the Eighth Missouri Infantry (Confederate)*. Edited by Michael E. Banasik. Iowa City, IA: Press of the Camp Pope Bookshop, 1999.

Porter, David Dixon. *Incidents and Anecdotes of the Civil War*. New York: D. Appleton, 1886.

Prushankin, Jeffery S. "To Carry Off the Glory: Edmund Kirby-Smith in 1864." In *Confederate Generals of the Trans-Mississippi*, edited by Lawrence L. Hewitt, Arthur W. Bergeron Jr., and Thomas E. Schott, 1: 57-90. Knoxville: University of Tennessee Press, 2013.

Rives, Judson (member of the Mansfield Cemetery Association). Telephone interview with author. October 9, 2023.

Robertson, Henry O. *The Red River Campaign and Its Toll: 69 Bloody Days in Louisiana, March–May 1864*. Jefferson, NC: McFarland, 2016.

Sage, Leland L. *A History of Iowa*. Ames: Iowa State University Press, 1974.

Sandburg, Carl. *Abraham Lincoln: The Prairie Years and the War Years*. One volume edition. New York; Harcourt, Brace, 1954.

Schneider, Paul. *Old Man River: The Mississippi River in North American History*. New York: Picador, 2014.

Scott, John. *Story of the Thirty-Second Iowa Infantry Volunteers*. Nevada, IA: self-published, 1896.

Sears, Stephen W. *Lincoln's Lieutenants: The High Command of the Army of the Potomac*. Boston: Houghton Mifflin Harcourt, 2017.

Sesser, David. "Sterling Price (1809–1867)." *Encyclopedia of Arkansas*. Updated April 9, 2022. https://encyclopediaofarkansas.net/entries/sterling

-price-2815/#:~:text=Sterling%20Price%20was%20a%20farmer,and%20 during%20the%20Camden%20Expedition.

Sherman, William T. *Home Letters of General Sherman*. Edited by M. A. DeWolf Howe. New York: Scribner and Sons, 1909.

———. *The Personal Memoirs of William T. Sherman*. 1885. Reprint. New York: Da Capo, 1984.

———. *Sherman's Civil War: Selected Correspondence of William T. Sherman, 1860–1865*. Edited by Brooks D. Simpson, Jean V. Berlin. Chapel Hill: University of North Carolina Press, 1999.

Snell, Mark A. *From First to Last: The Life of Major General William B. Franklin*. New York: Fordham University Press, 2002.

Sprague, Homer B. *History of the 13th Infantry Regiment of Connecticut Volunteers during the Great Rebellion*. Hartford, CT: Case, Lockwood, 1867.

Stewart, William H. Diary. Southern Historical Collection, Wilson Library, University of North Carolina at Chapel Hill.

Sutherland, Daniel E. "1864: A Strange and Wild Time." In *Rugged and Sublime: The Civil War in Arkansas*, edited by Mark K. Christ. Fayetteville: University of Arkansas Press, 1994: 105-144.

Swain, Craig. "C.S.A. Brigadier General Tom Green." Historical Marker Database. Updated April 24, 2022. https://www.hmdb.org/m.asp?m=7575.

Symonds, Craig L. *Joseph E. Johnston: A Civil War Biography*. New York: W. W. Norton, 1992.

Taylor, Richard. *Destruction and Reconstruction: Personal Experiences of the Late War*. New York: D. Appleton, 1883.

Texas in the Civil War. Austin: Texas Historical Commission, 2013.

Thomas, William G. *The Iron Way: Railroads, the Civil War, and the Making of Modern America*. New Haven, CT: Yale University Press, 2011.

Tyson, Carl Newton. *The Red River in Southwestern History*. Norman: University of Oklahoma Press, 1981.

United States Census Bureau. 1860 Census: Population of the United States, State of Texas. Updated December 16, 2021. https://www2.census.gov/library/publications/decennial/1860/population/1860a-34.pdf.

United States Department of the Interior. "History & Culture—Vicksburg Military Park." National Park Service. Updated July 26, 2019. https://www.nps.gov/vick/learn/historyculture/index.htm.

United States Government Printing Office. *Report of the Joint Committee on the Conduct of the War: Vol. 2, Red River Expedition*. Washington, DC: United States Government, 1865.

United States War Department. *The War of the Rebellion: Official Records of the Union and Confederate Armies*, 69 vols. Washington, DC: United States Government Printing Office, 1874–80.

———. *The War of the Rebellion: Official Records of the Union and Confederate Navies*, 30 vols. Washington, DC: United States Government Printing Office, 1874–80.

"U.S. Custom House, New Orleans, LA." United States General Services Administration. Updated August 13, 2017. https://www.gsa.gov/historic-buildings/us-custom-house-new-orleans-la#overview.

Warner, Ezra J. *Generals in Blue: Lives of the Union Commanders*. Baton Rouge: Louisiana State University, 1964.

———. *Generals in Gray: Lives of the Confederate Commanders*. Baton Rouge: Louisiana State University, 1959.

"Welcome to the Grand Ecore Visitor Center." US Army Corps of Engineers, Vicksburg District website. Accessed July 9, 2023. https://www.mvk.usace.army.mil/Missions/Recreation/Grand-Ecore-Visitor-Center/.

Williams, Richard Brady. *Chicago's Battery Boys: The Chicago Mercantile Battery in the Civil War's Western Theater*. New York: Savis Beatie LLC, 2005.

Winters, John D. *The Civil War in Louisiana*. Baton Rouge: Louisiana State University Press, 1963.

Woodworth, Steven. "General A. J. Smith's Guerrillas and the Battle of Nashville." Talk presented at 1864: The Western Theater symposium, Civil War Center, Kennesaw State University, Kennesaw, GA, March 22, 2014. C-SPAN—the Civil War Series, American History TV. https://www.c-span.org/video/?318492-2/general-aj-smiths-guerrillas-battle-nashville.

Wooster, Ralph A., and Robert Wooster. "People at War: East Texans during the Civil War." *East Texas Historical Journal* 28, no. 1 (1990): 3-16.

INDEX

Numbers in **boldface** refer to illustrations

Abbreviations:
Adm = Admiral
Capt = Captain
Co = Company
Corp = Corporal
DotTM = Department of the
    Trans-Mississippi
GIC = General In Chief
JCCW = Joint Committee on the
    Conduct of the War
Lieut = Lieutenant
Reg = Regiment
Rr. Adm = Rear Admiral

Act to Establish and Protect National
    Cemeteries, 175
Alabama, 3, 24, 99, 122, 131
Alabama River, 131
Alexandria, LA, after Mansfield/
    Pleasant Hill, 1, **33**, 103, 112,
    118, 119; Baily's Dam, 2; before
    Mansfield/Pleasant Hill, 19, 31, 34,
37, 41–53, 65, 73, 93; Confederate
    communication, 12, 180; Decisions
    Tour, 129, 138–43, 147, 149, 153, 156,
    158, 164, 168, 182–84; Union com-
    munications, 145, 146
Allegheny River, xii
Allen, Robert T. P., Col., CSA, 116
American Battlefield Trust, 167
Anaconda Plan, xii
Angelina County, TX, 99
Angola, LA, xii
Appalachian Mountains, xi
Arizona Territory, 5, 15
Arkadelphia, AR, 60, 110, 139, 176, 186
Arkansas, xii, xix, 86; military actions
    prior to the Red River Campaign,
    22, 38, 56, 169, 180, 182; Camden
    Expedition, 19, 25, 26, 43, 58–62,
    105, 119; Confederate actions
    during the Red River Campaign,
    74, 87, 89, 90, 106, 109–12, 115, 118;
    Decisions Tour, 127, 134, 160,

Arkansas (*cont.*)
174–78, 183–86; Department of the Trans-Mississippi, 18; Union communications, 132, 135, 162
Arkansas Post, Battle of, xi, 86, 92
Arkansas River, 86
Army of Tennessee, CSA, 13, 16, 17, 41, 122, 179
Army of the Cumberland, USA, 22
Army of the James, USA, 3
Army of the Mississippi, CSA, 16
Army of the Potomac, USA, 3, 4, 13, 141, 179
Army of the Southwest, USA, 56
Army of the Tennessee, USA, 3, 29, 31, 92, 123, 144, 145, 165
Atchafalaya River, xii, 45, 72, 112, 114, 119, 138, 176
Atlanta, GA, 3, 21, 22, 24, 29, 30, 41, 123, 131, 132
Atlanta Campaign, 22, 24, 132
Augusta, GA, 32
Austin, TX, 116, 179

Bailey, Joseph, Col., USA, 119
Bailey's Dam, 119, 147, 148
Ball's Bluff, Battle of, 12
Banks, Nathaniel P., Maj. Gen., USA, 4; actions after Mansfield/Pleasant Hill, 1, 2, 108–14, 118–21; actions at Alexandria, 45, 183, 119, 138; actions at Grand Ecore, 50–55, 118; actions at New Orleans, 44–49, 130, 137–43; actions at the Battle of Mansfield, 63, 68–81, 167–71; actions at the Battle of Pleasant Hill, 87–89, 91–96, 116, 160–66; actions before the Battle of Mansfield, 50–55, 63–70, 147–55; after-action report, Banks, 158–59; after-action report, Brig. Gen. Andrew Jackson Smith, 166; after the Red River Campaign, 121; commands before the Red River Campaign, 3–5, 9; communication from David Dixon Porter to Sherman, 150; communication from Grant to Sherman, 30, 132, 133; communication from Sherman to A. J. Smith, 145; communication from Banks to Halleck, 139; communication from Grant to Banks, 141; communication from Halleck to Grant, 131, 132; communication from Halleck to Sherman, 136; Confederate communication from Taylor to Kirby-Smith, 170, 171; life after the War, 121; life before the War, 3; letters to his wife, 1, 65; relieved of command, 119; retreat from Mansfield, 79–87, 171–74; retreat from Pleasant Hill, 100–106, 108, 155–59, 175, 176; testimony before the JCCW, 100, 153–155; the Union advances up the Red River, 11, 22–26, 29–32, 37–44, 57, 59–62, 132–36, 144–46, 184
Bastrop, TX, 116
Baton Rouge, LA, 119, 129
Bayou Bourbeux, Battle of, 115
Bayou Pierre, LA, 87, 150
Bayou Teche, LA, 5
Beauregard, Pierre Gustave Toutant, Gen., CSA, 92
Bee, Bernard, Brig. Gen., CSA, 12
Bee, Hamilton P., Brig. Gen., CSA, 12, 119
Benedict, Lewis, Col., USA, 94, 164
Black Hawk, USA, 48, 118, 141, 156
Blair's Landing, 87, 106, 118, 156, **157**, 161
Blair's Landing, Battle of, 78, **107**, 156
Blessington, Joseph Palmer, Corp. CSA, 70, 71
Boggs, William Robertson, Brig. Gen. CSA, 32–35, **34**, 37, 181–83
Bonaparte, Napoleon, 79
Boyce, LA, 93
Boyd, J. Mitchell, Sgt., USA, 123

Bragg, Braxton, Gen, CSA, 2, 7, 13, 15–17, 22, 41, 179, 180
Brashear City, LA, 45, 138. *See also* Mogan City, LA
Bristoe Station, VA, 4
Brownsville, TX, 5
Bucks County, PA, 92
Bullock, John, Brig. Gen, CSA, 94, 164
Bull Run, Battle of, 4, 8, 13, 28
Butler, Benjamin F., Maj. Gen., USA, 3, 44, 137

Cajun Prairie, 45, 139
California, 28
Camden Expedition, **58**, 62, 184
Cameron, Robert A., Brig. Gen., USA, 68, 80, 154, 72
Camp Chase, OH, 86
Camp Franklin, 123
Camp Sumter, 87
Canal Street, New Orleans, LA, 129
Canby, Edward, Maj. Gen., USA, 20, 119, 122
Cane River, 106, 118, 183
Carr, Eugene Asa, Brig Gen., USA, 59, 186
Cedar Mountain, Battle of, 4
Chancellorsville, Battle of, 21, 130
Chapman's Bayou, 80, 83–85, 172, 131
Chattanooga, TN, xi, 2, 22, 29, 39
Chickamauga, Battle of, 22, 29
Chickasaw Bayou, Battle of, 29, 96
Childers, Maria, 116, 117
Churchill, Thomas James, Brig. Gen., CSA, **86**; after-action report, 162–63; Battle of Pleasant Hill, 89–91, 94, 108, 115, 160–62, 164; communication from Taylor to Kirby-Smith, 171; life prior to the Red River Campaign, 85, 86; return to Arkansas, 112, 176
Citronelle, AL, 122
Clark, John Bullock Jr., Brig. Gen. CSA, 94, 162, 164

Comanches, 12
Corinth, MS, 92
Cumberland River, xii, 22

Dalton, GA, 22
Davidson, John Wynn, Brig. Gen., USA, 59
Davis, Jefferson, 5, 8, 13, 15–19, 107, 109, **109**, 130, 179, 180
Davis Administration, CSA, 17, 18, 107
Dawson, Joseph G., 20
Delhi, NY, 55
Department of Alabama, Mississippi, and East Louisiana, 122
Department of Arkansas, USA, 25, 26, 56, 62
Department of North Carolina, CSA, 15
Department of Texas, CSA, 18, 19, 24, 26, 74, 133, 180, 182
Department of the Cumberland, USA, 28
Department of the Gulf, USA, 3, 4, 22, 24, 26, 31, 45, 70, 130–32, 138; Corps d'Afrique, 26, 69; Fifty-Eighth Illinois Regiment, 94, 164; Grover's Second Division, 65, 103, 153, 158; Landram's Fourth Division, 80, 172; Lee's Cavalry Division, 54, 68, 69, 70, 101; Mississippi Marine Brigade, 26, 48, 65, 153; McMillan's Second Brigade, xvi, 89, 162; Mower's Division, 123, 125; Nineteenth Corps, xvi, 45, 65, 68, 69, 80, 83, 89, 94, 103, 105, 138, 153, 158, 162–65, 171–73; Seventeenth Corps, 31, 66, 100, 103, 106, 118, 123, 145, 153, 158; Sixteenth Corps, 31, 68, 89, 145, 158, 162; Shaw's Second Brigade, 89, 116, 123, 162, 165; Thirteenth Corps, 45, 68, 69, 77, 80, 92, 94, 138, 159, 164, 171, 172; Thirty-Eighth Massachusetts, 89, 172; Thirty-Second Iowa, xvi, 123, 165

Department of the Mississippi, USA, 28, 29, 38
Department of the Missouri, USA, 21
Department of the Shenandoah, USA, 4
Department of the Trans-Mississippi, CSA, 18, 20, 178; Bee's Cavalry Division, 4; Churchill's Division, 87, 89–94, 108, 115, 160–65, 171; Crawford's Brigade, xvi; Crescent Consolidated Louisiana Regiment, 81, 172; District of Western Louisiana, 7, 8; Eleventh Texas Infantry, 99; Gray's Brigade, 81, 172; Green's Cavalry Corps, 48, 49, 69, 73, 74, 87, 94, 99, 101, 115, 118, 156, 161, 164, 168; Marmaduke's Division, xvi, 62, 110; Maxey's Cavalry Division, 74, 169; Mouton's Division, 77, 78, 81, 101, 115, 157, 171, 172; Polignac's Brigade, 73, 87, 161, 168; Seventeenth Texas Volunteer Infantry, 116; Sixteenth Texas Infantry, 70; Texas Division, 46, 62, 70, 71, 73, 87, 89, 112, 115, 116, 123, 143, 161, 162, 168, 176; Twelfth Texas Infantry, xvi
Department of the West, CSA, 16
Department of Western Louisiana, CSA, 18
DeRussy, Lewis G., Col., CSA, 143
Des Moines, USA, 124
Desoto Parish, LA, 175
Dickey, William H., Col., USA, 68
District of Southeast Missouri, 56
Dripping Springs, Battle of, 15, 180
Dubuque, IA, 123
Dwight, William, Brig. Gen., USA, 89, 105, 162, 173

Eastport, USA, 38, 117
Eighth Iowa Infantry, 56
Elkin's Ferry, Battle of, 111,

Emerson, Frank, Col., USA, 80, 172
Emory, William, Brig. Gen., USA, 84, 105, 154, 172, 173
Essex, USA, 124
Ewell, Richard S., Maj. Gen., CSA, 4, 8, 28
Ewell's Division, CSA, 28
Ewer, James Kendall, 63

Fair Oaks. *See* Seven Pines, Battle of
Farragut, David G., Adm., USA, 40
Fifteenth Corps, USA, 29, 56
First Arkansas Mounted Rifles, 86
First Dragoons, 92
First Kentucky Cavalry, 85
First Manassas. *See* Bull Run, Battle of
Florida, 7, 12, 28
Forrest, Nathan Bedford, Lieut. Gen., CSA, 93
Fort DeRussy, LA, 19, 34, 73, 115, 123, **144**, 168, 182; the capture of, 45, 46, 93, 96, 139, 143, 164
Fort DeRussy State Historic Site, LA, 143, 144
Fort Donelson, TN, xi, 123
Fort Henry, TN, xi, 123
Fort Hindman, AK, 86
Fort Smith, AR, 59, 60, 110, 176, 185, 186
Forts Randolph & Buhlow State Historic Site, LA, 143, 147, 148, **148**
Fort Sumter, SC, 3, 16, 79
France, 151
Franklin, Benjamin, 79
Franklin, William B., Maj. Gen., USA, 41, 54, 55, 79, **80**; actions at Mansfield and Pleasant Hill, 68, 69, 80, 104–6, 172, 173; testimony before the JCCW, 97, 105, 153, 154
Fredericksburg, Battle of, 13, 21, 179
Frémont, John C., Maj. Gen., USA, 3
Front Royal, Battle of, 4

Galveston, TX, 5
Georgia, 22, 28, 32, 33, 41
Gettysburg, Battle of, 2, 21, 130
Gilmer, James, 35, 182
Gooding, Oliver P., Col., USA, 69
Grand Ecore, LA, **51**, **56**, 143, 151, **152**, 156, 179; after Battles of Mansfield and Pleasant Hill, 61, 81, 83, 87, 104, 105, 112, 118, 158, 159, 161, 175, 177; before Battles of Mansfield and Pleasant Hill, 32, 48, 50, 53, 65, 68, 93, 141, 149, 164, 172, 183; testimony before the JCCW, 154, 155
Grand Encore Visitor Center, 151, 155
Granger, Gordon, Maj. Gen., USA, 12
Grant, Ulysses S., Lieut. Gen., USA, **39**, Battle of Shiloh, 28; Battle of the Wilderness, 50; Chattanooga Campaign, 2, 22, 29; communication from Banks to Halleck, 139; communication from Halleck to Sherman, 134; coms from Grant to Banks, 31, 50, 51, 141, 149; communication from Grant to Sherman, 30, 31, 41, 132, 135, 145; communication from Halleck to Grant, 30, 31, 39, 40, 131, 144; the command of the Union operation, 39, 40, 135; early commands, 21; promotion to GIC, 39, 42, 134, 136, 144; reactions to Mansfield and Pleasant Hill, 119; the Union's spring 1864 offensive plans, 3, 21–25, 41, 131, 132; the Union advances up the Red River, 26, 29, 57, 144, 185; Vicksburg Campaign, 13, 29, 83, 179; West Point, 55
Gray, Henry, Col., CSA, 73, 81, 168, 172
Green, Thomas, Brig. Gen., CSA, actions at Bayou Pierre, 87; actions at Blair's Landing, 118, 156; actions at Mansfield, 69; actions at Pleasant Hill, 87, 94, 115, 161, 164; actions at Wilson's Farm, 69, 101, 156; death, 118, 156; and Harvey C. Medford, 99; march from Texas, 48, 49, 73, 74, 168
Grover, Cuvier, Brig. Gen., USA, 65, 103, 153, 158
Gulf of Mexico, xxi, 101, 123, 131, 157

Hahn, George Michael Decker, 47, 48, 139, 140
Halleck, Henry, Maj. Gen., USA, **21**, 130; Battle of Corinth, 92; communication from Banks to Halleck, 48, 139; communication from Grant to Sherman, 132; communication from Halleck to Banks, 25; communication from Halleck to Grant, 29–31, 39, 131, 144; communication from Halleck to Sherman, 39, 134, 135; the command of the Union operation, 29–31, 40–43, 47, 57, 135, 136; demotion from GIC, 39, 134, 145; early commands, 21; life before the war, 20; the Union advances up the Red River, 2–26, 29, 131, 133; the Union's spring 1864 offensive plans, 21, 22, 26
Halleck, Joseph, 20
Hardee, William, Lieut. Gen., CSA, 92
Harvard University, 7
Hatch, John, Maj. Gen., USA, 12
Hemphill, TX, 48
Hempstead, TX, 70
Henderson's Hill, Battle of, 93, 96, 164
Henry, C.A., Capt., USA, 187
Henry Cheautau, USA, 124
History of the Nineteenth Army Corps, 79
Holmes, Theophilus H., Lieut. Gen., CSA, 15–20, **20**, 179, 180
Hood, John Bell, Maj. Gen., CSA, 107, 33
Houston, TX, 70, 99
Hunt, Henry, Maj. Gen., USA, 20

265

Illinois River, xii
Indian Territory (Oklahoma), 5, 18, 74, 169
Ingalls, Rufus, Maj. Gen., USA, 55
Iowa, 123, 125
Ireland, 70
Irwin, Richard Bache (Biddle), Lieut. Col., USA, 79, 84

Jackson, Andrew, 137
Jackson, MS, 29, 180
Jackson, Thomas Jonathan "Stonewall", Lieut. Gen., CSA, 4, 8, 34, 76, 181
Jackson Square, New Orleans, LA, 129, 136, 137, **138**, **142**
Jefferson, Thomas, xii
Jefferson, TX, 25
Jenkins Ferry, Battle of, 110, 113, 177, 184, 187
Jenkins Ferry Battleground State Park, AR, 127, 183, **185**
Johnson, Bushrod R., Maj. Gen., CSA, 28
Johnson, Ludwell H., xx, 97
Johnston, Joe, Lieut. Gen., CSA
Joiner, Gary, xx, 31, 51
Joint Congressional Committee on the Conduct of the War, 44, 70, 97, 100, 105, 121, 153

Kentucky, 7, 13, 17, 28, 85, 86
Kentucky Campaign, 13, 17, 179
Kirby-Smith, Edmund, Lieut. Gen., CSA, **13**; after-action report, 113, 178; Battle of Jenkins Ferry, 184; Battle of Mansfield, 78–81, 109, 171; Battle of Perryvile,17; Battle of Richmond Kentucky, 13, 86; Battles and Leaders article, 181; command staff, 33; communication to Magruder, 74; communication from Taylor, 72, 75, 81, 169–71, 172; communication to Taylor, 72; communication to Jefferson Davis, 11, 18; Confederate defensive plans for the Red River Campaign, 34–35, 50, 168, 181–83; Confederate manpower, 91, 143; Confederate strategy for the Red River Campaign, 19, 20, 24, 33–37, 42, 43, 48, 57, 73, 113, 136, 184; early commands, 12–13; the Kentucky Campaign, 17; life before the war, 12; moves forces to Arkansas, 105, 106–14, 175–78; ordering reinforcements from Arkansas, 86, 160, 169; reaction to Steele's advance, 61, 62; reactions to Banks's retreat, 106; relationship with Richard Taylor, 7, 19, 74, 121; relieving Taylor of command, 122; taking command of the Trans-Mississippi, 11–19, 179–81; Union communication on, 30, 119

Lancaster, OH, 27
Landram, William J., Col., USA, 69, 80, 172
Lee, Albert L., Brig. Gen., USA, advance at Mansfield, 54, 68, 69, 70, 78; Battle of Mansfield, 69; Battle of Wison's Farm, 69, 101, 156; relieved of command, 119; testimony before the JCCW, 153, 154
Lee, Robert E., Gen., CSA, 2, 3, 13, 15, 179
Leola, AR, 183
Lexington, USA, 118
Lincoln, Abraham, **44**; assassination, 121; command of the Union operation, 40; comments on the Red River Campaign, 55; political strategy in Louisiana, 45, 138; promotion of Banks, 3–5, 44; promotion of Halleck, 21; promotion of US Grant, 2, 29, 144; support of Banks, 119; the outbreak of war, 123; the Union advances up the Red

River, 3, 21, 24, 131, 133; views on Vicksburg, 130–31
Lincoln Administration, xiii; the command of the Union operation, 31; operational objectives, 25–26; political strategy in Louisiana, 44, 48, 121, 137; support of Banks, 3, 119; the Union advances up the Red River, 8, 9, 22, 25, 26, 31, 131
Little Missouri River, 72, 110, 112
Little Rock, AR, 180–87; Battle of Jenkins Ferry, 184; the Camden Expedition, 57–62, 106, 109, 113, 169, 177, 184–87; Confederate headquarters in the Trans-Mississippi, 15, 19, 180; Confederate reaction to the Camden Expedition, 74; Confederate reinforcements, 111; Confederate strategy during the Red River Campaign, 182; Decisions tour, 179, 183; prior to the war, 86; Union capture of, 56; Union's fall 1863 campaign plans, 22
Loggy Bayou, 37, 118, 183
Louisiana Department of State Parks, 167
Louisiana Purchase, xii
Louisiana State Seminary of Learning & Military Academy, 28, 41
Louisiana State Senate, 7
Louisiana State University. *See* Louisiana State Seminary of Learning & Military Academy
Louisville, USA, 184
Lynch, William, F., Col, USA, 91, 94, 164, 165

Magruder, John B., Maj. Gen., CSA, 24, 25, 72–74, 131, 133, 168
Major, James Patrick, Brig. Gen., CSA, 99
Mansfield, Battle of, xv,11, 54, 60, 62, 63, **71**, **78**, 79, 85, 87, 99, 101, 115, 135, 151, 167; military actions after the battle, 1, 55, 70, 79, 82, 84, 89, 103, 118, 160, 164; actions at dusk, 80; actions before the battle, 27, 32, 37, 68, 42, 49, 75–77, 147, 152, 170; afternoon actions, 69, 70, 94, 164, 171; Churchill's after-action report, 162; comments on, 79, 96; Confederate casualties, 81, 172, 175; Decisions tour, 156, 160; Grant's reaction to, 119; morning actions, 69, 72; testimony before the JCCW, 153; Union casualties, 80, 172, 175; Union retreats from, 102, 147
Mansfield, LA, 48, 54, 72, 74, 75, 152, 165, 169, 170, 174, 175
Mansfield Cemetery, Mansfield, LA, 174, **174**, 175, **177**, 178
Mansfield State Historic Site, xix, **43**, 167, **168**, **173**, 174
Mansura, Battle of, 78
Marksville, LA, 45, 143
Marmaduke, John S., Brig. Gen., CSA, 111, 112, 176
Marshall, TX, 25
Maryland, 3
Maryland Campaign, 4
Massachusetts, 3, 7, 63, 84, 93, 20, 121, 164
Massachusetts State Senate, 121
Matagorda Bay, TX, 49, 73, 167
Maxey, Samuel B., Brig. Gen., CSA, 74, 169
Maximilian I, Ferdinand, 25
McClellan, George, B., Maj. Gen., USA, 3
McClernand, John A., Maj. Gen., USA, 41, 65, 86, 133, 153
McDowell, Irvin, Maj. Gen., USA, 92
McMillan, James W., Brig. Gen., USA, xvi, 89, 162
McPherson, James B., Maj. Gen., USA, 33, 154

Meade, George, Maj. Gen., USA, 3
Medford, Harvey C., 99
Memphis, TN, 134, 141, 147
Meridian, MS, 22, 132
Meridian Campaign, 22, 29, 132, 139
Mexican War, 7, 12, 16, 17, 56, 85
Mexico, xii, 5, 12, 16, 17, 25, 177, 131
Michigan, 56
Milliken's Bend, Battle of, 115
Mills, Clark, 137
Minneapolis, MN, xi
Minnesota, xii
Mississippi, 92, 130
Mississippi River, 63, 72, 115, 122, 130; Chattanooga, 22; command of the Union operation, 42, 136; communication from Davis to Kirby-Smith, 107–8; communication from Grant to Banks, 141; communication from Grant to Sherman, 132; communication from Halleck to Banks, 25; communication from Halleck to Grant, 131; communication from Halleck to Sherman, 135–36; communication from Kirby-Smith to Johnson, 18; Confederate command of the Trans-Mississippi, 15, 16, 179, 180; Confederate strategy for the Red River Campaign, 12, 19, 35; Decisions tour, 129, 137; history of, xi–xiii; Port Hudson, 2, 72, 130; the Union advances up the Red River, 3, 5, 26, 30, 133; Union control of, 108; Vicksburg Campaign, 2, 130
Mississippi River System, xii
Missouri, 5, 18, 89, 115, 160, 162
Missouri, CSA, 147
Missouri River, xii
Mobile, AL, 3, 21–29, 51, 131, 132, 142, 144, 149
Monett's Ferry, Battle of, 1, 78, 106, 118. *See also* Cane River

Monroe, LA, 12, 22, 59, 159, 178, 186
Moore, Risdon M., Col., USA, 165
Morgan City, LA, 45, 138. *See also* Brashear City, LA
Morganza's Bend, LA, 124
Mount Elba, Battle of, 111
Mouton, Alfred, Brig. Gen., CSA, 73, 81, 101, 157, 168, 172
Mower, Joseph A., Brig. Gen. USA, 93, 124, 125, 164
Myers, John R., Private, USA, 124, 125

Nashville, Battle of, 32
Nashville, TN, 22
Natchitoches, LA, 50, 63, 64, 68, 146, 149–52, **155**, 158, 179
New England, 3, 5, 103, 173
New Falls City Riverboat, CSA, 35, 182
New Mexico, xii
New Orleans, Battle of, 137. *See also* War of 1812
New Orleans, LA, xi, xii, **8, 49, 130, 137, 138, 142**; after the war, 122; capture of, xi; command of the Union operation, 29, 38, 144; communication from Grant to Banks, 51, 141, 149; Confederate spies, 73, 168; Confederate strategy for the Red River Campaign, 74, 169; Decisions tour, 127, 129, 152; Jackson Square, 136; Kirby-Smith B&L article, 182; Nathaniel Banks, 1, 3, 4, 44–48, 138, 139; Richard Taylor, 7; US Customs House, 129; the Union advances up the Red River, xiii, 26, 27, 134; Union's fall 1863 campaign plans, 22; Union occupation of, 3; Union political strategy, 3
New York, 20, 55, 56
New York Tribune, 79
Ninth Louisiana Infantry Regiment, CSA, 8

Ohio, 27, 86
Ohio River, xii
Oklahoma, xii, 5
Old Pleasant Hill. *See* Pleasant Hill, LA
Old River Control Structure, xii
Opelousas, LA, 8, 146
Osage, USA, 118
Ord, Edward, Maj. Gen., USA, 20

Parsons, Mosby Monroe, Brig. Gen., CSA, 87, 90, 162, 163, 171
Pea Ridge, Battle of, 56, 86
Pemberton, John C., Lieut. Gen., CSA, 96, 180
Pennsylvania, 79, 92
Perryville, Battle of, 13, 17, 179
Petty, Elijah Parsons, Capt., CSA, 116, 117
Pine Bluff, AR, 59, 86, 185, 187
Pineville, LA, 28, 41, 143, 147, 148
Pleasant Grove. *See* Chapman's Bayou
Pleasant Hill, Battle of, xv, 11, 27, 32, 62–64, **85**, **97**, 156, **166**, 175; actions after, 43, 99, 108, 118, 151, 153, 175; actions before, 55, 69, 147, 150; Banks's retreat from, 100, 101, 102–5, 111, 147, 157; Blessington's wounding, 71; Churchill's attack, 85, 87, 89, 161–64; death of Elijah Parsons Petty, 115–17; Decisions tour, 152, 156, 167; Grant's reaction to, 119; Smith's counterattack, 92, 94, 97; Taylor's description of, 91; Taylor's plan of attack, 94, 164; Thirty-Second Iowa, 123; Testimony before the JCCW, 153–54; Union retreat from, 43
Pleasant Hill, LA, 1, 69, 79, 81, 83, 84, 87
Pleasant Hill Battlefield Park, 92, 160, 161

Polignac, Camille Armand Jules Marie, Brig. Gen., CSA, 73, 77, 87, 94, 115, 161, 164, 168, 171
Porter, David Dixon, Rr. Adm, USA, **27**, **65**; actions at Alexandria after April 9th, 1, 108, 109, 111, 114, 158, 161, 175, 176; actions before April 8th, 37, 43, 48, 50, 54, 55, 64, 83, 138, 181, 183; the advance above Grand Ecore, 67, 68, 147–150; Bailey's Dam, 119; Banks's retreat from Mansfield, 87; Banks's retreat from Pleasant Hill, 103, 104; Battle of Pleasant Hill, 87; Blair's Landing, 118, 156; capture of Fort DeRussy, 45; Chattanooga, 39; the command of the Union operation, 40; communication from Banks to Halleck, 140; communication from Grant to Banks, 31; communication from porter to Sherman, 150; communication from Sherman to Smith, 145; Confederate defense of the Red River, 34, 35, 37; navel losses during the campaign, 121; Taylor's view of Union forces, 102; the Union advances up the Red River, 26; Vicksburg Campaign, 39, 130; views on the campaign, 118; and Wellington W. Withenbury, 51
Porter, Fitz-John, Maj. Gen., USA, 12
Port Hudson, LA, xi, 2, 21, 48, 130, 139
Port Hudson, Siege of, 5, 40, 72
Prairie D'Ane, AR, 112
Prairie Grove, Battle of, 15, 180
Prescott, AR, 112
Price, Sterling, Maj. Gen., CSA, **86**; actions prior to the Red River Campaign, 74, 86, 169; after-action report, A.J Smith, 165; Battle of Jenkins Ferry, 177, 184; Churchill's command, 160; Camden Expedition, 60, 109, 112; communication

Index

Price, Sterling, Maj. Gen., CSA (*cont.*) from Halleck to Grant, 131; communication from Taylor to Kirby-Smith, 170; Kirby-Smith moves forces to Arkansas, 111–13, 176; promotion to command, 19; Union communication, 25

Proclamation of Amnesty and Reconstruction, 45

Ransom, Thomas E. G., Brig. Gen., USA, 68, 69, 80, 154, 172

Richmond, KY, Battle of, 13, 86

Richmond, VA, 3, 8, 11, 15, 108, 113, 178, 180

Ricketts, James B., Maj. Gen., USA, 20

Rosecrans, William, Maj. Gen., USA, 22

Russell B. Long Lock and Dam and Picnic Ground, LA, 155, 157, 160

Sabine Crossroads, 69, 79, 154. *See also* Mansfield, LA

Sabine Pass, Texas, 5, 22

Saint Charles Hotel, New Orleans, LA, 137

Saint Charles Parish, LA, 7

Saint Louis Republican, 174

Salomon, Frederick, Brig. Gen., USA, 59, 185

Schofield, John M., Maj. Gen., USA, 33

Scott, John, Col., USA, 123

Scott, Winfield, Maj. Gen., USA, xii, 2, 3

Scurry, William R., Brig Gen, CSA, 115, 116, 70

Second Bull Run, Battle of, 4, 8, 13

Second California Cavalry, 92

Second Corps, USA, 4

Second Manassas. *See* Second Bull Run, Battle of

Second Seminole War, 16

Second US Infantry, 56

Seven Days, Battles of, 8, 15, 180

Seven Pines, Battle of, 16

Seventh Corps, USA, 56

Shaw, William T., Col., USA, 89, 116, 123, 162, 165

Shenandoah Valley, VA, 3, 4, 79, 81

Shenandoah Valley Campaign, 8

Sheridan, Philip H., Maj. Gen., USA, 33

Sherman, Mary Hoyt, 27

Sherman, Robert, 27

Sherman, William T., Maj. Gen., CSA, **28**; actions prior to the Red River Campaign, 22; A. J. Smith's command, 27, 30–32, 70, 92, 144, 145; Battle of Chickasaw Bayou, 96; command of the Union operation, 39–42; communication from Banks to Halleck, 139; communication from Grant to Banks, 51, 141, 149; communication from Grant to Sherman, 41, 132, 135; communication from Halleck to Grant, 132; communication from Halleck to Sherman, 39, 134, 135; communication from Porter to Sherman, 149, 150; communication from Sherman to A. J. Smith, 112, 145; commands prior to the Red River Campaign, 28, 29; comment on the Red River Campaign, xiii; life before the war, 27; March to the Sea, 123; the Union's spring 1864 offensive plans, 3; Vicksburg Campaign, 56; the Union advances up the Red River, 24–26, 132

Shiloh, Battle of, 16, 28, 123

Ship Island, Battle of, xi

Shreveport, LA, xix, 11, 86, 121, **179**; A. J. Smith counterattacks, 93, 164; availability of A. J. Smith's command, 144, 145; Banks changes his line of march, 50–55, 148–50; Banks remains in New Orleans, 47–49; Banks retreats to Pleasant Hill, 79, 81, 83, 172, 173; Banks withdraws to the Red River, 104, 105; Banks's order of march, 63–70, 152, 153; capture of, 1, 26; Churchill fails to find the Union flank, 86, 87, 89, 160; command of the Union operation, 31, 32, 42, 43; communication from Banks to Halleck, 139, 140; communication from David Porter to Sherman, 150; communication from Grant to Banks, 141; communication from Sherman to A. J. Smith, 145, 146; communication from Taylor to Kirby-Smith, 170; Confederates divert the Red River, 32–37, 181, 182; Confederate stand at Mansfield, 72–79, 168–71; Decisions Tour, 127, 129, 160, 167, 175, 178, 183; headquarters of the DotTM, 19; Kirby-Smith moves forces to Arkansas, 107–14, 176, 177; path of the Red River, xii; Steele advances at Shreveport, 55–62, 183–86; testimony before the JCCW, 100; the Union advances up the Red River, xiii, 24, 25, 29, 133

Shreveport-Natchitoches Stage Line Road, 55, 64, 70, 83, 89, 152, 162

Sibley, Henry H., Brig. Gen., CSA, 92

Sigel, Franz, Maj. Gen., USA, 3

Simmesport, LA, 119, 123

Sioux City, USA, 124

Smith, Andrew J., Brig. Gen., USA, xvi, **93**, 112, 121, 123; actions before April 8th, 43, 45, 66, 68, 70, 138, 147, 148, 153; after-action report, 165–66; Banks withdraws to the Red River, 103, 105, 106; Battle of Mansfield, 81, 83, 84, 172; Battle of Pleasant Hill, 87, 90–97, 102, 103, 115, 116, 161–66; command of the Union operation, 31, 32, 42, 50; communication from Grant to Banks, 141; communication from Grant to Banks, 51, 145–47; communication from Sherman to A. J. Smith, 145–47; Decisions Tour, 160, 143; testimony before the JCCW, 154; the Union advances up the Red River, 26, 138, 144, 157

Smith, Thomas Kilby, Brig. Gen., USA, 66, 100, 101, 103, 105, 118, 153, 158

Smith, William "Baldy", Maj. Gen., USA, 12

Smith's Gorillas, 70, 92

South Carolina, 28

Springfield, KY, 7

Springfield Landing, 64, 152, 158

St. Augustine, FL, 12

Steele, Frederick, Maj. Gen., USA, **57**; after Mansfield/Pleasant Hill, 119, 121, 177; Banks withdraws to the Red River, 105, 106; Battle of Mansfield, 169; Battle of Pleasant Hill, 78; Camden Expedition, 110–13; command of the Union operation, 30, 38, 41–43, 134; commands prior to the Red River Campaign, 55–56; communication from Banks to Halleck, 139–42; communication from Capt. Henry to Steele, 187; communication from Grant to Sherman, 133; communication from Halleck to Banks, 25; communication from Halleck to Grant, 30, 131, 132; communication from Halleck to Sherman, 136; communication from Kirby-Smith to Taylor, 72; communication from Sherman to Steele, 30; communication from Taylor to Kirby-Smith,

Steele, Frederick, Maj. Gen., USA (*cont.*)
74, 169, 170; Confederate stand at Mansfield, 74, 75; Decisions Tour, 127, 184; Kirby-Smith moves forces to Arkansas, 109, 110, 176; Steele advances at Shreveport, 55–62, 183–86; the Union advances up the Red River, 26, 46, 48

Stevens, Isaac, Brig. Gen., USA, 20

Stone, Charles P., Brig. Gen., USA, 12, 41

Stoner Avenue Park, Shreveport LA, 178, 179

Stones River, Battle of, 13, 21, 179

Story County, IA, 123

Tappan, James Camp, Brig. Gen., CSA, 48, 87, 162

Taylor, Richard (Dick), Maj. Gen., CSA, 1, 7, 11, 123, 168; actions after April 9th, 108, 118, 119; actions before April 8th, 49, 50, 55, 64, 65, 93, 139, 143, 149, 151–53; after the Red River Campaign, 121, 122, 123; Banks retreats to Pleasant Hill, 81, 83–85; Banks withdraws to the Red River, 101, 103, 104, 106, 156, 157, 158; Battle of Blair's Landing, 156; Battle of Mansfield, 63, 69, 70, 72, 75–78, 80, 81, 157, 171, 172; Battle of Pleasant Hill, 85, 87, 89–91, 94, 96, 160–64, 166; communication from Kirby-Smith, 72; communication to Kirby-Smith, 72, 75, 77, 121, 169, 170, 171; communication to Magruder, 72; commands prior to the Red River Campaign, 4, 7, 8; comments on the Campaign, 101, 102; Confederate defensive plans for the Red River Campaign, 18, 19, 24, 27, 33, 34, 37, 73, 74, 133, 169, 170, 181, 182; Decision tour, 167; Kirby-Smith moves forces to Arkansas, 108–14, 175–77; life before the war, 7; relationship with Kirby-Smith, 18–19; relieved of command, 113, 122; Steele advances at Shreveport, 55, 57, 60–62, 105, 184; the Union advances up the Red River, 26; views on the Battle of Pleasant Hill, 108

Taylor, Zachary, Maj. Gen., 7, 85

Tennessee, 2, 13, 29, 116, 131, 179

Tennessee River, xii, 22

Texas Military Institute, 116

Thayer, John Milton, Brig. Gen., USA, 59–61, 110, 111, 176, 185, 186

Third Corps, CSA, 13

Thomas, George H., Maj. Gen., USA, 22, 28

Through the Howling Wilderness, 31, 51

Tones Bayou, LA, (Tone's Bayou), 35, 37, 182, 183

Trinity, TX, 73, 168

Tullahoma, TN, 13, 179

Tupelo, Battle of, 32, 93

Twelfth Corps, USA, 4

Tyler, TX, 25

United Daughters of the Confederacy, 167

United States Army Corps of Engineers, xii, 151, 156

United States Custom House, New Orleans, LA, 129, 130, 136, 137

United States House of Representatives, 3

United States Military Academy, 12, 16, 20, 28, 32, 40, 55, 92

Valley Campaign, 1862, 8

Vance, Joseph W., Col., USA, 69, 80

Vicksburg, MS, 22, 45, 65, 112, 130, 133, 138, 139, 147, 153, 180, 182; surrender of, 2, 5, 21, 130

Vicksburg Campaign, 13, 15, 29, 39, 56, 74, 79, 83, 123, 130, 169, 179
Virginia, 3, 4, 8, 122
Virginia Polytechnic Institute, 33
Virginia Tech. *See* Virginia Polytechnic Institute
von Clausewitz, Carl, 44

Wabash River, xii
Walker, John G, Maj. Gen., CSA, 46, 73, 87, 89, 112, 161, 162, 176
Walker's Greyhounds. *See* Department of the Trans-Mississippi, CSA: Texas Division
Walker's Texas Division. *See* Department of the Trans-Mississippi, CSA: Texas Division
Waltham, MA, 3, 121
War of 1812, 20, 92. *See also* New Orleans, Battle of
Washington, AR, 61, 72, 110, 186
Washington, DC, 2–5, 21, 24, 38, 121, 130, 134, 137
Washita River, 12, 145
Western Theater, xi, 8, 16, 21, 123
West Point. *See* United States Military Academy
Wilderness, Battle of, 50
Williams, Alpheus, Maj. Gen., USA, 4
Wilson's Creek, Battle of, 56, 86
Wilson's Farm, Battle of, 69, 156, 101
Winchester, VA, 122
Wisconsin, 119
Withenbury, Wellington W., 51, 53, 149

Yellow Bayou, Battle of, 78, 106, 114, 119, 123

www.ingramcontent.com/pod-product-compliance
Lightning Source LLC
Chambersburg PA
CBHW030512080526
44586CB00011B/159